More Praise for
A New Evangelical Manifesto

"*A New Evangelical Manifesto* is a timely and important book that refuses to shrink back from the pressing moral issues of our time. As rising generations shake off the scales of the religious right, many Christians are looking for fresh approaches to modern problems. While readers may not agree with every word contained herein, they'll find much to learn from and even more to rejoice over."

> **JONATHAN MERRITT,** author of *A Faith of Our Own: Following Jesus Beyond the Culture Wars*

"Evangelical Christianity has long had outside critics. The criticism in this book is much more powerful because it comes from within. But this book is far more than simply an indictment of certain practices and patterns within evangelical Christianity. It also sets forth a hopeful vision for what evangelical Christianity can and should be. Everyone who cares about the Christian witness in the world will want to read this book and join this important conversation."

> **MELISSA ROGERS,** Center for Religion and Public Affairs, Wake Forest University Divinity School

"As I read *A New Evangelical Manifesto*, I kept thinking of Martin Luther King's description of the freedom movement, from his 'Letter from a Birmingham Jail' in 1963—the movement was standing up 'for the best in the American Dream' and 'the most sacred values in our Judeo-Christian Heritage,' bringing 'the whole nation back to the great wells of democracy' from the nation's beginnings. So too, this Manifesto and the movement it represents. This is a bold, compelling, passionate statement for Christians—and all Americans—to move beyond the blame games, hatreds, and demonizations which so warp our capacities to act across differences to build a sustainable, just, and participatory democratic society. The authors embody the Holy Spirit at work in the world, in a tempestuous and crucial moment in time."

> **HARRY C. BOYTE,** Center for Democracy and Citizenship, author of *CommonWealth: A Return to Citizen Politics*

"This collection of important, provocative, and challenging essays has the potential to be a 'game changer' in the life of the Church and its public persona... If change is to truly occur, the church universal must take a sober look at itself and courageously seek to bring the Kingdom Ethic to all the world regardless of race, creed, gender or nationality. The authors in this collection are to be commended for the courage and faith in announcing to us all that we need to examine ourselves and our motives. *A New Evangelical Manifesto* challenges us to reconsider long held assumptions and bravely seek the guidance of the Holy Spirit in our journeying toward the 'beloved community.'"

SEAN SMITH, pastor, New Horizon Baptist Church, Atlanta

"*A New Evangelical Manifesto* is a historic declaration by Christians determined to get Jesus back into Christianity. It challenges the older white men who lead the church, who yearn to take back the power they had before Americans of color so multiplied. Men who are the face of loss, fear, anger and destructive partisanship. Almost half the authors are under 35; many are women. They want to give Christianity one more chance. To reject patriarchal power over women, to care about the poor, the marginalized, the sick and the dying. To see God in the face of all his creatures regardless of faith, color or economic status. They miss Jesus of Nazareth, the original bleeding heart liberal."

JOSEPH V. MONTVILLE, George Mason University

A New Evangelical
MANIFESTO

*This book is dedicated to "good news" evangelicals
in the United States and in all the world*

A New **Evangelical**
MANIFESTO

A Kingdom Vision for the
Common Good

David P. Gushee, EDITOR

CHALICE
PRESS

ST. LOUIS, MISSOURI

Cover design: Elizabeth Wright
Cover art: BigStock

www.chalicepress.com

PRINT: 9780827200340 EPUB: 9780827200357 EPDF: 9780827200364

Library of Congress Cataloging-in-Publication Data

A new evangelical manifesto : a kingdom vision for the common good / David P. Gushee, editor.
    p. cm.
Includes bibliographical references.
ISBN 978-0-8272-0034-0
1. New Evangelical Partnership for the Common Good. 2. Evangelicalism. I. Gushee, David P., 1962-

BR1640.N473 2012
277.3'083--dc23

2012019271

Printed in the United States of America

Contents

Introduction

The New Evangelical Partnership for the Common Good (henceforth, NEP), was founded in January 2010 by Richard Cizik, Steven Martin, and myself. This book aims to explain who we are and what we believe—"we" meaning not just the three of us, but the substantial part of the American evangelical community that we inhabit and that speaks alongside us in this powerful collection of essays.

The organizational history of NEP can be outlined with merciful brevity.

I first encountered Steven Martin more than a decade ago through his brilliant documentary films related to the German Church Struggle during the Nazi era, to which I had the chance to contribute a comment or two and to show in numerous courses on the Holocaust. Steve really understands Christian moral collapse (and resistance) during the Nazi era—and his films offer profound clues for understanding our own Christian failures (and faithfulness) today as well.

I first crossed paths with Richard Cizik in the late 1980s, when he served as Vice President for Governmental Affairs at the National Association of Evangelicals and made a visit to the Union Theological Seminary campus in New York, where I was a doctoral student. Richard and I worked together on several important NAE initiatives before his tenure in that pivotal role was so abruptly terminated in 2008—a story he tells within these pages, in detail, for the first time.

When, beginning in 2006, I became engaged in the fierce struggle against U.S. detainee abuse as president of Evangelicals for Human Rights, Steve and Richard and I found ourselves working together as a team, along with others, attempting to stand fast against torture in the face of broad evangelical complicity or silence. We agreed in late 2009 that our shared vision and combination of interests and gifts might make for a great synergy, and so we decided to combine our organizational efforts and found NEP together. Our first initiative was a (successful) call for international debt relief for Haiti after the terrible earthquake of January 2010.

We are deeply grateful that Chalice Press reached out to us to ask us to put together a book-length manifesto outlining our vision. We are grateful to Brad Lyons and the team at Chalice Press for their great interest in NEP and their belief that we have something important to say, and that Chalice Press should be the host. Chalice Press's commitment to us, and their sense that our voices need to be heard especially clearly during the bitter 2012 election season, motivated them to move with extraordinary speed to produce the volume you now hold in your hands.

What exactly are these "new evangelical" voices saying? The paragraphs below are how we have framed our efforts from the very beginning. This statement can still be found on our website (http://www. newevangelicalpartnership.org/?q=node/18):

Christians by definition are those who bear witness to our faith in Jesus Christ, including his identity, his teachings, and his mission in the world. We bear witness in many ways. One way is to offer proclamation and action concerning the moral will of God for human communities.

The Bible teaches that every human being is precious in God's sight (Ps. 8). All are the beloved objects of God's creating, sustaining, and redeeming grace. What happens to human beings matters immensely to a God who "so loved the world that he sent his only Son" (Jn. 3:16) to redeem it. Christians are called to embody and articulate God's love for the world in all that we do. This is the heart of Christian evangelistic and moral witness and is critical for our calling to proclaim the Gospel to all the world.

Much Christian moral witness takes place quietly in families, local congregations, and local communities, as Christians simply go about their daily lives and seek to live as faithful followers of Christ. This is the responsibility of all Christians.

But some Christian moral witness occurs at national and international levels, where many significant challenges to human well-being are often created and addressed. Christians have no choice but to engage religious, economic, cultural, and political institutions with our best efforts to articulate and embody the love and justice of Jesus Christ for the well-being of God's world. These arenas will be the focus of the New Evangelical Partnership.

This is what we see, and what we want to see:

We see Jesus Christ, our Lord and the world's Savior, whom we love—he is the center of our lives.

We want to see more Americans choose to believe in Jesus and live as his disciples.

We see that the evangelistic and discipling work of American Christianity has been badly damaged by a generation of culture war-fighting—some doubt Jesus… because of Christians.

We see the allegiance of America as a whole to Christian faith slipping a little bit more each year, partly as a consequence.

We want to see a renewed Christian public witness in America for the sake of the Gospel.

We want to see an engagement of Christians in American public life that is loving, rather than angry; holistic, rather than narrowly focused; healing, rather than divisive; and independent of partisanship and ideology, rather than subservient to party or ideology.

We see in many sectors a Christian public engagement that calls itself Christian while often damaging the work of Christ and violating the teachings of Christ.

We see other excellent examples of Christian public engagement that need to be celebrated and encouraged.

We want to see a Christian public witness that reflects the actual life, ministry, and teachings of the Jesus Christ we meet in Scripture and experience in the church at its best.

We want to see the incarnation of the teachings and example of Christ, not just the articulating of those teachings in word alone.

Readers will have to decide for themselves whether the twenty-two essays gathered in this volume fulfill the promise embedded in this founding NEP vision. Perhaps I am biased, but, as the editor of this collection, I think these essays do indeed accomplish that goal. I hope that you find them as enormously encouraging as I do. Without giving away too much, let me say a few words about what you are about to read.

It might be hard to notice in an election season in which the word evangelical means little more than "right-wing social conservative Republican voting bloc," but evangelicalism is actually a religious community. It is—we are—one part of the global Christian family and a more-or-less identifiable part of the Christian landscape in the United States. Representing nearly a third of Americans,[1] evangelicals are spiritually serious, theologically orthodox, evangelistically engaged, morally earnest Protestant Christians, members of hundreds of particular denominational traditions and tens of thousands of congregations all over the country. (You will find other ways of defining evangelicals in this book. But that's good enough for now.)

So this volume begins with seven essays related to the church. We start there because we think the ills of what goes by the name "American evangelicalism" (and they are legion) are rooted in profound problems in our churches. Different authors will say it in different ways, but the way I say it is that far too often American evangelicals are more American than Christian, more fixated on nation than on church, and more loyal to sub-biblical American values and practices than to the living biblical Word or the way of Jesus Christ. The first part of the book, then, offers some discussion of what has gone wrong with American evangelicalism as a branch of the universal Christian Church, and some clues as to how to get healthy again.

Many observers describe four decades of politicized culture wars on our right flank as "evangelicalism." In this viewpoint, evangelicalism is characterized by, among other things, a tendency toward constant attacks on perceived enemies of God, the church, and America. These are all blended together, of course, in an idolatrous religio-political mashup. We have become, in Rodney Clapp's words, "bad news evangelicals."[2] We have been known for our polemics, for whom we are against—for whom we want to oppose, defeat, smash to smithereens.

Section II of this volume lifts up groups of people who surely could use some good news—and some good, godly love. Several authors in this collection return to *evangelion,* the root Greek word for evangelical. *Evangelion* means "Gospel," or the "Good News." These authors call for an evangelicalism that brings good news to (all!) people, and indeed, good love to (all!) people. These creative essays address marginalized and often victimized groups such as trafficking victims, children, women, poor people, those suffering preventable diseases, people of non-white races, and the dying. Several essays point to specific Christian initiatives that don't just talk about but deliver good, loving care to these and other suffering ones in our broken world. That's an evangelicalism about which one need not be ashamed, in contrast with an "evangelicalism" that mainly bashes, wounds, and excludes. A few of these essays are a bit edgy, and I personally do not agree with every word; but it is about time that evangelicals created communities of free, faithful inquiry rather than fearful boundary-guarding.

The final section seeks to name redemptive approaches in public life. This is the most public-policy oriented section of the book. It demonstrates that "new evangelicals" care about a holistic array of cultural and policy concerns that include abortion but extend to torture, peacemaking, nuclear weapons, consumerism, the death penalty, and global warming.

Polling shows that younger evangelicals are much less enamored of the Christian Right and much more attracted to the kind of center-left (if one must label us) evangelicalism represented here. We will be eager to hear the responses of younger evangelicals to see whether we have represented you well. More than half of these essays are written by Christians under the age of thirty-five. We also have a strong representation of women writers in this volume. One of our goals in NEP is to help break the stranglehold of the older white male power structure in evangelical life—you know, the guys in suits who try to tell everyone else what it really means to "count as" an evangelical, and while they are at it, who gather to determine who "true" evangelicals will vote for in November. You may also notice here a stronger representation of Pentecostal Christians than has been typical among "card-carrying evangelicals." We seek the democratizing of the evangelical world as well as the biblical work of gift-identification. Hopefully this collection offers at least a start in the right direction.

Anger seeps out from this collection, but we hope that anger does not dominate its spirit. A person has the right to be angry at that part of the evangelical leadership in the U.S. that has damaged the very word evangelical and whose politics has actually driven people away from our loving Lord Jesus Christ. Some of our authors, especially the younger ones, are not at all sure they want to apply the term "evangelical" to themselves. They agreed to write for this collection maybe because they see NEP as "all right" despite the "E" in our name. Who knows, maybe the response to this collection will settle the matter of whether the Christian Right has damaged the term "evangelical" in this country beyond repair.

At least the three founders of NEP—aging white males as we may be—hope to believe that the long, proud tradition of "good news evangelicalism" so well-represented in contemporary voice here should be defined and defended one more (one last?) time.

We think you will enjoy this powerful expression of Christian faith, Christian vision, and Christian love. NEP Advisory Board member and well-known Christian leader Brian McLaren will get you started. You are in for a treat.

David P. Gushee

SECTION I

A New Kind of Evangelical Christianity…

The Church in America Today

Brian McLaren

For many decades, church researchers (in evangelical circles at least) created a cliché referring to evangelical growth and mainline decline. Evangelical growth rose from vibrant conservative theology and piety. Mainline decline resulted from institutional bureaucracy and liberal theology. Catholic growth, if it was acknowledged, was due to two different sources— big families augmented by immigration. Now those clichés have become threadbare, and a clearer assessment of the church in America today is showing through.

More recent and more accurate assessment reveals that decades of evangelical growth derived largely from two sources: a clearer sense of message and mission and a more entrepreneurial "need-meeting" approach to ministry.[1] Ministry was facilitated by less denominational bureaucracy and more local autonomy, yielding more freedom to innovate. Innovation resulted in large numbers of Catholic and mainline Christians being won over to evangelicalism, much as the patrons of Home Depots and Wal-marts were won over from their old neighborhood hardware or dime stores.

The inflow of unsatisfied mainline Protestants and Roman Catholics was a limited "market." Now this market seems to have run its course. If we subtract growth through immigration, the fastest growing religious group in America today is the spiritual-but-not-religious–people who are dropping out of "organized religion" entirely, whatever its brand. Diana Butler Bass summarizes:

> According to *Newsweek*, these polls found that the percentage of self-identified Christians has fallen 10 points since 1990, from 86 to 76 percent, while the percentage of people who claim they are unaffiliated with any particular faith has doubled in recent years, rising to 16 percent.[2]

Evangelical church attendance appears to have plateaued. The coming decline may mirror that of mainline Protestants, just thirty or forty years later—just as Catholic Church attendance continues to fall among the nation's non-immigrants.[3]

At this moment, we are poised to realize that all sectors of Christianity in the West, not unlike all sectors of religion in general, are experiencing similar pressures and facing similar challenges, four of which deserve special attention. How we respond to those four challenges will determine whether our descendants look back on our times as best or worst, good or bad, a hopeful new beginning or a sad and depressing end.

The first of those challenges is the *cultural shift from what many call the modern/colonial/industrial world to the postmodern/post-colonial/post-industrial world.* Just as postage stamp and post office are losing ground to e-mail and Facebook, and just as the bookstore and the record label are giving way to new digital counterparts, and just as banking and journalism are being transformed by new technologies, the familiar worlds of church, worship, and spiritual development are similarly being challenged. Will the traditional brick-and-mortar church go the way of the travel agency and telephone booth? Will our denominations prove to be dinosaurs?

Just as the Christian faith was deeply embedded in medieval culture to such a degree that modern expressions of the Christian faith were considered heretical, so today Christian faith is deeply embedded in modern culture to such a degree that postmodern explorations are considered heretical. Just as the emergence of Christian faith from its medieval context was gradual and diverse, so the current emergence of Christian faith will take time to develop and will take many forms. What those forms will look like is impossible to predetermine. We can be confident that Christian faith will adapt robustly to the emerging culture, just as it has done so creatively in the past.

The second challenge is the *reality of pluralism.* I don't think my grandparents ever met a real live Muslim, Buddhist, or Hindu. Back in their day, a mixed marriage meant a Presbyterian marrying a Methodist. I don't think my children will ever pass a week without interacting with many people of many varied faiths and philosophies. Each religious identity is affected by increasing encounter with others. Some react with defensiveness and aggressiveness, seeing other faiths as threatening competitors and hostile invaders. Others react by minimizing religious identity altogether, seeking to minimize friction by minimizing difference.[4] In between those extremes, nearly everyone negotiates old prejudices and beliefs with the daily practicalities of getting along and getting acquainted. As a result of the growing pluralism of the postmodern world, each new generation has a radically expanded range of options in maintaining, changing, modifying, or rejecting the religious heritage of its upbringing, and that freedom to choose is already having profound impacts on our faith communities. To put it in the language of business: if customer loyalty is taken for granted, religious communities face the real possibility of going out of business.

Third is an internal reality: *apathy or inflexibility in relation to the first two challenges*. In light of the postmodern shift and the new reality of pluralism, we might expect that our churches would be energized and eager to respond, but that is not always the case. Thankfully, the percentage of people awake to these challenges seems to be growing. Nearly all our Christian communities have a core that is conservative and change-averse in one of two ways. Those who are liberal theologically tend to be conservative and inflexible methodologically, and those who are liberal methodologically tend to be conservative and inflexible theologically. If the first two areas of change are as real and profound as many of us believe them to be, both groups will have some serious adjusting to do.

Theologically, this challenge to change isn't simply that old answers are being rejected in favor of new answers. For example, it's not that free-willers are becoming predestinarians or vice versa, although both are occurring. No, it's that new questions are being raised—questions that render the concepts of predestination and free will equally irrelevant or uninteresting. The question is no longer, "Are we saved by faith alone, or by faith plus works?" The question is, "What is salvation in the first place? What are we being saved from and for?" The question isn't, "Are you an exclusivist, an inclusivist, or universalist?" but rather, "How do we join God in God's saving work in history?" The question isn't, "Are you an inerrantist?" or, "Who has the right form of church government?" The question is, "What, in light of the complexities of hermeneutics, does it mean for any text to have authority in a community?" and, "How can the church be better shaped by mission?"

The same upheaval confronts our churches in terms of pragmatic issues. The debates of recent decades might be summarized as charismatic versus noncharismatic, megachurch versus small church, traditional versus contemporary, seeker-friendly versus believer-friendly, attractional versus missional, and so on. The new questions go much deeper: What kind of future do we believe God desires? What kind of people are we seeking to form, to help build such a future? What practices will help form such people to build such a world?

These questions are being asked, in many locales, against more urgent pragmatic questions—questions of survival. On a local level, the costs of operating a single congregation have risen dramatically in recent decades.

Where a congregation of eighty attenders was financially viable a generation ago, a two-hundred-attender congregation now may feel marginal. These fiscal challenges are complicated by demographic shifts—whether rural to urban, urban to suburban, suburban to regentrified urban and exurban, or rust belt to sun belt. As a result, many congregations are closing their doors or anticipating having to do so, often after running at a financial loss for many years, exhausting savings that accumulated over generations. It's no wonder that, on a regional and national level, the downsizing of many denominational structures is well underway.

Since appropriately energetic and creative responses are not yet forthcoming to the first three challenges, it is not surprising that, by and large, those who remain in our churches—whether Roman Catholic, mainline Protestant, or evangelical—are on average older, with younger generations increasingly joining the ranks of the spiritual but not religious. Too often, the loyal remnant blames the young for their defection rather than taking responsibility themselves. Too often, when the remnant takes responsibility, they feel a sense of resignation and failure that paralyzes rather than energizes. Either way, the result is apathy.

Sometimes denial is in play: people simply avoid facing the trends. Sometimes apathy is based on a rather selfish hope that the church will stay in operation long enough for the current generation of tithers' funerals to be appropriately conducted. Often, apathy is encouraged by the existence of thriving megachurches whose localized vitality masks the larger realities of shrinking numbers and wrinkling members.

The fourth challenge is *political*. Large sectors of the church have become the religious expression of partisan voting blocs. These wings of the church find identity is decreasingly centered in Jesus and his gospel and increasingly centered in a political, social, or economic ideology instead. In a 2011 *New York Times* column, Eric Weiner explained why this partisan politicization drives younger generations away from the church: "[W]e've mixed politics and religion so completely that many simply opt out of both; apparently they are reluctant to claim a religious affiliation because they don't want the political one that comes along with it."[5]

This politicization is sometimes left-wing/progressive but more often right-wing/regressive. In the latter case, Christian identity takes on three characteristics:

1. *Nostalgic:* The language of "going back" or "taking back" suggests a widespread longing for a former golden era when America was a more Christian nation—notably when divorce, abortion, and homosexuality were

less common and when the institutional church and state were less separated. This nostalgia is remarkably similar in feel whether it occurs in evangelical, mainline, or Catholic settings.

2. *Nativist:* That lost golden age was also an age when white Christian males, and especially white Protestant heterosexual males, were in the clear majority and represented the center of power. That power seems to have eroded—first with women, then with African Americans, then with Asians and Latinos, then with the LGBT community, and increasingly with people of other faiths, especially Muslims. As traditional power hierarchies collapse, people often respond with feelings of loss, fear, and anger. In that context, a desire grows for the old majority to resurge and reclaim its lost power and privilege.

3. *Negative:* Loss, fear, and anger create a general tone of negativity, expressed in harsh rhetoric toward "the other" and in calls for increasingly desperate measures under threat of increasingly dire consequences if those measures don't succeed. Under this regime of negativity, groups define themselves increasingly by what they're against. For example, the very term "evangelical" has come to mean—among both outsiders and insiders— against abortion, against gay marriage, against government-sponsored social programs, against government regulations on business, against demilitarization and the prohibition of torture, against full acceptance of Muslims in American society, and against sustainable statehood for Palestinians. The less fervently one maintains these "againsts," the less secure one's conservative Christian identity.

Nostalgia, nativism, and negativity have proven powerful and motivating memes in Christian broadcasting, publishing, and political organizing— especially among older generations in evangelical and Roman Catholic circles. But they are singularly distasteful to people of the emerging culture who find the "three N's" depressing and repulsive. They seek instead an ethos of hope, diversity, and creative collaboration.

1. *Hope:* People of the emerging culture know they face monumental global crises—economic, ecological, social, political, and spiritual. They judge it irresponsible and unfaithful to talk about the good old days in such a time of crisis when constructive action is needed. That's why they seek a message of hope, and that's why they are not satisfied with an evacuation plan that leaves the earth behind to be destroyed. Emerging culture participants would rather seek a transformation plan that proclaims the possibility that, through faith, contemporary crises can be faced and overcome. They dare believe that with God better days are possible for their children and grandchildren.

2. *Diversity:* In the emerging culture, a monoculture is not desirable. Diversity is respected as a strength, and intolerance is suspected as a weakness. That's why people in this emerging culture seek a Christian vision that moves toward the other in hospitality and neighborliness. They avoid demonizing the other and comparing "our" best with "their" worst. They seek instead to build bridges and work with others for the common good.

3. *Creative Collaboration:* In the emerging culture, the gospel must lead to empowerment—not the traditional concept of seizing and wielding power over others, but rather discovering power with others to address our common threats and to seek the common good. It's not enough to stop others ("liberals" or "progressives") from doing harm; they want to work creatively with others to do what is good, beautiful, true, and necessary.

In my travels, I constantly encounter not only young adults for whom 3-N Christianity has become unacceptable, but also older adults, including surprising numbers of pastors. They frequently speak to me of "the machine" and "the system" that they have lost confidence in. Joining it, supporting it, or even reforming it are not options for them.

Rather, these creative collaborators seek an escape from this system and an alternative to it. For some, the only alternative is to leave the Christian faith entirely. Every expression of the Christian faith in their experience is hostile to an ethos they could hold in good conscience. Some become faith-hostile, and others join the ranks of the spiritual but not religious.

Some continue to show up at conventional churches, enjoying what they can and enduring the rest, but they will never be fully engaged "true believers" in the way their parents were...unless substantial change comes. They simply ignore "the machine" and "the system" and explore ways of life that seem to them authentic, honest, and faithful, nourished in their search by Web sites, books, podcasts, conferences, cohorts, and small groups. Some of them gravitate away from 3-N evangelicalism and Roman Catholicism to find a home in mainline Protestant, progressive Catholic, new monastic, and emergent communities. Others simply try to "live it," foregoing involvement in traditional congregational life entirely, forming circles of friends among whom their questions can be asked, their dissatisfactions acknowledged, and their hopes explored.

These dynamics are especially evident in evangelicalism, my own heritage. I dare to hope that there could be, within the bounds of traditional evangelicalism, some space for the disillusioned and disaffected to rekindle hope. But I see little evidence that sufficient space will be opened up, at least not before several more generations are lost to the movement. Most evangelical gatekeepers in media centers such as *Christianity Today*, CBN,

TBN, Salem Radio, and Moody Radio are temperamentally and historically connected to the conservative wing. The best they can do is support updated revivals of their conventional ethos, embodied in groups such as the neo-Reformed.

Even if a few are personally sympathetic to change (often because their own children and grandchildren have left the evangelical community), they are nearly always afraid of offending those to their right who wield advertising and donor clout. With much to lose by being labeled "liberal" and much to gain by retaining the conservative label, few leaders show the courage to speak out about the stranglehold the nostalgic, nativist, negative wing has on the movement. The only way they can resist extreme voices to their right is to paint voices to their left as equally extreme. They can thus take the posture of being moderates or centrists, but their moderate center becomes smaller and less robust the more it drives away its more progressive voices and defers to its most conservative wing. Because this so-called center can only welcome those deemed acceptable by the right wing, it is in truth neither moderate nor a center.

Evangelical colleges and seminaries are especially conflicted in this environment. Their mission sensitizes them to the struggles and needs of young people, but their funding depends on older people. Often, the better job they do in exposing their young charges to a more hopeful, diverse, and creative vision of the faith, the less their charges will feel at home in their parents' churches after graduation. Youth and mission organizations face similar struggles.[6]

Groups within evangelicalism that challenge the status quo hold promise in creating and defending an alternative space for a "minority report" among evangelicals—building an ethos characterized less by the three N's and more by hope, diversity, and creative collaboration.[7] As an alternative space, these groups do not claim to represent the majority in the present, nor do they present themselves as a moderate center of power. Rather, they occupy a leading edge—which is necessarily a marginal rather than central space. From that marginal space they advocate for a future that is different from both the nostalgic past and the embattled present.

One question these groups will face is whom they will seek as their partners. If they only seek partners among identified evangelicals, their influence will only be able to build very slowly, since the majority of evangelicals are deeply committed to their current ethos, and change is seen as infidelity to God. But if these groups seek partnership with others who share their commitment to hope, diversity, and creative collaboration, then their partnership could quickly expand. That partnership could include mainline

Protestants, Roman Catholics, Eastern Orthodox, members of the historic peace churches, and many ethnic churches that have never felt fully welcome within traditional evangelicalism. This would shift the term "evangelical" away from its more popular sense—meaning a socially, theologically, and politically conservative demographic—and would reclaim its more historic sense—that is, rooted in the gospel or evangel of Jesus Christ.

Exciting partnerships are indeed forming—around Jesus and his gospel of the reign or commonwealth of God. These energetic ventures include established groups such as Sojourners and Evangelicals for Social Action, along with newer groups such as Red-Letter Christians, the emergent/emerging church conversations, the missional movement, the new monastics, the Wild Goose Festival, and many others. It remains unlikely that these partnerships will take the form of traditional modern/colonial-era institutions with their hierarchies, their rules of order, and their clear and well-guarded boundaries and borders. They will more likely mirror the networked world of the Internet, where power is decentralized, where assets are open-sourced, where borders and boundaries are blurry and intentionally porous, and where rapid change is expected, not resisted.

Eventually, networks and movements leave their mark on institutions. But institutional change is slow, and so in our dynamic context, there is likely to be more volatility and fragmentation before a new coherence emerges.

If we are truly centered on the living Jesus and his dynamic "new-wine" gospel, we are not bound by the grim determinism of current trends projected into the future. The future for us is not a predestined inevitability that we must resign ourselves to. It is, rather, a possibility that we can participate in creating. So, whatever the status quo, we draw strength for today and bright hope for tomorrow from the great and liberating faithfulness of God. Empowered by that strength and hope, what new coherence might emerge through new creative partnerships in these challenging times? The voices in this book are among the best people, I believe, to answer that question.

2

Where the Church Went Wrong

Steven Martin

Then Peter got down out of the boat, walked on the water and came toward Jesus. But when he saw the wind, he was afraid and, beginning to sink, cried out, "Lord, save me!" Immediately Jesus reached out his hand and caught him. "You of little faith," he said, "why did you doubt?" (Mt. 14:29–31)

For most of my life a recurring nightmare has plagued me. It comes in two versions. In one I am back in college, living a carefree existence. Suddenly, I dreadfully realize I had signed up for one class but had forgotten to attend every day since the beginning of the term—and an exam is coming up! Not only have I not studied for it, I've never attended a single lecture. Panic sets in, and then I wake up.

Another version of that dream involves, well, a day back in elementary school. I realize I forgot to put on an important article of clothing. Yes, you guessed it. It's usually something pretty significant—like pants. I call this dream "the unprepared dream." Some exercise of my subconscious confesses that I'm woefully unprepared for something going on in my life. I have had this sensation often, and I'm wondering if you've had it too.

That same panicked feeling engulfs me when I compare the life of the modern-day church to the biblical vision of Jesus with his disciples. Too often my experience in worship echoes Jeremiah's complaint: "They dress the wound of my people / as though it were not serious. / 'Peace, peace,' they say, / when there is no peace" (Jer. 6:14). Something is missing—some note no one is hitting.

Newcomers to the faith notice it easily. Even lifelong Christians are aware that something is wrong. One senses a disconnect. On the one hand stands the deeply inspiring, powerful vision of the church in the book of

Acts. On the other hand we have life in the church as we know it today. *Here* Jesus teaches, heals, exorcizes, and calms the storms at the shores of the Galilean Lake. *There* sits…the church we know. At best, even in the most vibrant congregations, one cannot escape the feeling that something is not as it should be. At worst, the church is, and has been, full of downright evil.

Where did it go wrong? Where did the church take a detour that led it to where it is today? In this chapter we will look the problem of a broken church straight in the eye—its causes and its effects. Facing this reality is difficult, and we ask you to face it with courage and with hope. The church continues to be, and always will be, the very Bride of Christ. The marriage bond between Jesus and his church is strong, but one partner has remained faithful while the other has not.

You face the temptation to skip over this chapter, to move on to more inspiring, motivating material. Before you do so, understand that the thoughts expressed here will add to the background necessary to understand our call to a radically better church, one able to learn from the past and move courageously into the future. In facing the dark, we are able to see the flicker of light more clearly. That light is the hope that the kingdom of God can be experienced in the life of the Christian congregation.

The Church as Followers of Jesus

I often sit in my comfortable living room chair on Sunday mornings trying to decide if attending worship is going to be worth all the hassle. Should I wake the kids, or should I let them sleep? My coffee is warm, and the house is quiet. Will the act of disturbing this peaceful moment pay off in spiritual benefits if I load the family into the van and head to Sunday morning worship? Will I be led on a great adventure if I join with my sisters and brothers for worship, or will I be left hungry, unfed, longing for nourishment? I'm sure you've struggled with this question from time to time.

It's hard to imagine Paul contemplating this dilemma as he languished in prison for three years. Or Esther as she put her life on the line for her people. Or Jairus as he watched his daughter come back to him. The Bible supplies us a vision of life as it should be: not as a list of do's and don'ts; or as advice on raising kids, making investments, or carrying on with daily life. The Bible offers a life deeply infused with the holy, miracle-filled life found when we follow Jesus with reckless abandon.

We evangelicals have often been found guilty of drifting off-message. Let's face it: it's easier to trade "blessed are you who are poor" (Lk. 6:20) for the Prosperity Gospel, or "'Truly I tell you, whatever you did for one of the least of these brothers and sisters of mine, you did for me'" (Mt. 25:40) for elaborate end-time theories. The Prosperity Gospel fuels our dreams of living like the Kardashians (however dismal that may be), and end-times theories make for better late-night reading. In a world in which it is very difficult to "love your enemies" and "consider the lilies of the field," it's easier to base one's life around convoluted, mind-bending, counterintuitive theologies than to simply do what Jesus calls us to do.

My proposition is this: *to follow Jesus is to routinely, intentionally do what the world deems impossible.* One of the most amazing gifts of my United Methodist heritage comes in the second of three questions asked at baptism: "Do you accept the freedom and the power God gives you to resist evil, oppression, and injustice in whatever forms they present themselves?" Impossible. Everyone knows that resisting evil, oppression, and injustice will get you killed (in one form or another). We rarely fear death, yet we bargain away Jesus because of all the little "deaths" we imagine we might suffer. But look at the beautiful language used in this vow: consider the words, "accept," "freedom," and "power." To resist the power of darkness and evil in the world is not an achievement, ability, or the product of training. God's power to resist evil is a gift. It might be *the* gift. It's available freely to all who reach for it. Reaching for it will certainly require death, or at least a lot of little "deaths." That's okay, for the promise of resurrection awaits.

Which Side Are We On?

The church has consistently made choices through the centuries, sometimes uncritically, to side with worldly forms of power instead of God's power. The beleaguered early church, after suffering decades of soul-crushing persecution, welcomed Constantine's decree that Christianity would rise to dominance in the Roman Empire. Bishops suddenly lost their status as fugitives and became respected members of the imperial court. Worshipers abandoned their clandestine house church assemblies and built marvelous basilicas. The shift was as fundamental to the substance and practice of the faith as it could possibly be.

In this context, isn't it fascinating that the Apostles' Creed skips over Jesus' life and teachings completely? "Born of the Virgin Mary, suffered under Pontius Pilate…" When Jesus' whole life is a critique of power, religious authority, and occupation, how can that life be properly institutionalized into an empire concerned with armies, borders, security, uniformity, and public welfare? It becomes much more convenient to squabble over trinitarian theologies and the presence of Christ in the sacraments than to disciple a church that follows the Sermon on the Mount.

The seduction of the church by Constantine has brought some of Christendom's greatest glories, but also its deepest horrors. Catalogues of the church's failings always include the Crusades and the Inquisition. For this author, the most formative set of questions arose in the midst of making three films on the role of the church in the rise of Hitler and Nazism, and ultimately in the Holocaust. This twelve-year period has become a plumb line in history, a demarcation between the past and the future that forever demands a refocusing of the church's energies toward following Jesus rather than Constantine and his disciples. As Dietrich Bonhoeffer remarked in 1934, "National Socialism has brought an end to the church in Germany."[1] Perhaps Bonhoeffer's words were more universal than once thought.

The End of the Church: Nazi Germany

Paul Althaus was a professor in the small Bavarian town of Erlangen. Althaus was the most widely published interpreter of the life and works of Martin Luther, the great reformer of the church; it is difficult to read Luther today without doing so through the lens of Althaus's formidable work. He served as a pastor in Lodz, Poland, during the difficult years following World War I. His preaching during that time reflects the agony and soul-searching of so many in the years following Germany's humiliation: he saw his nation's loss as its crucifixion and longed for its resurrection as a great world power.

In 1933 Althaus saw that resurrection in Adolf Hitler and the ascension of the Nazi party to power. In a widely distributed booklet in Erlangen, Althaus proclaimed: "We Protestants have seen the turning year of 1933 as a gift and miracle of God." He went on in this tract to praise the "renewal" of Germany under Hitler as exactly the resurrection he was looking for. Althaus saw Hitler as a new Luther, a great German who would reform the church and nation and put her back on the stage as a world power.

Karl Themel was a pastor in Berlin when the Nazis came to power. He joined the Nazi party one year before Hitler became Chancellor and was looking forward to the changes that would come under his leadership. Soon after Hitler's rise, Themel's old friend, Ludwig Müller, was appointed Reichsbishop. Themel quickly realized the benefits of being on the right side of power. One of these benefits was to receive an appointment to a prestigious position within the Berlin church. He had arrived, using political friendships and connections to further his career. He was a man of power and purpose.

In the tumultuous years of 1933 and 1934, the political winds were not always in Themel's favor. Soon his friend, Reichsbishop Ludwig Müller, found himself sidetracked by a government that no longer needed the church's good favor. As a result Themel lost his prestigious position, and quickly went looking for a way to write himself back into power. He had a few extraordinary skills: he was a gifted administrator and organizer, he understood the kind of information kept in church records, and he completely identified with the Nazi ideology. He knew he could be useful to the Nazi government, which was growing more powerful every day.

Themel knew that church baptismal records held secrets that, if uncovered, would be pleasing to Nazi officials. According to newly enacted laws, if a person had Jewish grandparents, baptism did not make them into non-Jews. Themel organized an office, with the church's blessing, that would organize the information contained in hundreds of thousands of baptismal certificates. Over the course of several years he did so, identifying thousands of baptized Christians living in the areas surrounding Berlin as having Jewish racial heritage. Themel handed this information over to a powerful friend in the Nazi SS, and over 2,700 people went to the camps as a result.

Themel failed his denazification trial in 1945. He was banned from service in any German churches until the mid-1950s, when he resumed pastoral service. He never renounced his Nazi views and set about reconnecting with colleagues. Themel labored unsuccessfully to produce works that would defend his racist positions as the product of the true Protestantism.

Gerhard Kittel was the son of Rudolf Kittel, a world-renowned figure in Hebrew Bible scholarship. His own fame and importance grew as he became a professor at the prestigious University of Tübingen. Editing the *Theological Dictionary of the New Testament*, a work still in wide use today, he became the world's leading authority on the Jewish background of the New Testament.

In 1933 Kittel gave a speech entitled, "Die Jüdenfrauge," or "The Jewish Question." In this speech, published widely in the months after it was given, Kittel spoke to the popular concept that Jews were behind everything bad happening in Germany. Kittel suggested steps that could be taken to "solve" this "question." One solution would be to deport all Jews to the East, where they could live together and reform themselves into a renewed and vital community. Another would be for Jews to assimilate into German society, but that was not a viable option because this was the cause of the "Jewish problem" itself. Another solution, he said, would be to exterminate all of the Jews everywhere. But this, he said, was not an option, for it was impractical—it had been tried before, and had never worked.

For his expertise and reputation, Kittel was employed by the Nazi Reich as a founding member of the "Research Section on the Jewish Question," a committee charged with forming the theological rationale for the elimination of Jewish life in Europe. Functioning in various capacities, he stayed a part of this committee through the entire Third Reich, even when the intentions of the Reich were revealed in November 1938 in the event euphemistically known as "Kristallnacht," or the "Night of Broken Glass."

Captured by French forces in 1945, Kittel was imprisoned as a war criminal and died humiliated and broken just a few months after.

Why this dreadful litany of horrors? Because these brief biographies illustrate the dramatic failures of a church that sides with power rather than with Jesus. These well-known figures were pious Christians who read the Bible, prayed at meals, held family devotions, served their churches, attended worship, and upheld their communities. They carried the marks of the redeemed in ways socially acceptable in their time. But they committed horrific crimes: Althaus, using his formidable voice to proclaim that God's work in the world was manifest in the rise of Adolf Hitler; Themel, using baptism as a weapon of fear and death against the vulnerable; and Kittel, using his intellect and reputation to turn the goodness of Christian faith against an imagined enemy.

I also believe these biographies should not be surprising to us. What are we to expect from a church that, for over 1700 years, has found its home with Caesar rather than with Jesus? As we read these stories and seek to learn from them, I hope they will instill in us what they have provoked in me: a sense of urgency about building a new kind of Christianity, one that reflects the whole of the gospel instead of one that reflects the world.

Water-Walking and Christian Living

I offer this proposal: *the basis for Christian life is the act of following Jesus.*

To this point, let us lift out of the gospels a story that has always been central, if not profoundly puzzling, to many of us: the story of Peter and his journey out of the boat and onto the water.

The disciples are out on the Sea of Galilee in their boat in the early morning hours. A high wind has whipped up the sea. Jesus takes a stroll on the water, and Peter asks to join him. It's a simple tale told in Sunday School classes across the world. Deceptively simple.

For some this is a cute story, a clever (and unbelievable) miracle. Christians through the centuries have found this story so unbelievable that we have either confined it to the realm of art or dismissed it altogether. English architect John Nelson Darby (1800–1882) used stories like this to construct his theology of Dispensationalism, so problematic for the church and world today: God *must* deal with human beings in different ways in different ages ("dispensations"), for miracles like these surely never take place today.

My premise is that such miracles surely *do* take place today, and the loss of this insight is at the core of what's missing from the adventure of Christian living! In fact, to settle for a life in which we are incapable of leaving the boat to step out on the water is to deny the very power of Christ himself. Assignment of the ability to walk on water to a specific time in history when God so empowered humans, but no longer does so, lies at the root of the modern church's pessimism and hopelessness. Loss of this water-walking narrative is the basis for the church's inability to meet the challenges of the present and future. Recovery of it could fuel a remarkable future.

Peter's walk on water was a micro-experiment in what Jesus did in macro: he faced the impossible and put his body on the line. Peter saw in Jesus how powerful life could be, and he had the courage to believe he could have that life for himself. The only thing that stood between his life and that of Jesus was the boat! No one could blame him if he wanted to stay in the boat. After all, the wind was blowing, the waves were crashing, and to get out of the safety of the boat would mean disaster for him and for the gospel itself! (What would readers think if Peter, "the Rock," died or disappeared in the middle of the narrative?) To stay in the boat would have been the perfectly natural, normal choice.

Then, like today, loving your enemy could get you killed (paradoxically, not by the enemy but by your "friends"). Turning the other cheek could only get you further humiliated than you already are. Hanging out with lepers, tax collectors, and prostitutes would not help your social standing and your ability to earn a healthy living for yourself and those who depend on you. No one would blame you if you followed a more conventional, in-the-boat lifestyle. Do you see how the boat symbolizes the world in which we live, and the water the treacherous, difficult, risky life of following Jesus in the kingdom of God?

Yes, Peter sank in that water. It happens. But he got back on top again. Yes, Jesus died an agonizing death for challenging life in the metaphorical "boat" and demonstrating the necessity of doing so. Let's be clear: Jesus didn't live forevermore after dying from old age or getting killed in an accident. He was executed for demonstrating the power inherent in a completely truthful life, and received life again because his life was based in truth, and his life *is* truth uncompromised.

To follow Jesus, then, is to live truthfully, with the knowledge that to do so means to get out of the boat and walk on the water. This is what it means to accept Jesus as Lord and Savior: to accept Jesus as Lord is to follow and obey him. To accept Jesus as Savior is to know that when we follow him, he will rescue us. "Blessed are those who persevere under trial, because when they have stood the test, they will receive the crown of life that God has promised to those who love him" (Jas. 1:12). Where did the church go wrong? When it stopped teaching people to walk on water?[2]

3

A Disenchanted Text: Where Evangelicals Went Wrong with the Bible

Cheryl Bridges Johns

Christianity in the United States is no longer a "Scripture haunted landscape."

The Bible is a book that continues to sell well, but fewer and fewer people are bothering to read any one of the many versions they own.[1] Ignorance about basic Bible stories is commonplace, and it seems that these days no one loses sleep over the Bible. Americans, in the words of Gary Burge, "are in danger of losing the imaginative and linguistic world of the Bible."[2]

In 1970, James Smart described, "The Strange Silence of the Bible."[3] He warned that "the voice of Scripture is falling silent in the preaching and teaching of the church and in the consciousness of Christian people, a silence that is perceptible even among those who are most insistent upon their devotion to the Scriptures."[4] In 1970 the silence of the Bible was a worrisome issue; in 2012 that silence is deafening. Even among evangelicals—those who are most insistent upon their devotion to the Scriptures—the rate of biblical illiteracy continues to climb. And as biblical illiteracy climbs, evangelicals are failing to realize that the problem does not lie primarily with people who do not read the Bible. The problem rests with the *way* evangelicals read the Bible.

The modern version of the Bible, be it evangelical or mainline, is one that offers little power to enchant the lives of people. It is a text that has ceased to be, in the practices of the Christian church, the lively oracles of God. Therefore, it should not be surprising that people do not read this sacred text. Furthermore, we should stop making them feel guilty for this neglect.

The modern version of the Bible—the Bible as it is conceived in modernity—is quite different from the Bible of generations ago. Even the words we use to speak of Scripture reveal this disparity. Words such as

17

"holy," "sacred," "mysterious," are long gone from our vocabulary. Instead, evangelicals use words such as "inerrant," "factual," or "principles." More liberal-minded Christians use other words such as "historical," or "myth." In both camps our language reveals that our understanding of the Bible suffers from an acute case of "Enchantment Deficit Disorder." As naturalized citizens of the modern era, we are all carriers of this disease. The symptoms are everywhere—an intense craving for mystery and wonder but an equally intense skepticism of the supernatural, a severe lack of sacred spaces in both public and private life, and the disappearance of sacred words.

The disenchantment of Christianity is a result of Protestantism's long love affair with the Enlightenment project. Max Weber, in his astute study of the rise of the modern world, was one of the first to note the close connection between Protestantism and the fate of "rationalization and disenchantment." "The fate of our times," observed Weber in an address to science students at Munich University in 1918, "is characterized by rationalization, and above all, by the disenchantment of the world."[5] Weber went on to warn students that joining the modern world meant that they should be willing to bear this burden of disenchantment, letting go of magical beliefs and superstition. If they could not do these things, noted Weber, they could quietly go away from the university and back to where "the arms of the old churches were willing to take them."[6]

In 1918 no rational person wanted to be found in the arms of the old churches where superstition and magical thinking prevailed. Many people were more than willing to bear the burden of disenchantment for the trade-off of progressive science. Throughout the twentieth century the message was quite clear: one has to let go of superstitious faith to fit in with the modern project. During the twentieth century many university students heard (and heeded) this warning.

Protestants, in particular, having broken with the old churches and their magical view of nature, helped fuel the turn to rationalization. Furthermore, they helped the world make the great ontological turn to the human subject. What a turn! The rational power of the individual became a hallmark of Protestantism as well as modernity. Corresponding to this turn, there was the objectification of the world and everything in it. Following course, the objectification of the world became a Protestant agenda as much as a modern agenda. This dual move—the turn to the human subject and the objectification of the world—sealed the fate of the Bible.

Scholars of the Bible were more than willing to bear the burdens of rationalization and disenchantment. In their quest to be scientific, liberal Protestants turned to the higher criticism offered in the German universities.

The German model emphasized a "neutral scrupulous objectivity," and a "commitment to science" in organic (naturalistic) evolutionary terms.[7] In this context, the Scriptures came to be understood as historical human documents. These documents could be studied in order to gain a better view of the layers and contours of history.

Many conservative Protestants were just as determined as liberals to be scientific. Instead of the German model of science, they chose the earlier Baconian model that stressed nature itself as a model for science. Known as "Common Sense Realism," this form of thinking argued that the world could be known directly, and through careful observation it could be studied. It was a system of "self-evident first principles." These principles, such as the existence of God, are the starting point from which all other knowledge would be built.

The new science (the one the liberals followed), argued conservatives, was not a "true science." For conservatives such as Charles Hodge and B.B. Warfield, the Bible could be scientifically proven to be valid. Their logic of proof rested in the premise that in the original autographs (*autographa)*, the Bible was penned without human error. This lack of error was *scientific proof* of divine inspiration. Because the Bible was factual and without error, it was "true." Working with biblical facts, conservative biblical scholars could, like other scientists, "collect, authenticate, arrange and exhibit [these facts] in their internal relation to each other."[8]

What both liberals and conservatives of the twentieth century shared was a twofold belief: the Bible as object of scientific inquiry and the power of the human subject *over* the text. Both groups robbed the Bible of its status as having any *subjecthood*. These "scientific" approaches left no sense of the Scriptures containing real presence. Such a sacramental view belonged back with the old churches! God in the Bible was replaced with God who authored the Bible or the God who is described in the Bible. Truth was disjoined from presence, and Spirit was disjoined from Word.

Fundamentalists developed a particular distain for the enchantments of the old churches and seemed determined to erase any vestige of magical thinking. Speaking to a group of students at Columbia Seminary in 1918 (the same year that Weber gave his lecture to the students at Munich University), Warfield warned the students of the old churches that were so little instructed in the "true forces of nature."[9] In other words, the old churches were nonscientific and superstitious. Warfield also warned the students regarding the "new churches" that were offering another updated version of superstitious faith. For Warfield, the fledging Pentecostal movement, just like Roman Catholicism, was an example of "counterfeit Christianity."

In the minds of the fundamentalists, Christianity needed no mystery or miracles. Those things were taken back to heaven when Jesus ascended. The apostles (who retained some vestiges of the miracles) gave the church a perfect historical witness to the ministry of Jesus. This Bible was factual and accurate. The role of the modern reader was to accept the factual record, believe it, and follow its precepts. Human reason guided the reader to note the truth of the Scriptures, and reason led people to believe in the God of these truths. Faith, in this paradigm, was part of a respectable package. It had a rational quality to it that was in line with "the true forces of nature."

Such a strange irony! The fundamentalist doctrine of Scripture developed in the early part of the twentieth century resulted in a *very low view of the Bible*! It was a low understanding because the Scriptures were reduced to history and removed from the life of God and the economy of God's mission in the world.

The ferment of the 1940s and the emergence of the National Association of Evangelicals provided opportunity to revisit the doctrine of Scripture. Pentecostals were brought into the mix, but they were looked upon with suspicion for "putting experience over Scripture." Anxious to gain acceptance, this group did nothing to defend their pneumatic reading of the text. In fact, many Pentecostals went to great lengths to adopt a fundamentalist reading of the Bible. It was an ill-fitted arrangement, but they made it work.

From the beginning evangelicals went wrong on their doctrine of Scripture. Evangelical leaders and biblical scholars felt compelled to fight the Scripture wars of an earlier generation. They could not operate out of a different epistemological lens other than modernity. So, they too went to battle for the Bible.[10]

With the rise of the religious right during the 1980s, "culture warriors" emerged. Both sides of the culture wars made the other objects of derision and aversion. Each accused the other of wrongly using the Bible. James Davison Hunter, in his assessment of these battles, notes that both sides of the culture wars used the same language against the other, so that "it is nearly impossible to distinguish which of the two coalitions is speaking."[11]

Toward the end of the twentieth century, the "biblical worldview" movement came on the scene with its own idea of how to engage culture. "A biblical worldview," notes George Barna, "...is a life lens that provides a personal understanding of every idea, opportunity, and experience based on the identification and application of relevant biblical principles so that every choice we make may be consistent with God's principles and commands."[12] It means that we "think like Jesus" because thinking like Jesus means that one will act like Jesus. Jesus was able to focus on God's principles, evaluating all information and experiences "through a filter that produced appropriate choices."[13]

Biblical worldview ideology represents the height of Enlightenment thinking and modernity's emphasis upon rationalism. People are primarily "thinking beings" who operate out of information and principles. In fact, in the biblical worldview camp Jesus was primarily led by his power of reason and his ability to draw from his biblical foundation that was "clear, reliable and accessible."[14] Jesus was the ultimate Thinking Being. His Bible was a list of clear principles.

Barna notes that when Jesus was instructing his disciples, "He would anchor his teaching to core scriptural principles."[15] Barna fails to realize that his Jesus is more Greek than biblical. Barna fails to understand how the Bible is much more than a repository of principles and commands. No wonder the biblical worldview camp does little to combat biblical illiteracy! Really, who would want to read *this* Bible or follow *this* Jesus?

Now, in the early years of the twenty-first century, after years of battling for the Bible, battling with the Bible, and engaging in a war with culture, Christians find themselves not only alienated from the Bible but also alienated from their own children. The strident rhetoric of the culture wars has created a wave of refugees. These young people are fleeing the killing fields of the churches and denominations in growing numbers. They are "post-evangelical" or "post-fundamentalist," "emergents" or the "spiritual but not religious."

Some of these refugees have their Bibles with them and are searching for new ways to read this text. They are looking for what Tim Conder and Daniel Rhodes, pastors at the Emmaus Way Church, describe as "a textual hermeneutic that moves beyond the trench lines and polarizations of the mainline/evangelical cold war."[16] Others have abandoned their Bibles, equating Scripture with the culture from which they are fleeing.

Many of these refugees are biblically illiterate. They are what Phyllis Tickle calls "scriptural innocents." Tickle makes the point that this new generation's lack of knowledge of Scripture pushes them in one of two directions. "Either innocence of scriptural experience is propelling them to seek ever more eagerly for structural engagement with it, or else a total lack of prior exposure is propelling Scripture itself farther and farther into the attics of life where all antiques are stored for a respectful period of time before being thrown completely away."[17] For Tickle, either situation has the possibility of danger, for "naifs of every kind are vulnerable at every turn... easily exploited, easily crippled, easily sacrificed."[18]

Deep inside most of these young adults is a hunger for enchantment. They are the generation that devoured Harry Potter, Tolkien, and the *Vampire Diaries*. They seek what the ancient Christians called the *mysterion*, the ever-widening mystery of Christ that beckoned believers into the life of God.

Now, the time is ripe for revisiting the doctrine of Scripture. It is time to stop talking about biblical worldviews and making people feel guilty for not reading the Bible. While modern translations may prove helpful to some, we do not need one more biblical translation that is "accessible to the modern reader." Evangelicals do not need to get back to the Bible; they need to get back to God in the Bible. This move calls for a major ontological turn and a radical reorienting of ourselves, the Bible, and the world in which we live. Everything must change.

Reclaiming Holy Scripture

The identity "Christian" will continue in the land that lies ahead; but unless the Bible is reclaimed as Holy Scripture, "Christian" will cease to reference a biblical religion. Evangelicalism, in particular, will fall prey to what James Smart called "the cultural subversion of the biblical faith."[19] We are a long way down the road toward this subversion of the biblical faith. Evangelicals are more and more associated with a particular political ideology, rather than a particular theological belief. We have become people of culture rather than a people of "The Book."

Many young evangelicals are seeking to read the Bible in a new way. Rejecting the foundationalism of a previous generation, they seem to be moving toward viewing the Bible as a catechetical, community-forming text that frames the world with meaning. What they do not want is a text that reduces the Bible into propositional truths. Conder and Rhodes make clear that they are rejecting "a foundationalism that holds the possibility of a sacred, abstract Bible—a Bible that can exist as God's Word apart from the people to whom it was revealed as a gift is shaky ground."[20] For them, "The Bible, identified and received as a loving word, demands the presence of faithful community to interpret and embody the texts."[21]

John McClure identifies the Bible within the post-foundational communities as being "primarily centrifugal; it pulls those within its orbit inward—inculturating, shaping, forming and constructing identity."[22] This communitarian approach to reading the Bible has many strengths. First, it removes the Bible from the hands of the so-called experts and brings it back into the hands of the people. Second, a communal reading of the text acknowledges the presence of God in and among the people of God. Third, communities are better able to discern how the Bible speaks directly to their particular cultural context.

However, within the post-foundational reading of the Bible lies a haunting missing element: namely, the Bible as Holy Scripture. The community retains the modernist vision of the human subject as over the text and as the final arbitrator of truth. Instead of there being one subject, now we have a community of subjects. The text continues to be the object, and we the people retain our modernist right to be the subjects in control. In other words, many of the young want to journey with the Bible, but do not want to be deconstructed by the Bible. Actually, they have seen no model of deconstruction. Their parents had already tamed the Bible.

Literary theorist Wesley Kort points out that while the non-foundational approach to reading the Bible appears as a good alternative to a propositional reading, this reading does not fully appreciate the true theological gift that Scripture offers to human communities. That gift is the "movement away from self and world toward their divestment and abjection."[23] In other words, reading the Bible should be an act of deconstruction.

Deconstruction reasserts the Bible *as Scripture*. It frames the text in a manner that the reader recognizes "the distance and the uncertainty that always exist between the reader and the saving knowledge that may be received in and by reading scripture."[24] Kort asserts: "Where there is no question that reading can always be dominated by already formulated cognitive and institutional conclusions, it is precisely the possibility of delivery from such domination that reading the Bible as scripture holds out."[25]

Kort points in a direction of reading the Bible in which the human subject(s) read as an act of radical dislocation and divestment of position and identity. This type of reading stands in stark contrast to how the Bible has been read in modernity and in postmodernity. McClure makes a good point when he observes that "the tension between reading the Bible in order to foster identity and reading the Bible as subversive of identity cannot be easily resolved."[26] The Bible is a text that helps shape communal identity. In this sense, Conder and Rhodes' understanding of the Bible as a community-forming text is helpful. On the other hand, "*As scripture* the Bible refuses over and over again to close itself as a book, to secure its connotations to a single self-referential tautology."[27] In the end, a post-foundational reading of the Bible does little to re-enchant the text. It gives to the community a power that it does not rightfully have, namely the power of "Word." At best, a communal reading of the text can testify and point to the Word. In the end, however, the community has a secondary, interpretative role.

Most people hunger for a biblical Word that is more powerful, more mysterious, and more transformative that the one being offered by either those in the older propositional camp or those in the post-foundational camp. This hunger goes across the board. It is not a liberal hunger or a particularly evangelical hunger. Beyond the trenches of the culture wars, somewhere in the margins, I believe we can discover a Word that will feed us all.

In light of the above assessment, I want to offer a Pentecostal reading of the text as a way of moving forward. This hermeneutic is derived from a confessional Pentecostal stance, but in itself is not uniquely Pentecostal. I understand Pentecost as the Great Feast of the church catholic. Its ongoing fruit does not belong to any particular faith confession.

The Feast of Pentecost not only offers humanity a new vision for community and empowerment, but it also brings something else: a fund of knowledge that is held within the embrace of the Holy Spirit. This fund of knowledge leads to all truth. It is not tied to some domesticated form of "inspiration," but comes to us in the full force of revelation of the Triune God. As John Webster notes, "God's revelation is God's spiritual presence. God is the personal subject of the act of revelation, and therefore revelation can in no way be commodified."[28]

Moderns have so commodified the Bible that we have forgotten that revelation brings us the very presence of God and not merely teachings about God. We have forgotten what it means to be afraid. We have so objectified the biblical text that we do not recognize our own position as object under the Word of God. Therefore, we believe that it is possible to promote truth about God without realizing that God's truth and God's presence are a package deal. We believe that the truth we are somehow promoting can be neatly packaged, arranged, and presented in a form that is easy to manipulate.

Because we are not afraid, we have failed to discern God's economy of salvation as it extends into creation and as it intersects into the lives of the marginal. The deconstructive power of the Scriptures brings grace and judgment into the world, beginning first with the people of God.

If the Holy Spirit is "God's outreach to the creature, and also the way back to God (Eph 2:18),"[29] then pneumatology becomes central to discussions of Scripture. I agree with Webster, who says that the primary ontology of Scripture is "defined out of the formative economy of the Spirit of God."[30] The modern Bible divorced Spirit and Word, making the Bible a static entity that was starkly separate from God's life. As evangelicals revisit the Bible, we will have to give it back over to the Holy Spirit. That will be hard going for most of us, for we are used to our role as the subject over the text.

The modern project has emphasized the agency of humankind. Now is the time to see how this agency has led to control, domination, and the commodification of life. Submitting to the agency of the Holy Spirit means that we give up control and allow, as did Jesus, the Spirit to drive us toward proclaiming a full, liberating gospel: "The Spirit of the Lord is on me because he has anointed me to proclaim good news to the poor..." (Lk. 4:18).

What would happen if evangelicals began to read the Bible in the presence of God? First, I believe it would mean that we would stop judging the world and begin to judge ourselves. Actually, we could currently use some deconstruction. We need some tearing down and an infusion of humility.

Second, conviction would fall upon us for our failings to follow the gospel. We would begin to see how selectively we read the Bible and how we use it for our own agendas.

Third, courage would infuse us as we came to fear God above all else. We would not fear cultural marginality that always comes when you begin to dance with the Spirit. This courage would give us the ability to stand for those who cannot stand for themselves. We would answer Steve Martin's invitation to "walk on water."

Pardon my Pentecostal musing, but I long to be part of an evangelical revival of the Word of God. I long to hear people weep when the Scriptures are read. I long to tremble as the Word of God dances over the congregation, and I long to hear the poor find voice and proclaim a God who scatters the proud, drags strong rulers from their thrones, and puts humble people in places of power (Lk. 1:51–52). I long to see the Holy Spirit using the Word to sweep us into the ecstatic life of God. Then, and only then, I believe, will we cease to be a cultural entity and truly be those who proclaim the *evangelion*, the good news of the gospel.

4

My Journey toward the "New Evangelicalism"

Richard Cizik

If you've never changed your mind about something, you may be dead. Spiritually, intellectually, and even politically, if new facts and realities don't ever prompt you to alter your way of thinking, you might as well be dead. To not learn and change, especially spiritually, is a form of death.

But change is hard. It's also risky.

I know about the consequences of changing one's thinking. I was fired from my position as Vice-President for Governmental Relations of the National Association of Evangelicals. That's right, I was asked to resign for comments made on a nationally syndicated radio show called "Fresh Air." I provided too much "fresh air" for my bosses to handle. Officially, I was asked to resign. But the reality is that I was fired.

This event devastated me and my family. We were shocked that such a drastic action had been taken. "Please have your office cleared out within a few days"—these were my instructions. That wasn't an easy thing to do. I had worked for the Association since 1980, and this was 2008. So, for twenty-eight years I had faithfully represented the organization, the last ten as Vice President. I loved it and the people I had worked with.

Being axed in such a fashion proved hard. As if to dramatize their dissatisfaction, my "going away" severance was three months of salary. It was a clear message: please, just go away. Or as one editor wrote: "Evangelicals, one surmises, aren't always against divorce."

I was heartbroken. The nation's newspapers, including *The Washington Post* and *The New York Times*, as well as small dailies such as my hometown *Free Lance-Star*, ran stories with these headlines: "Evangelical Leader Quits Over Gay Union Remark," and "Truth Breaks a Fall."

In a broad-ranging conversation about my work to educate my fellow evangelicals about the impacts of climate change, I told Terry Gross, the host of NPR's "Fresh Air," that I could support "civil unions" for gays and lesbians and that government funding of contraception was morally acceptable as a way to avoid abortion.

Perhaps most offensive to the board of the National Association of Evangelicals, which had given speaking platforms for Republican candidates for the presidency going back to Ronald Reagan, and whose officials I had joined for election campaigns for these Republican candidates, was that I said I had voted for candidate Barack Obama in the Virginia primary (against Hillary Clinton) for the presidency. Implied, of course, was that I had voted for Obama in the general election of 2008. And Barack Obama is a Democrat.

The impacts were felt personally and professionally. It prompted the president of Houghton College to write and cancel my graduation speech. It prompted Denver Seminary, where I had graduated, to drop me from the Advisory Board of the Grounds Institute of Public Ethics. It prompted the head of a family ministry, Marriage Savers, which I had served as a board member, to call me and tell me, "We're dropping you from the board of directors."

Sadly, it prompted friends and colleagues to shun me and no longer inquire about my health and well-being. Even our friends from church, where we had attended faithfully for a decade, didn't understand.

A poll by America On Line (AOL) asked its readers to weigh in on this question: "Did the National Association of Evangelicals do the right thing in firing Richard Cizik?" Nearly 50,000 cast ballots. By a slim majority the consensus was "yes."

So who's to blame? I had lived on the edge of American evangelicalism, speaking out on the need to broaden the movement's agenda to include issues such as climate change, and, if you will pardon the flat-Earth imagery, tumbled over the edge.

While I didn't represent the NAE in the interview with Bose-like fidelity, I did represent millions of evangelicals—especially the younger ones. Friends such as Dr. David Gushee at Mercer University and Katie Paris of Faith in Public Life posted a website where one hundred evangelical leaders signed a letter affirming my ministry and principles, and the need for the Association to carry on with these principles.

However, for most evangelicals who dare to differ with their fellow evangelicals over issues of politics, there's no one to come to their defense. Personal friendships or relationships are frayed, sometimes even broken.

How did this rigid political conformity happen? Sociologist Robert Putnam has argued that most evangelicals now choose their local church based upon its political views, not theology. Within the unique evangelical subculture, the prevailing beliefs are conservative. To be politically liberal, and express that viewpoint, can get you fired. Politics is the new orthodoxy.

Should the NAE be blamed? Arguably, it did what it had to do to preserve its reputation for conservative Christianity. Did it really do the right thing? What message did it send?

Inescapably, the message is this: "We are controlled and intimidated by the Religious (that is, Political) Right and will do whatever it takes to avoid their criticism."

That's why the evangelical church in America is in big trouble. It has lost its center: the Gospel. It is a movement that has been captured by conservative politics and treats that message as more important than the Gospel. It will do anything, literally anything, to maintain the conservative status quo. Throw anyone overboard. Avoid taking a stand on controversial topics, such as climate change. Even refuse to confront racism, Islamophobia, or anti-gay bigotry. No matter the heresy, or bad judgment, organizations such as the National Association of Evangelicals will choose to walk away from a controversy before they will confront the major figures of the Religious Right.

This is why I often say, "We need to put the protest back in Protestantism." Not against Catholicism as in Martin Luther's day, but on behalf of the holistic Gospel. Why do I say this? We who are evangelicals have allowed ourselves to be co-opted by a pale substitute of the real thing.

What's a "New Evangelical"?

On a bright sunny day not long after leaving my position with the NAE, I was crossing a sidewalk between the Capitol and the Cannon House Office building and ran into an old friend, Rep. Frank Wolf (R-VA). He and I had been involved in many campaigns, including anti-religious persecution.

The congressman says, "Richard, how are you and what are you doing?" I replied, "Creating the new evangelicals." To which Rep. Wolf responded, "What's wrong with the old evangelicals?"

Since we were in the middle of a busy street and the light was turning green, I replied, "Let's get together to talk about it, but it's not about one's age." He seemed relieved to hear that, smiled quizzically, and we rushed off in different directions.

So, what is a "new evangelical"? The fitting place to begin is with "the heart of the Bible, the Gospel in miniature," as Martin Luther put it. Here it is: "For God so loved the world, that he gave his only begotten son, that whosoever believeth in him should not perish, but have everlasting life" (Jn. 3:16, KJV)—probably the first verse you memorized and certainly one of the most familiar verses in all of Scripture. Sometimes you see people at televised sporting events holding up a poster with that reference on it: John 3:16. I saw it last Friday, on the back of a truck rolling down Interstate 95—"John 3:16"—as if you could do evangelism just by citing chapter and verse. But if you're going to do it, John 3:16 is not a bad verse to cite.

It wasn't even a word before Jesus came along. You could have good news, but not *the good news* until Mark entitled his Gospel *the* good news, the *evangelion,* from which we get the words *evangel, evangelism,* and *evangelical.* All of these are derived from the good news about Jesus, which brings me to my personal story or witness, as evangelicals say.

The community of faithful in America who should be about the "good news" are the evangelicals. We want to tell the story of Jesus to the whole world, but instead we have become "bad news evangelicals."

Former *Christianity Today* editor and blogger Rodney Clapp wrote about my being fired from my evangelical post. He claimed the firing revealed "conservative evangelicalism's deeply reactionary tendencies." He listed five main points:

1. The movement we call *fundamentalism* was a reaction against late nineteenth-century biblical criticism and biology.
2. These same fundamentalists later reacted against the social gospel movement so strongly that they practically ignored the Bible's teaching on caring for the poor and oppressed.
3. In the middle of the last century conservative evangelicals were galvanized by strong anti-communist sentiments, and, as a predominantly white movement, both then and now, they were slow to support civil rights for blacks.
4. In the 1970s Hal Lindsey wrote a book called *The Late Great Planet Earth,* which was at least in part a reaction against the Soviet Union, European unification, and the ecumenical movement. More recently the *Left Behind* series sought to rescue American conservative Christians from Arab terrorists, one-world government, and moral decline.
5. Aside from all that, "the evangelical media has been playing defense for years—arming the faithful against religious cults, then the New Age movement, then feminism, then secular humanism, and so on and so on."

Clapp concluded, "American evangelicalism appears to be strong. But it is in deep trouble." "It is in deep trouble," he says, "because it faces a significant cultural and generational shift. Identifying itself with the political right, the movement cannot easily shake the image of being primarily negative and destructive… Indicators show that it is losing attractiveness not only among unconverted fellow Americans but among its own young." More significantly, "evangelicalism is in deep trouble because the gospel really is good news, and reactionaries are animated by bad news, by that which they stand against."[1]

John Howard Yoder, the late evangelical scholar and pacifist, said:

> For a practice to qualify as 'evangelical' in the functional sense means first of all that it communicates news. It says something particular that would not be known and could not be believed were it not said. Second, it must mean that this 'news' is attested as good; it comes across to those whom it addresses as helping, as saving, and as shalom.[2]

So what qualities or characteristics make someone a "new evangelical"? As with all evangelicals, we are orthodox in the usual sense. We believe in (1) the authority of Scripture as the Word of God; (2) the virgin birth, saving death, and bodily resurrection of Jesus; (3) the call by our Lord to be born again; and (4) the command to share that faith with others.

But here is where the "new" parts with the "old":

First, we are committed to reaching out beyond our own constituency to be "bridge-builders" with others for the sake of the public good. Surely the culture war—and the narrow list of concerns, such as opposition to abortion and same-sex marriage that fuel this societal conflict—is a sign of the general collapse of a vision for the common good. Reaching out to scientists, for example, to address climate change is a fitting example of such bridge-building.

The old guard of American evangelicalism responded to the "Evangelical Climate Initiative" (2006) and a subsequent statement entitled "An Urgent Call to Action: Evangelicals and Scientists Unite To Protect Creation" (2007) with an *ad hominem* argument. James Dobson told his listeners on his *Focus on the Family* radio show that "Richard Cizik has an underlying hatred for America." On the *700 Club*, Pat Robertson joined in, denouncing creation care and demanding to know why "God-fearing conservatives like Richard Cizik" were teaming up with "far-left environmentalists."

These two responses to what the late Francis Schaeffer dubbed "co-belligerency" are paradigmatic of "old evangelical" thinking. In the vernacular, the religious right simply doesn't "get it." It is committed to working only with those who are in the corner by themselves. These "corner-dwellers" are doomed to fail in their misguided attempts to change public policy because they don't understand how to be bridge-builders.

Second, we are committed to not politicizing the church. "An Evangelical Manifesto" (2008) explains it this way: "The politicization of the faith is never a sign of strength but of weakness."[3] We are for vigorous dialogue within the evangelical church about what constitutes the "common good," and the pursuit of that end, but we do not want the church wracked by politics.

As Vice President for Governmental Affairs at the NAE, I assisted in drafting and then championed the whole spectrum of issues enumerated in the document "For the Health of the Nation: An Evangelical Call to Civic Engagement" (2006). You can embrace all these issues without turning them into a political cudgel that divides the church. This idea of a bigger agenda of Christian duty is not a call to politicize the body of Christ but to faithfully reflect Christ and his concerns for the whole world in all of our public engagement.[4]

These two essential characteristics of "new evangelicals" are controversial, even shocking, to millions of our fellow believers here in the United States. They regard both principles as offensive, even heretical. That's surely a sign of just how badly reform within the evangelical movement is needed.

A Moment of Truth

Now I serve as President of the New Evangelical Partnership for the Common Good (NEP). Wherever I speak now, someone always comes up to say something like: "I'd never heard of you until I was driving down the highway listening to your interview on National Public Radio. I want to commend you for your courage in speaking out."

The agenda for my ill-fated interview on "Fresh Air" focused on my views about American evangelicalism and my role as a lobbyist for the NAE. Terri Gross hosted the interview. She had been following my efforts to educate the movement on what we had begun to call "creation care," a term designed to help frame biblical truth about the need to care for the environment.

In the course of the interview Gross asked about newly elected President Barack Obama; civil unions and gay marriage; about whom I had voted for in the 2008 election; abortion reduction methods, including contraception; and a host of other topics related to evangelical advocacy and our movement's political engagement. Unbelievably, the interview cost me my career and calling of twenty-eight years with the Association.

Leading figures of the Religious Right had been attacking me for years. In 2006 the Evangelical Environmental Network released the "Evangelical

Climate Initiative," which I had helped formulate and market to our movement. The following year, radio broadcaster and child psychologist Dr. James Dobson became so disturbed by what he called my "relentless campaigning" about the reality of climate change that he and twenty-five other leading figures in the conservative movement essentially demanded my resignation. At that time, the NAE's President Leith Anderson backed me, suggesting that my work as a spokesman for the NAE was equally balanced between a host of duties and issues, none of which were related to global warming. But that support would evaporate in late 2008.

The actual events of early December 2008 that led to my being asked to resign are now three years old, but not something I've previously written about.

I'd held the position of Vice-President for Governmental Affairs for ten years, and labored in the government relations office for eighteen years before that. All of that time I was, like the NAE, a faithful ally of the Religious Right on almost all the hot-button social issues. What precisely had I said or done to warrant being asked to resign? The best explanation is that I revealed some of my personal thinking, ideas not previous expressed publicly but which had been percolating in my mind for some time.

I spoke mostly on the environment in that December 2, 2008, interview with Terri Gross, but did respond to her questions about same-sex civil unions, gay marriage, and my support for Barack Obama in Virginia's presidential primary. In a short portion of the program, Gross asked me, "Two years ago, you said you were still opposed to gay marriage. But now as you identify more with younger voters, would you say you have changed on gay marriage?" I responded, "I'm shifting, I have to admit. In other words, I would willingly say that I believe in civil unions. I don't officially support redefining marriage from its traditional definition, I don't think."

My colleagues in the office, attempting to understand my actions, exclaimed: "You've never mentioned some of these views to us before." So what explains my sudden reversal of opinion? Was it, as one critic suggested, that Terri Gross seduced me with her liberal bias into saying something I didn't believe? Hardly. I was a spokesperson with over twenty-five years of experience in interviews with the national media. A more plausible explanation leans on something described by scientific researcher Benjamin Libet: "At least for some actions that we believe we have consciously 'decided' on, neuroscience experiments show that our brains begin to prepare to take a particular action long before we are conscious of having decided or chosen to act."[5]

The uproar that followed forced Leith Anderson, President of the Association, to explain: "The NAE is not an advocate for civil unions and the role of an NAE spokesperson was primarily on behalf of what we have said, not on behalf of what we have not said. It's also to represent our constituency, and our constituency does not favor civil unions." (It should be noted that the NAE had never taken an official policy position on the topic of civil unions.)

I had been weighing the controversy over the years and come to the private conviction that it was not possible for me to hold that the country could deny constitutional rights, such as "equal protection" and "due process" to an entire class of people (gays, lesbians, and trans-genders) just because of tradition or because their behavior constituted sinful behavior in the minds of Christian evangelicals. Needless to say, this view was a minority view among evangelicals in 2008, though much less so in 2012. The political pendulum has swung quite rapidly toward equality of rights regardless of sexual orientation. For example, I personally approve of the lifting of the "Don't Ask, Don't Tell" policy in the military, and military brass now have testified that doing so has not been a problem for "unit cohesion."

I also told Gross that I had voted for Obama in the primaries, but stopped short of saying whom I voted for in the general election. I thought this was a way of giving some political cover to all those evangelicals (38 percent, if you count black and Latino evangelicals) who voted for Barack Obama in the 2008 election. Having traveled around the country and visited more than forty campuses (many in the Council of Christian Colleges and Universities), I have routinely heard students and adults confess: "To say I voted for President Obama will only provoke a fight or challenge, so I keep my mouth shut."

To leaders of the Religious Right, my interview on NPR was too much. They rose up to demand my resignation. "For better or for worse, Rich became a great, polarizing figure," said the late Charles Colson of Prison Fellowship. "Gradually, over a period of time, he was separating himself from the mainstream of evangelical belief and conviction. So I'm not surprised. I'm sorry for him, but I'm not disappointed for the evangelical movement." In other words, I was no longer staying comfortably within the Republican mainstream. My views were characterized by Tony Perkins, head of the Family Research Council as "off the reservation." In my mind, however, I was simply trying to avoid politicizing the Gospel.

Some evangelicals also complained about my response to a question on abortion: I said: "Two-thirds of younger evangelicals say they would still vote for a candidate even if the candidate disagreed with them on the issue of abortion, and that's in spite of the fact that younger evangelicals are decidedly pro-life. In fact, health care is just as important to younger evangelicals as is abortion." I also spoke in favor of the government supplying contraceptives in response to Obama's campaign promises to reduce unintended pregnancies.

At the time, I didn't view my comments as all that controversial, certainly not something that would force me out of my job. Yet a few days later, having flown back from Paris after the founding meeting of Global Zero, Leith Anderson explained that the controversy was not going to go away. The Executive Committee of the NAE had met by conference call that morning and wanted my resignation. I signed a resignation letter already prepared. Another page-long "non-disparagement agreement" had also been typed up for my signature. On that one, I told Leith to wait for a response. I decided a few days later there was no need. Disparaging the NAE, for whom I had worked for twenty-eight years, was not something I was going to do. Nor have I done so in the intervening years.

It was a painful experience. No one works nearly three decades for a ministry they've loved, even come to embody, and walks away overnight without a great deal of emotion. Should I have said what I said? Maybe not, but it happened. The reality is that I had been thinking about these topics— civil unions, gay marriage, family planning strategies to reduce abortions, as well as the presidential vote of 2008—for a long time.

Terri Gross of "Fresh Air" is a very good interviewer, the best there is. I told her what was really on my mind. I went back a year later and did a second interview, not apologizing for anything I said previously—indeed, reaffirming my original comments. They are what I believe.

The difficulty, as I see it, is that the evangelical world is unable to tolerate dissent. Unity has become uniformity. Authority cannot be questioned. However, on matters of politics, particularly, which are so subject to personal judgment or prudence, we need to grant some freedom.

Setting aside my role as spokesman for evangelicals and whether or not I should have admitted to some personal changes of mind, a larger truth is at stake. Will we use the Gospel for political purposes, or make it hostage to any political person or cause? Some sixty times in the New Testament the death and resurrection of Christ are described as liberating, and the Christian life as one of freedom. The apostle Paul declared, "It is for freedom that Christ has set us free. Stand firm, then, and do not let yourself be burdened again by a yoke of slavery" (Gal. 5:1).

A demand for political conformity is a form of legalism that must not characterize the body of Christ. Neither should any judgmental or unloving attitudes over differences of opinion. Disagreements, moreover, should not be regarded as off limits but as legitimate and even healthy. They offer the opportunity to discuss conflicting ideas with a spirit of prayer, openness to the Holy Spirit, and unconditional submission to God's Word. In this way the church is a community that transcends, while never denying, its internal differences. Here is victory over the last great temptation (as the book of Revelation intimates): that of making politics more than itself.

The story of my dissent from the "evangelical mainstream" (as Colson put it) goes back to 2002. That year I attended the Oxford Conference on Climate Change, against the wishes of my fellow NAE Executive Committee members, especially my (late) good friend Diane Knippers, who was then President of the conservative Institute for Religion and Democracy. I not only attended, but came away from the event persuaded that climate change was real, and that the fledgling evangelical creation care movement ought to be willing to address it.

Walking in the gardens of Blenham Palace, not far from Oxford, I received counsel from Sir John Houghton, an evangelical scientist who was a co-chair of the Intergovernmental Panel on Climate Change. He advised me to speak out about what I had decided. I told him, "It could cost me my job." He acknowledged as much, but suggested that it was a risk worth taking if the evangelicals in the United States were to ever join their fellow believers from around the world in the fight against global warming.

Speak out I did. Evangelical political leaders outside the organization which I worked for were incessant critics, even going so far as to use manipulative tactics to sabotage my goals as director of public policy. No good deed goes unpunished.

Those who hired me, and supported me for a long period of time, eventually wilted under the pressure. They lost their nerve. They feared that the Religious Right leadership would engage in a never-ending fight to remove me from my post.

In a private admission to me, NAE president Leith Anderson told me that it was not just my creation care advocacy and call for action on climate change that were my undoing. The full panoply of issues and concerns prompted the decision to ask for my resignation.

Two years earlier, in 2006, thirty top Religious Right leaders had called for me to be "silenced or fired." It didn't help, according to Anderson, that when the host of the "Fresh Air" program asked me, "What next?" I replied that I was going to Paris for the Founding Director's conference of a movement to abolish nuclear weapons called "Global Zero."

Over a sad Outback dinner, Anderson told me that if I had replied to Gross "that I was going to fight abortion," then I might have saved my job.

Alas, fighting abortion by funding family planning and contraceptives, the lack thereof being the main reason there are hundreds of thousands of abortions annually in America alone, was not perceived as being sufficiently "anti-abortion." But this misunderstanding is common among evangelicals. What the Executive Committee of the NAE really wanted to hear me say on the program was that my next agenda was to go back to fighting the Democrats and the "culture wars."

At the time, I was too shell-shocked to want to say anything to the press, wisely concluding in hindsight that anything said might be misunderstood or perceived as self-serving. Now a number of years have passed, and the lessons learned from my experience might be of some assistance to the body of Christ, which is still the uppermost consideration in my decision to write about it here.

So what might be of a salutary nature to say to my fellow believers? Is it possible that the condition of the evangelical movement has changed so much that the lessons of my experience no longer apply? I don't think so. We're in a presidential race, and the temptations toward partisanship abound with even more ferocity. The Religious Right has a visceral dislike for President Obama and wants to defeat him, no matter what. Pastors didn't hesitate to endorse certain Republican candidates for the GOP nomination.

All the more reason to speak out now, before this election cycle gets even more heated. The actual details of my departure from the NAE are not as important as the lessons that might be learned from my painful departure from the organization.

And what might those lessons be?

I believe three primary lessons can be learned from my experiences: to see and think more clearly; to care more deeply; and to act more boldly. Let me elaborate.

The Vision: God calls us to see and think more clearly.

I believe that God still gives us a "vision" of what he calls us to do, and we need to be able to see it. Cal DeWitt, a biology professor at the University of Wisconsin, the grandfather of the creation care movement, calls it being able to "behold" the world and events around us in a new way. From the cross, Jesus said, "Mary, behold thy son," and, "John, behold thy mother." Each would have to see the other in a new way.

We need to see the evangelical movement with a new set of lenses. The assumption is that evangelical Christians won't change their allegiance to a narrow set of litmus-test values—opposition to abortion and gay marriage—and that those issues still define what it means to be an evangelical.

Au contraire. A group of "new evangelicals" have already left the political right. Theologian Scott McKnight calls this "the biggest change in the evangelical movement," nothing less than the emergence of "a new kind of Christian social conscience."[6] These new evangelicals focus on such startlingly different types of issues as economic justice, environmental protection, immigration reform, militarism, and consumerism.

We're not saying the Religious Right is not a potent political force, just that the evangelical movement no longer sings in one voice, but rather in robust polyphony. According to a June 2008 Pew Forum on Religion and Public Life study, devout Christians who don't think of themselves as part of the Religious Right come to roughly 24 percent of the population.[7]

This growing constituency has a vision for evangelicalism that will rescue it from the narrow-mindedness of the Religious Right. It sees a world and has a vision beyond what Michelle Goldberg, a *Salon* reporter and author of *Kingdom Coming: The Rise of Christian Nationalism*,[8] describes as a "totalistic political ideology" that encompasses a wide variety of conservative groups.

Goldberg captures a truth that I experienced all too clearly working within the evangelical political subculture: "You're either with Jesus [meaning the totalistic political ideology], or you're with the liberals." Need I elaborate on the dangers and consequences of this kind of either/ or, black and white, good versus evil, Manichaean thinking? This kind of spiritual myopia damages the work of the church and violates the teaching of Jesus Christ.

Evangelicals need a different vision: We need to see Jesus Christ, our Lord and the world's Savior, whom we love. We want to see more Americans choose to believe in Jesus and live as his disciples. We see that the evangelistic and discipling work of American Christianity has been badly damaged by a generation of culture-war fighting. We see the allegiance of America as a whole to Christian faith slipping a little bit more each year, partly as a consequence of our own mistakes.

Very importantly, we want to see a renewed Christian public witness in America for the sake of the Gospel. We want to see an engagement of Christians in American public life that is loving rather than angry; holistic rather than narrowly focused; healing rather than divisive; and independent of partisanship and ideology rather than subservient to party or ideology.

We want to see a Christian public witness that reflects the actual life, ministry, and teachings of the Jesus Christ we meet in Scripture and experience in the church at its best. We want to see the incarnation of the teachings and example of Christ, not just the articulating of those teachings in word alone.

The Strategy: God calls us to care more deeply.

I've said in many college chapels, "A vision without a strategy is a hallucination." Unless you have a strategy that appropriately complements your vision, that noise you hear is the sound of defeat. The evangelical church is losing the challenge to see and think more clearly because it is way too calloused about how it operates in "the world." Thus, we need to care more deeply about the vision we espouse.

Maybe one of the reasons is that vision is not just the ability to see things differently and the effect of that ability on one's functioning—whether in religion, art, government, or science. The kind of vision I am talking about is not just an intellectual thing; it's an emotional phenomenon.

Vision is having some sense of where you begin and end, and where others in your life begin and end. It is the capacity to get outside the emotional climate of the day. It is being willing to be exposed and vulnerable. Your imagination will be limited if you're afraid of standing out. It is not just the fear of criticism; it is the fear of standing alone, and not having anyone you can rely on. Until you come to the place where you will relish having to take responsibility for your own actions and your own responses, you will likely wilt under the pressure. What do people do under this pressure? They walk away from the job or the vision given them.

One thing is clear. I didn't walk away from the vision given me. I was fired, told my vision was the wrong one for the organization. They may have been right, but I wouldn't give up the vision of what God has told me to do. It continues today.

Leaders are often misunderstood and called all sorts of names. I was called "anti-American, anti-capitalist," and was said to be "divisive" and possessing an "underlying hatred of America." This didn't bother me as much as it did my family. Nonetheless, when you're in a bind and have to choose between continuing a relationship and giving up your goals, better to choose goals over camaraderie, consensus, or team-building. This is a tough choice, but the one we must sometimes make in life.

I had been persistent in the face of downright rejection by many others and didn't want to give up the fight. Success, after all, depends on a relentless drive that won't take refuge in working a mere forty-hour week, or in cynicism. The resistance leaders meet also comes from inside, the voice that asks, "How can you have it right, and everyone else be crazy?" A kind of self-differentiation is needed at times to separate oneself and one's vision from the naysayers, and without that strength of character many a believer will give up the battle.

It is this quality of tenacious "caring" for the welfare of the church of Jesus Christ, tenacity in the face of opposition, that the new evangelicals must embody if we are to succeed. My sense back in 2008, and confirmed even more by the events that followed my departure from the NAE, is that if we are winsome, respectful of the other's viewpoint, and always loving, we will win back the evangelical church to a more Christlike stance.

The Tactic: God calls us to act more boldly.

It is my judgment that America generally, and the church in particular, has lost its nerve. We need a kind of holy boldness.

My favorite illustration of boldness is Daniel. He was a servant to King Darius, who sought to create a Medo-Persian empire in the sixth century B.C.E., ruling over the kingdom of the Chaldeans (Dan. 6:1—28). Darius became duped by unworthy satraps who were jealous of Daniel, whom the King intended to appoint over the entire kingdom.

These commissioners got the King to sign a decree that "anyone who prays to any god or human being during the next thirty days, except to you, Your Majesty, shall be thrown into the lions' den" (Dan. 6:7). Well, Daniel knew that the document had been signed and yet continued kneeling on his knees three times a day "and prayed, giving thanks to his God, just as he had done before" (Dan. 6:10). This landed him in a den of lions.

Though Daniel was himself a target for hate and jealousy, so was Darius, who was put in the terrible position of having to make a tragic moral choice. Darius could condemn his servant Daniel and save the Empire and his leadership, or he could save his friend Daniel and sacrifice the Empire.

Darius ordered Daniel cast into the lions' den, saying:"May your God, whom you serve continually, rescue you!" (Dan. 6:16). Much disturbed by this state of affairs, the king "spent the night without eating and without any entertainment being brought to him. And he could not sleep" (Dan. 6:18).

In the morning, Darius arose at dawn and went to the lions' den, to discover Daniel very much alive. To which Daniel said: "May the king live forever!" (Dan. 6:21). The king then brought those who had accused Daniel and cast them into the lions' den. Darius then made a decree that "in every part of my kingdom people must fear and reverence the God of Daniel. For he is the living God and he endures forever; his kingdom will not be destroyed, his dominion will never end. He rescues and he saves; he performs signs and wonders in the heavens and on the earth" (Dan 6:26–27a).

The point here is not just that Daniel was faithful, but that Darius had to choose between difficult options—saving his kingdom or his friend.

The political significance of this story was suggested to me by Rep. Paul Henry (R-MI), the late son of the famous evangelical theologian Carl F. H. Henry. The younger Henry used the story to indicate the conundrums that political leaders face all the time. Defense weapons designed to defend are used to make war; poverty programs aimed at providing help can produce dependence, and so on.

Henry's point was that as a member of Congress he had to make choices all the time, often between two less than perfect options—hence the need for not just godly wisdom but for bold leadership even amidst difficult choices.

Bold leadership is also humble. One need look no further than Mary. When told of her impending, supernatural pregnancy by the angel, Mary responded, "Let it be to me as you say." She embraced her destiny in faith, believing that God would do as he said and accepting that he had chosen her for a mission. She did not dither like Moses, nor did she reject the calling as Jonah did. Because she had surrendered her life to God, she was humbly able to accept her role. It was a role that Simeon later prophesied would cause her heart to be pierced as with a sword.

The Magnificat (Lk. 1:46–55) also reveals that Mary was exceedingly humble. To both the angel and to Elizabeth she refers to herself as a "handmaid," best translated today as "servant" or "slave." It wasn't false modesty, as she would never come to wealth or a life of ease. But she is venerated to this day for her willingness to be obedient and accept her role.

We are all called in some way to serve God in this world, and to do so with no expectation of any life of comfort. The choices we make may pierce our hearts in such a way that the wound stays for years. The pain may be in our very own souls. We act anyway to do the right thing, as best we know it. I know that pain, and yet I also experience the presence and direction of the Lord.

I say it again: "If you've never changed your mind about something, pinch yourself: you may be dead." It's the last line in the documentary film *Countdown to Zero*, released in 2010 by Participant Films. In that case, with the danger being nuclear weaponry, the *double entendre* is obvious. But all of us will die a bit internally whenever we should take a stand, but don't; when we simply must speak out, and won't. There's always a cost to be paid, now or later, if we shirk our duty.

This kind of boldness requires old-fashioned courage. We must be both the "Daniels" and "Danielles" to speak up. It requires being what others will criticize as being "divisive" or a "disturbance." Why is this necessary? Leadership is not just about vision and strategy. It is equally about "creating a climate where the truth is heard and the brutal facts confronted,"[9] to quote Jim Collins. Collins explains that "there's a huge difference between the opportunity to 'have your say' and the opportunity to be heard. The good-to-great leaders understood this distinction, creating a culture wherein people had a tremendous opportunity to be heard..." [10]

We must understand this truth and boldly assert the right within our churches for the "new evangelicals" to be heard. Changing the status quo also demands that we understand that the most powerful force for altering the internal psychological structure of a human being is discontinuity between one's prevailing thinking/behavior and one's most deeply held values and aspirations.

We're courageously challenging the evangelical movement toward what is right—an unpoliticized, holistic Gospel. For this higher value and aspiration to break into the prevailing thinking requires the followers of Jesus to be courageous and speak out. This means: be prepared to suffer the consequences. This requires courage.

Join me in a bold reassertion of what the Gospel of Jesus Christ stands for, and what the Church so desperately needs from evangelicals—an ongoing commitment to renewal and reformation; to self-examination, reflection, and a willingness to be corrected and to change whenever necessary.

5

A Theology That "Works"

Paul N. Markham

Writing this chapter is both a pleasure and a challenge. I'm excited to be writing this for Christians—or those interested in Christianity—who just want to talk straight about living a life of faith that makes a difference. We all know how important theology is and that a healthy reading of the Bible is essential to understanding our faith. A significant number of us, however, just want our faith to "work." We want to live passionately for something that leads to a better world for us and those around the world.

From the outset of this chapter, I'll confess that this isn't just about "those" new evangelicals out there somewhere. In many ways, it is about me as well. For a long time, I thought that my own experience with Christianity was somewhat unique. Despite the many friends and co-workers I found in the church, I somehow just didn't "fit." A few years back I began to suspect that I might not be alone, so I put my background in theology and sociology to work investigating what I called the "new evangelicals." I learned a lot, and, in 2010, I published this research in an academic journal.[1] This chapter is an attempt to "sit down" with you, the reader, and talk through what I learned and why it is important to this manifesto. Going forward, I've decided to shy away from talk of "them" and adopt the "us" language when talking about this new generation of Christians. Part of the journey for you will be to decide whether you are numbered among the "us" I describe.

Another thing I will be honest about is that while I use the term "new evangelicals," I'm not sure those I'm describing would accept this label. I use the term because, despite our differences with contemporary evangelicals, we do share a common historical narrative. (I talk about this in my article.) One of the most interesting things I discovered about the new evangelicals is that we are so difficult to identify because we don't like to be labeled.

This is why pollsters have such a difficult time nailing us down. After giving several opportunities for my interviewees to group themselves politically and religiously, I found they just couldn't be cornered that easily.

These young new evangelicals don't necessarily want to be seen as Democrats or Republicans, though they are very political—albeit in a nuanced sense of the term. The new evangelical vision cuts across traditional partisan lines. New evangelicals do not fit neatly within either progressive or conservative camps. We value family and local community, but are leery of large systems—whether government or corporations—that purport to have the answers we seek. This doesn't stop at political labeling. Most even reject denominational labels, choosing to be identified as "followers of Jesus." The academic in me admits the need for ongoing social scientific analysis, but the big picture is clear: a lot of people in the United States are deeply committed to their Christian faith but have trouble finding a home in the options they have available to them.

I'm excited to be a part of this manifesto. The creation of this collection of essays is giving a voice to a great number of Christians who embrace their vibrant faith, but find difficulty fitting within an evangelicalism recently dominated by the Religious Right. As some of us in this volume have described, evangelicals have a rich history of seriously engaging both their personal religious faith and the social responsibility to which that faith calls them. Through this chapter I will share a *new* evangelical vision about how we can work together to make a real difference in the world. This is more than just a feel-good message. It is a present-day fleshing out of Jesus' kingdom of God message.

The Kingdom of God and the Common Good

New evangelicals are about working for the kingdom of God. What does it mean to have a kingdom vision for the common good? Why does it matter? While the authors of this manifesto will surely not agree on every theological point, we are committed to both the possibility of a world that reflects the nature of God and to our own roles in co-creating that world. The kingdom of God vision we support pays serious attention not only to what Jesus did some two thousand years ago, but also to what *we* are called to do and be as a result of the life Jesus lived. Our view of God is one of a loving and just Creator, and it only takes a brief look around to see that the world is not what God would have it be. This is a problem. It's *our* problem—and we see ourselves as workers with God to do something about it.

As exciting as the mission is, writing about it is a challenge because of the many tendencies to privatize a personal but necessarily public faith.

Describing the common good can be a formidable academic exercise, but my gut tells me that those of you reading this need little convincing. New evangelicals care less about the language used to describe our engagement—faith-based, democratic, civic, public, etc.—than we do about the actual outcome of our efforts. New evangelicals are committed to living our personal faith in a very public way—that is, to work for the common good. This means not just the good of the individual Christian or church, but the good of the world in all of its diversity. For this reason, new evangelicals will not shy away from terms such as democracy or public engagement, because they simply refer to means of involving a broad range of people in efforts that affect us all.

Over the decades, we have seen some faith-based groups expand from outreach-style charity or service to much more politically engaged forms of advocacy and organizing around social justice issues. Through my research, I learned that the single most unifying issue among young new evangelicals is concern about social justice issues. Struggling for social justice is fundamental to how we act out our Christian faith. This manifesto speaks to this new generation of Christians in America. This is what we mean by "public witness"—not shouting in the public square about how pious we are, but engaging in the hard work of addressing problems and systems that affect a wide range of people. In this sense, topics such as education, economics, and foreign policy become *spiritual* issues.

Why Partnership Matters

Any public successes I've had, in ministry or otherwise, have never been due to my personal ability to solve the problem myself. Success has come when and because I figured out that the skills and talents of people working together achieve far more than I ever could alone. Partnership is about understanding that we must depend on others to meet our goals. As personally connected to God as we might feel, the world is big and our problems are so complex that we must come to grips with our inability to fix things on our own. This doesn't mean we give up and look to "experts" to fix things for us. It means we must come to a deeper understanding of what it means for everyday people to work together for a just society.

While partnership is common in religious congregations, the kind of collaborative work driving new evangelicals is much more likely to draw on a broader base of creative potential. This includes both formal organizations and the "ordinary people" affected by the problems we face. It is fairly common for churches to partner with other congregations or parachurch organizations, but new evangelicals are willing to expand these partnerships to include public and interfaith collaborations. We see our faith and passion for the common good to be a value-added feature of partnerships that work. Our public witness is not limited or threatened by those that hold different views.

Aside from partnership with formal organizations, one of the greatest things we can do in our church communities is build a deeper relationship between what we think of as "professional" ministry and the everyday activities of those who participate in congregational life. Most clergy are trained to teach and administer the basic features of the church community, but few are prepared to truly understand the power of laity to address problems beyond the church walls.

The young Christians that I interviewed in my research had a remarkable understanding of commitment to community. Their attitude reminded me of stories I heard growing up about the "old folks" sharing meals together and gathering on front porches for stories of work and family. Despite the high-tech nature of our society, these young people refuse to abandon our "high-touch" human nature. This focus on community has a strong effect on the potential for meaningful partnerships. Most often faith-based partnerships are the result of formal agreements between organizational leaders—e.g., the pastors of two churches agree to partner for a holiday food drive, a church partners with a local nonprofit to raise money for families in need, etc. However, new evangelicals see greater potential in partnership.

During my interviews, I commonly probed for insights into how people pursued their social justice goals. It was unanimous that partnership was essential to their efforts. Interestingly, they didn't wait for formal partnerships to be formed by their pastors or ministry leaders and then figure out how they fit. Rather, they saw themselves as initiators of the partnerships. One respondent told me that she has a weekly meal with friends and members of the community. During this time they discuss common interests and connections, and how they might build networks to meet their goals. This "grassroots" approach to partnership-building values the diverse talents and capacities of ordinary people and their ability to contribute to the world around them. We can learn many lessons, but practically it means that new evangelicals are interested in being a part of organizations that focus on a rich community life and serve as catalysts for their own creative potential to partner for the common good.

A Theology of Public Work

For decades, engaged Christians have espoused what we might call a "prophetic politics" that combines personal conversion and efforts to transform society. In our current political climate, I understand why anyone might want to flee from involvement in politics, but I am using the term to refer to the basic processes of humans working together to achieve a desired goal. In this sense, politics is a necessary aspect of any human society, so the question is not *whether* new evangelicals will be politically active, but *how* we will exercise our politics. This means much more than how votes will be cast. It means how our voices will be heard and how our creative energies will be applied to the problems that plague our world.

As I processed the many narratives I heard through my research, I began to think of this new vision in terms of a very old story—Nehemiah and the rebuilding of Jerusalem's walls. Nehemiah has much to teach us about our contemporary challenges and how we might rise to meet them. The story shows a skillful politician who gained permission from the king of Persia in 446 B.C.E. to return to Jerusalem to lead the Jews in rebuilding the city walls that had lain in ruins for decades. Nehemiah's leadership was different from the model of Moses leading the people out of slavery in Egypt, or Solomon dispensing wisdom.

Nehemiah did not undertake the effort of rebuilding the walls of Jerusalem by first setting forth a program with clear goals and steps to get there. Nor did he formulate a detailed theory of wall rebuilding and encourage the citizens to study up before proceeding. I'm sure he faced dozens of reasons he could have listed not to entrust the building efforts to the people themselves. After all, where were the "experts"? What could ordinary people like a delicate-handed goldsmith know of bricks and mortar? How could bands of women and children be as effective in construction as Persian engineers? Fortunately, Nehemiah had a deeper understanding of expertise, efficiency, and the meaning of what he called "the good work."

Nehemiah understood that rebuilding the walls was not a mere construction project, but required bringing people together to rebuild relationships, renew their commitment to God, and in the process recover a sense of their great tradition, all in the service of renewing a common life together. Rather than pursuing the logical route of hiring laborers to rebuild the walls for the people, Nehemiah called the city's inhabitants to rebuild the walls for themselves. Rebuilding the walls became a religious and spiritual act of *civic* restoration. In other words, this action of working together to restore the city blurred the lines between secular and sacred, public and private. As the rebuilding took place, the people regained a sense of their common purpose and, despite their many differences, created a shared life together. I believe this new generation of evangelicals seeks similar acts of spiritual *and* civic renewal. We see God as bigger than ourselves, our churches, or our country. We believe building the kingdom of God involves people working together across our differences to create a better world for everyone.

So why the emphasis on "work"? Churches across the country meet urgent or one-time needs through volunteerism, financial assistance, disaster relief, etc.; however, many congregation-based social service efforts lack substantive engagement toward sustainable development—that is, they are rarely ongoing, extensive, and focused on addressing systemic causes of social problems. Perhaps no one in the world does service better than the religious. Our Christian traditions teach us about compassion and self-sacrifice. New evangelicals share the servant's heart of the evangelicals before them, but we are exercising a form of creative activism focused on empowering communities to become co-creators of the world, and not merely consumers of it.

Churches and individual Christians who share this new evangelical vision for the common good seek to be empowering both internally and to the communities around them. Simply understood, this kind of empowerment occurs when groups partner with others to work toward creating some common good rather than merely serving or delivering goods to a passive people. The empowerment approach emphasizes the ability to identify the skills and assets of others and the role they play in solving common problems. These kinds of partnerships honor the fact that all people are created in the image of God and have experiences and gifts that count toward building a better world.

The power of this partnership approach emphasizes what we might call the "Commonwealth of God." It is common to think of the world—and the societies that make it up—as God's creation over which humans have responsibility. This view is important, because it stresses the personal responsibility of individual Christians to care for the world that God has created. New evangelicals have a fervent sense of social responsibility, but it is reflected in interesting ways. The notion of the world as the Commonwealth of God engages humanity in a richer way. A commonwealth only exists as the product of what its members determine it to be. In the Commonwealth, we play a vital role as God's people in forming a just society. Furthermore, as with the rebuilding work of Nehemiah, the creative process itself generates a distinctive kind of responsibility in each of us. We are not simply caretakers in the world God created, but vital players in the creative process itself. The apostle Paul spoke about this by referring to believers as the "body of Christ"—the hands and feet of Jesus carrying out God's will in the world.

N.T. Wright explains, "We are invited—summoned, actually—to discover, through following Jesus, that this new world is indeed a place of justice, spirituality, relationship, and beauty, and that we are not only to enjoy it as such but to 'work' at bringing it to birth on earth as in heaven."[2]

A defining characteristic of a new evangelicalism is this distinct call to public faith. In this context, work is essential as it emphasizes the key theme of co-creation, which means that bringing the kingdom of God to its fullest reality requires both divine *and* human activity.

Work is also different from service in that it is organic and unscripted. As with rebuilding the walls of Jerusalem, work often doesn't have a set of ready-made instructions. Work requires cooperation and problem-solving skills. Work often requires that we start in the middle even when we might not be sure where we are. In other words, working for the common good requires an imagination that can only emerge through *acting*, and not through simply *thinking* about hypothetical scenarios. We do this by engaging in a form of meaningful partnership work that brings a diverse people together to produce something greater than the sum of its parts.

For example, a student once asked me how Christians and Muslims could work together on social justice issues. The assumption behind his question was that the two were so fundamentally different that before entering into any collaborative effort, they must first agree on some theory or approach to how people from different religions can work together. My suggestion to him was that he immediately dispense with the theory and enter directly into the work itself, because it would only be in the process of working together to create something of value that the Christian and Muslim would develop the imagination required to develop a "theory" in the first place. My point to the student was that work is unique in its ability to make another world possible. Of course, critical thinking is important, but my argument was that the thinking should always take place in the context of the collaborative action itself. It's within this human dynamic that new possibilities are discovered.

More often than not, only through engagement in this type of work can we begin to name the goal of the work itself. We see this exemplified in Jesus' Sermon on the Mount. His focus was not about providing instruction—be meek, peaceful, etc.—but about describing the characteristics of a meek and peaceful people that could only then understand God's nature and purposes in the first place. New evangelicals understand that living a vibrant Christian life is about more than simply *believing* in this or that doctrine. We are willing to "start in the middle" and work together to see God's will come to fruition in the world. We must learn to be like Nehemiah and see the richness of the people and resources around us as well as our collective ability to make a difference. As we build relationships through working together, we are not only transformed as individuals, but are enabled to together transform the world around us.

What Now?

If this new evangelicalism is to take hold, we must be serious about the kind of education we need. We must develop the skills and deep habits of partnership and working across differences. As with the builders of the walls in ancient Jerusalem, the work of rebuilding our world requires a revitalization of abilities to see beyond what *is* to what *can be*. The new evangelical public witness combines a sacred and public spirit with the work of culture change to rebuild the moral and civic fabric of our society. In this era marked by division, strife, and uprooted pursuit of individual success, we need prophets of the possible who can move the rhetoric of "working together" to the reality of a more just society. Sacred narratives such as Nehemiah help us understand essentials of the Christian faith and provide a framing story to sustain the work to which we are called.

My time with new evangelicals has helped not only to make sense of what is likely an emerging movement, but also to help make sense of myself and my own religious experiences. During my interviews, I asked for the respondents' thoughts on how many people there were across the country who shared their faith and passion for social justice. The responses were nearly unanimous—they felt certain that thousands must be committed to a similar cause, but they felt very alone in their struggles. If the new evangelicalism I've described in this chapter resonates with you, stand up and speak out. There are more of us than you think!

6

God's Vision for the Church—Kingdom Discipleship

Glen Harold Stassen

In 1992, several of my friends in academia participated in the International Dietrich Bonhoeffer Society Conference, which met that year at Union Theological Seminary in New York. I had then been teaching at Southern Baptist Theological Seminary for sixteen years. Even though I had been raised evangelical in a North American Baptist church to which I am still enormously loyal and grateful, I was thinking institutionally more as a Baptist than explicitly as an evangelical. I have been a North American Baptist, American Baptist, D. C. Baptist, National Baptist, Southern Baptist, Cooperative Baptist, and now again an American Baptist. But institutionally, I was at Southern Baptist Theological Seminary.

Even though Southern Baptists are categorized as evangelicals by the polling organizations, they have for a long time thought of themselves as separate and unique. They have a regional loyalty and a sort of established-church power position that does in fact make them somewhat unique. Often Southern Baptists had no representation in evangelical organizations.

I was surprised to notice that 10 percent of those present in the Bonhoeffer Society conference were Southern Baptists, including Barry Harvey of Baylor University, who later became chair of the American section of the Dietrich Bonhoeffer Society. Clearly, Bonhoeffer had articulated the vision and many of the corrections from which we were thinking Southern Baptists needed to learn.

So we Baptists met together for a meal to ask each other: Why is Dietrich Bonhoeffer speaking so powerfully to our denomination's particular needs and to our own emerging spirituality in our time? Today I contend that the vision evangelicals need to heed in our time of highly ideologized and polarized politics is the vision for the church for which we were seeking when Bonhoeffer spoke to us as Southern Baptists during our struggle in that time. David Gushee and Michael Westmoreland-White also resonated with the vision we were receiving, and, at Michael's suggestion, we saw similar themes in Martin Luther King, Jr. We published an article, "Disciples of the Incarnation," in *Sojourners* magazine in May 1994. That article has become programmatic for me and I think for all three of us.

The Programmatic Vision for Kingdom Discipleship

Let me articulate some dimensions of the programmatic vision that we set forth in 1994 and that I believe were not only right then, but all the more needed now.[1]

First, many mainline Protestant churches lack a clear direction and suffer from a crisis of identity or failure of conviction. Surely evidence since then about the decline of many mainline churches is confirming that diagnosis. Many evangelical churches reduce Jesus to a personal savior without discipleship, without following Jesus' teachings and example. Recent books by evangelical authors are echoing that theme, decrying the co-optation of a significant number of evangelical churches by an ideology that teaches individualistic pursuit of wealth and expresses disdain for policies that defend the human rights of the weak and the poor. So, we wrote, "The crying need of our churches is for faithful discipleship to Jesus as Christ and Lord, not creedal rigidity or groundless ethical commotion."

I have since been struck that others in addition to Bonhoeffer and King also focused on a thick and concrete understanding of Jesus' teachings on discipleship. This includes many who stood the test and made faithful witness during the Third Reich, the Civil Rights Struggle, and the Revolution of the Candles that toppled the dictator, Erich Honecker, in East Germany in 1998.

Second, Christ-centered churches that call for conversion, and share this evangelical commitment, "grow more than churches with an abstract and impersonal theology." But they often have "romantic or mythological Christologies that either sentimentalize Jesus or focus on Christ's divinity to the exclusion of his humanity, the ancient heresies of Docetism and Gnosticism." The result is a vague ethic ripe for co-optation by political ideologies that resemble the selfishness and greed of the atheist Ayn Rand more than the way of Jesus. Bonhoeffer and King had no patience with such Gnostic pictures of Christ.

Third, King and Bonhoeffer lived incarnational lives in the sense that they entered incarnationally into the experiences of other people and different cultures. Bonhoeffer was converted from German nationalism to peacemaking when he entered deeply into the experiences of African Americans in Abyssinian Baptist Church in Harlem and in Bible studies and homes there where he studied the writings of the Harlem Renaissance. King entered into studies in a predominantly white seminary and graduate school. Already in college King had turned to seeing whites as potential allies during intercollegiate work against racial injustice. He saw that to carry out effective change, we need to find allies who can walk with us, hand in hand.

Again, I am struck with parallels in the lives of Karl Barth, André Trocmé, Clarence Jordan, Dorothy Day, and Muriel Lester. They all entered into the lives of others different from themselves, though they were not martyred. We need "incarnational solidarity with the poor and others who are discriminated against, those who suffer, those who are different from us." These Christians demonstrated such solidarity.

Fourth, we need a strong emphasis on grace—not grace that makes us passive but *participative grace* that makes us active participants in what God is doing in Christ and through the Holy Spirit in our churches and our society. The grace that we need is not only participative grace, but also *Christomorphic grace:* it is not merely a vague feeling, but takes the form that we see revealed in Jesus Christ. For Bonhoeffer, "costly grace" meant that grace is not only forgiveness, but also empowerment to faithful obedience and to participation in the redemptive work of God in Christ.

King wrote similarly. His dissertation on God's matchless power; his wrestling with discouragement and depression, lifted by his sense of God's empowering grace; his cosmic vision that in the long arc of the universe God bends toward justice; and his commitment to the way of Jesus were not only absolutely crucial for his own staying power, but were the guidance that led the Civil Rights Struggle to be remarkably disciplined, remarkably nonviolent. I do not know of a single incident when the millions who marched in those many cities ever turned to violence. This was a key to the dramatic victories that they (we) won.

Fifth, my own Baptist tradition had picked up our secular culture's limitation of the Gospel to the private life of faith while the public culture is governed by secular forces that contradict the way of Jesus. Evangelicals want to be "biblical," but don't pay attention to the most important biblical teachings relevant to public life. So they often confuse loyalty to the Bible with an authoritarian ideology.

Sixth, both Bonhoeffer and King paid attention to the Bible's call for justice. Both explicitly advocated protection of such God-given human rights as religious liberty, equality before the law, and the right to bodily life. Both Bonhoeffer and King respected and drew upon American articulations of human rights such as in the Declaration of Independence and the Bill of Rights.

This American human rights tradition has led our nation in confronting segregation and discrimination, in calling the practice of torture to account, and in supporting religious liberty for Muslims as well as other minority groups. Muslims are now saying they are enjoying better lives and better acceptance in the United States than in European nations. This is so despite the huge challenge presented by the actions of a heretical and extremist Muslim sect, Al Qaeda, in its 9/11 attack. That Americans are not letting the actions of that heretical sect turn them to injustice against Muslims generally is a tribute to the American tradition of human rights and our hard work to overcome the racism and xenophobia against immigrants throughout our history. I am not saying America has no problems—ideologies of racism, militarism, and imperialist exceptionalism are still visible. I am saying that it is our tradition of human rights, of *e pluribus unum,* and our hard work to overcome the strains of injustice by supporting our better tradition of human rights and liberty and justice for all, that leads us to do better than we would otherwise do. This we can celebrate.

Bonhoeffer and King lead us in a kind of patriotism that celebrates the human rights and "liberty and justice for all" of American tradition, a patriotism that is better than imperialistic militarism. We need to participate in the struggle for this true American tradition, and not let it get distorted and perverted into a kind of nationalism that lacks love and compassion for less powerful groups in our country, including the poor as well as religious minorities.

Seventh, we need to focus on the huge importance of prayer for Bonhoeffer, as seen so clearly in his books. As for King, after his famous "kitchen encounter" with God, when he felt defeated and knew his life was threatened, King wrote movingly of prayer, and practiced fasting. Modern society is spiritually impoverished and needs the witness of Bonhoeffer and King to prayer, not in escape, but in the midst of the real struggles of life.

The Need Has Increased

Since the days of Bonhoeffer and King, David Kinnaman of the Barna research organization, together with Gabe Lyon, has published *Unchristian.*[2]

Their conclusions have been echoed by Christian sociologists such as Robert Putnam and others.

Kinnaman and Lyons report that Christianity's image has declined precipitously in the United States in recent years. Especially among the young who are outsiders to the church, Christianity has a negative image and is associated with intolerance rather than love and compassion.

More recently, Mike Slaughter, Charles Gutenson, and Robert P. Jones have published a striking book, *Hijacked*.[3] They present similar data and conclusions. The decades-long white evangelical marriage with conservative ideology and partisan identification has damaged the church's witness profoundly. It has tempted evangelicals to be less prophetic, and to be drawn toward efforts to exert political control and dominance. These efforts have created a backlash among many younger Americans. Meanwhile, white evangelicals are rapidly becoming more extreme through the well-known process by which ideological homogeneity produces greater and greater insularity.

The generational backlash is evident in the response among younger evangelicals to "The Manhattan Declaration," a 2008 conservative Catholic and evangelical manifesto. Jonathan Merritt has noted the absence of any "notable evangelicals under 40" among the signatories. He also chided the authors both for the condescending tone of the document and for their exclusive focus on a few hot-button issues that dovetail with a partisan agenda.

Older generations often speak as if a handful of issues are the only ones that deserve our passionate witness and concerted attention. But younger Christians believe that our sacred Scriptures compel us to offer a moral voice on a broad range of issues. The Bible speaks often about life and sexuality, but it also speaks often on other issues, such as poverty, equality, justice, peace, and care of creation. The problem we are identifying, the concern that we are addressing, is not Christian participation in the political process. It is co-optation of the Gospel by a partisan ideology.

Thus I think we are seeing several megachurch pastors, such as Bill Hybels, Rick Warren, Greg Boyd, and Joel Hunter, moving farther away from the ideology of the religious right, in a way similar to the argument by Mike Slaughter and Charles Gutenson above.

More recently, my evangelical friends have been expressing dismay at the media's labeling some of the extreme economically selfish, Ayn-Rand-influenced, anti-creation-care, anti-immigrant, pro-militarism views expressed in political debates during the presidential primaries as views intended to draw votes from "evangelicals." These seem to us so opposite to the caring that Jesus embodied and taught. We worry about the corruption of churches and corruption of the understanding of the Gospel of Jesus Christ if these views really do appeal to evangelicals. The good news is that these extreme views do not seem to have worked very well to draw evangelical voters. Maybe the politicians are misreading us. Maybe the media are misreading us. One can only hope.

The Trend toward Christ-centered, Thicker Jesus Discipleship

The good news is that Christian ethicists are trending toward paying more accurate attention to the way of Jesus. When David Gushee and I were planning *Kingdom Ethics*, we surveyed about thirty textbooks in Christian ethics. We found only a total of four pages affirming the implications of Jesus' Sermon on the Mount for Christian ethics. We were astounded. So we wrote a textbook in which the Sermon on the Mount sets the agenda—while also of course paying attention to other biblical teachings, to theology, social science, and some philosophy. And now there are textbooks by many other scholars that do significant exegesis of the way of Jesus.

Ryan Bolger and Eddie Gibbs studied over one hundred emerging churches that are attracting the very young adults who Kinnaman and Lyons say were being driven away by authoritarian and ideological kinds of Christianity. They published their results in *Emerging Churches*.[4] They identified nine practices that were crucial for these churches, and singled out three core practices that were most important in influencing the other six. These involved participating in activities that:

1. identify with the life of Jesus (and embody the kingdom);
2. transform secular space rather than accepting the modern split between sacred and secular;
3. live in community—both in the church community, and the community where we are.

Not every reader of this essay will affirm everything they think of when they think of emerging churches, but these themes strike a chord for young adults. They are making a difference where a difference needs to be made.

I am impressed by Robert Guelich's inaugural essay as professor of New Testament at Fuller Theological Seminary on May 9, 1989.[5] In "What Is the Gospel?" he wrestled with the connection between Paul's statement of the Gospel in 1 Corinthians 15:1–5 and Mark's statement of the Gospel in Mark 1:1, 14–15, echoed in the other three Gospels. Guelich develops his argument much more fully than I can here. But he concludes (as will I):

> Mark's understanding of the "gospel concerning Jesus Messiah, Son of God" corresponds to Jesus' own ministry and message. Jesus'

unique authority, whereby he exorcised demons, healed the sick, offered his rehabilitating fellowship to social and religious outcasts, and taught parabolically about the Kingdom of God, indicates that he viewed himself to be God's "anointed" of Isa 61, the one of Isa 52:7 who was to announce and effect the gospel of God's shalom, salvation, the promised rule which he openly proclaimed as the Kingdom of God…

The answer to our dilemma of how the gospel of the Kingdom and the gospel of the cross relate is that the gospel of the cross is integral to the gospel of the Kingdom in Jesus' ministry. But the gospel of the cross is only integral to the gospel of the Kingdom if we understand both to be an expression of the same "gospel," namely Isaiah's promised "gospel" of God. *The "gospel" then is the message that God acted in and through Jesus Messiah, God's anointed one, to effect God's promise of shalom, salvation, God's reign.*

7

Kingdom Community

Steven Martin

Books aplenty on church, community, ecclesiology, and other associated topics fill entire sections of libraries and bookstores. A quick search on the Internet reveals the vast and deep soul-searching taking place among scholars and leaders who care deeply about the church and seek its vitality. It would be a huge overstep to suggest that I am writing anything that has not been written already. As I consider the thought and prayer that has gone into the hundreds of thousands of churches and Christian communities, the struggles of pastors and leaders who care deeply about their people, who are constantly caught in the tensions of leadership, I feel quite unqualified to write this chapter. Twenty years of pastoral experience have raised many questions and very few answers. Perhaps personal struggle with such issues can produce some good thoughts to be offered here.

First, an autobiographical note: I am ordained in a mainline denomination. As with many of my sisters and brothers with a deep evangelical experience and conviction, I came to be sometimes at odds with fellow pastors and with my superiors. That conviction has been tempered and molded by the wisdom and practicality that comes from centuries of tradition. If we believe the Holy Spirit is present in the church, then we have to take seriously the idea that church tradition is in some way the repository of the Spirit's actions through the centuries, however tainted by human sinfulness. The fire of my evangelical experience has been profoundly shaped by the beauty of the Spirit's hand in things such as liturgy, the language of vows, and historical events such as the Protestant Reformation and the Wesleyan revival.

My life as a pastor came to a crisis point a few years ago. I realized I had a deep need to be liked, a need that often overpowered my willingness to provide prophetic counsel. What good is a pastor who only loves the sheep but never challenges them to live more faithfully? As the Iraq War loomed on the horizon, every cell in my body screamed that this was a horrible mistake and an abuse of our nation's overwhelming power, but I felt incapable of saying so. I wondered if, in fifty years, a historian read through church newsletters to see what I said about one of the greatest moral crises of our time, would she find anything? The answer, tragically, was no.

So I left pastoral ministry to seek a more faithful voice. Doing so has provided me with a wilderness experience richer than anything I could have imagined. Perhaps someday I might return if God calls; I never like to close doors unnecessarily. The view I now have of the Christian community as both a leader and participant might be helpful in the pages that follow.

What's the Purpose of Community?

Community. It's always been funny to me to hear people idealize a church as being like a family. Yes, the Christian community *is* just like a family, with all the joy, laughter, camaraderie, tears, longing, and heartbreak. Like families, churches have their share of abuse, stagnation, fear, dysfunction, and death. That will never change. Evangelicals can point blaming fingers at the Catholic child abuse scandals (and rightly so), but we have our share of scandals, too. The name Ted Haggard comes to mind, among countless others.

Community is a basic human need. Psychologists have shown that solitary confinement, as practiced in prisons through the complete removal of all human contact, destroys the human mind. Community, like food and water, is a basic human need and right. Christian community adds a layer to the life of the believer through the living out of the command of Jesus in Matthew 28 to "go and make disciples of all nations…teaching them to obey everything that I have commanded you," and of John 13:34, "A new command I give you: love one another." At its most basic level, kingdom community is about exactly that: making disciples, teaching people to follow Jesus (for a lifetime), and building a community on selfless love, the kind embodied in Jesus' own sacrificial love. Do this, and you shall live.

Many point to the church of Acts 2 and 4 as the standard of kingdom community. These were people who devoted themselves to the apostles' teaching, the breaking of bread and prayer, and the sharing of all things in common. Not bad. Many bristle when this vision of the church is raised. They claim that it smacks of communism and that those who suggest it as a pattern for church life would happily extend it to America herself. Honestly, this standard is practiced on some level in every congregation through simple acts of kindness and charity. It is one of the many signs of vitality we all see.

As we "new evangelicals" consider our unique contribution to the Christian landscape, I would like to propose this as a standard of measuring kingdom community: *I suggest that a church is not a church at all unless it produces at least a handful of people capable of following Jesus' most difficult teachings, such as the love of enemy.*

I do not believe that everyone in a church must be capable of this. After all, we are only human! We are all at various stages of development in our faith journey. Every true church must have a few "saints," if you will. Without them a church is only a club or civic organization.

Love of Enemy

In nearly any list of his sayings, Jesus' demand to "love your enemies and pray for those who persecute you" (Mt. 5:44) ranks among the most difficult and controversial. Enemy-love is a critical key to the kingdom. It is what can open the heart of the believer and renew the whole church. It can turn the world upside down and challenge every established maxim of community. Enemy-love can enrich the believer beyond measure as well as create extraordinary difficulty for those who practice it. Enemy-love is a hopeful, joyful opportunity rather than a dreadful "Thou shalt not…"

Discerning whether the original word in the Bible for "your" is singular or plural is a vital element of study. Without going into our Greek textbooks, let's think about the possibilities. Most of us consider this admonishment to "love your enemies" to be an individual matter, a one-on-one between persons in some kind of conflict. When you find yourself in an ongoing sparring match with a next-door neighbor who does not like your dog, you feel that Jesus would prefer that you take a plate of cookies to the troublesome neighbor instead of perpetuating the conflict. This would be one appropriate interpretation of the application of enemy-love. We can imagine that, even if the neighbor takes the cookies and still calls the police about your dog, eventually his heart will be softened and he will change his ways.

When the conflict becomes intractable, we begin to reconfigure the equation. Perhaps, like Pharaoh, God has hardened the heart of the neighbor. Perhaps this neighbor is like Paul's "thorn in the flesh" that serves to irritate and purify. Or perhaps we lump this teaching in with others that are just too difficult, too impractical this side of heaven, and we give up, devoting our energies to private prayer and reflection as the basis of the Christian walk.

Consider for a moment how revolutionary the phrase, "Love your enemies," becomes when we make "your" plural. What if Jesus is speaking to groups rather than to individuals? What if Jesus wants persons who belong to a group that defines itself over and against another to love each other? Then "you" are not being urged to make peace with a stubborn neighbor, but to step outside the boundaries of what your group, your tribe, your people deems acceptable. If we understand "your" to be plural, the saying becomes infinitely practical and powerfully subversive.

I grew up during the Cold War in a town at the heart of America's nuclear weapons manufacturing infrastructure. Secrecy and concern for security were so strong that few of us knew what our parents did for a living. Then, I never imagined that I would meet a Russian in my lifetime. Now my children go to school with kids whose Russian parents have come to work in the same city. As far as I can tell they're nice people, just as they likely were years ago. Yet we stood at the brink of mutual annihilation several times during the Cold War (and with missiles still easily retargetable, perhaps we still do), ready to choose up sides when our leaders told us to do so. Are Russians any different just because our leaders no longer tell us that they are our enemies?

If enemy-love is to be applied by members of one group to members of another, it means that I, a Christian, must love members of tribes my nation's leaders define as my enemy. In many parts of this country, people fear that Muslims are part of an enemy tribe infiltrating American life. Jesus, then, simply commands me to love Muslims. If my country has taken sides with Israel against the Palestinians, then I must not only love Israelis (which is easy for me to do), but also to reach beyond and love Palestinians as well (which, as it turns out, is also easy to do). If my tribe has determined that gay people, or homophobes, or global-warming believers, or SUV drivers, or fiscal conservatives, or Keynesians, or free-market libertarians, or socialists, or hedge fund managers, or union members, or nuclear weapons makers, or peace activists are my enemies, following Jesus means reaching beyond how my tribe defines those persons and loving them.

When we do this, we discover something radically new about people, God, and the nature of all things. This discovery proves transformative is countless ways.

Many fear that when we do too much of this enemy-love, we lose something. We lose our identity in some important way. To be honest, this is always a risk, but it is more important to follow God than to protect our borders.

I could point to other "difficult sayings" of Jesus as equally transformative when practiced in a believer's life. Let me just say again that kingdom community is experienced when we put these difficult teachings into practice. A church is not a church unless it has at least a few, if only a few, who can do so.

Matthew 25 as a Formula for Kingdom Community

Perhaps the most well-known facet of Matthew's apocalyptic vision in chapter 25 is the final judgment, the famous "Sheep and Goats" metaphor. I suggest that we take a look at the entire chapter as a blueprint for kingdom community, especially in this postmodern, post-Christendom, post-everything era. I do not suggest that it should be lifted out of Scripture in a way that denies parts that "don't fit" anymore, as such errors are rampant throughout the body of Christ and have led to our greatest catastrophes. Let us allow this chapter to serve as a lens through which we see Scripture, and the community based on it, more clearly.

Matthew 25 is composed of three sections that admonish the believer (1) to be vigilant, (2) to take great risks, and (3) to generously serve the poor and outcast. Let us consider each of these on their own, and then we will consider how a community based on these three dimensions of Christian living will live in the world.

Be Vigilant

Matthew 25:1–13, the "Parable of the Ten Virgins," sets two groups of wedding attendants against each other. Five of the girls brought enough oil to last through the night, and five did not. All would have been fine if the unexpected—the delay of the bridegroom—had not taken place. The shortage of oil only becomes a problem when the bridegroom takes longer to arrive than expected. When the five "foolish" girls leave to get more oil, they miss the arrival of the bridegroom. Vigilance and preparedness for the unexpected seem to be the lessons here.

Take Great Risks

This is followed by "The Parable of the Talents," or, in my copy of the New International Version, "The Parable of the Bags of Gold." Three servants are given their master's gold and are told to invest it. Two of them double their master's money, and one returns the original amount safely. Two are congratulated, and the third is cast out. How did the first two succeed in doubling their investment? We can only surmise that they did so by each taking a huge risk with their master's money. The only investment manager I can recall who was able to guarantee a large, steady return for investors was Bernie Madoff. Receiving such a large, 100 percent return on the master's money could only come through some high-flying schemes in which the servants risked *everything*. The servant cast into the "outer darkness"? He kept his master's money in a safe place where it couldn't be lost.

Before I go on to the third section of this triad, let me offer a few thoughts from these parables for the contemporary church. The first parable urges the church to be fully, completely prepared. For what? The parable seems to have been written for a church that was waiting for the imminent return of Christ, but we should not limit its meaning to only this crisis—or opportunity—for the church.

Many, many times the church has been caught off-guard and unprepared for the times in which it lived. During those times the church has always had folks who *were* prepared and vigilant, and the witness of the church has been maintained through the centuries because of them.

It is in the Parable of the Talents that we see, perhaps, the greatest indictment. Churches, generally, are not good at taking risks. This is why churches favor pastoral care and ministries of mercy rather than ministries of justice-making. Working for justice and fairness, as in the story of Paul, Silas, and the slave girl (Acts 16:16—24), often brings controversy. With large buildings, staff salaries, and big budgets, few churches seem to be able to rejoice when they are counted worthy of suffering disgrace for the name (Act 5:41).

Serve the Poor and Outcast Generously

Finally, we come to the Sheep and the Goats. As a seemingly infinite number of words have been written and spoken about this parable, it seems foolish to try to add to them. Allow me to point out a couple of features. The Sheep, of course, are those rewarded by God, those who did what God wants from his people. The Goats had failed to do what God desires. What does God want? Simply, God wants us to take care of each other. The strong must help the weak. A watching God awaits us, prepared to reward us for what we have and have not done.

Elisabeth Schmitz: A Model for Kingdom Community

Elisabeth Schmitz grew up in the town of Hanau just outside of Frankfurt, Germany, in the early part of the twentieth century. She read insatiably and often lectured her older sisters that they were not serious enough. When she went to college, she was dissatisfied with the university in nearby Bonn and sought the bright lights of Berlin instead. There she studied theology and history with some of the brightest minds in the world.

She became a fixture in the home of Adolf von Harnack, perhaps the greatest theologian of his day. She was among the very first women in all of Germany to earn a doctorate.

Equally influential was her circle of friends. She chose to live in the Jewish Ghetto in Berlin, an odd choice in those days for a fair-haired German girl. She sought out the culture and thought of those different from herself. She grew close to a physician, Martha Kassel, a friendship that would have profound implications for her life.

When Hitler and the Nazis came to power, Kassel lost her job due to the new anti-Semitic policies. To save money, Schmitz and Kassel moved into an apartment together. Germans were insulated from news of the persecution being suffered by Jews, but with Kassel in the house, Schmitz heard stories about it every day. She became increasingly alarmed that her church was doing nothing to stop this injustice. In 1935 she began writing a document that would be one of the clearest critiques of the Nazi regime given by any voice in all of the German church.

She finished this "Denkschrift" in the summer of 1936 when she proposed to regional church leaders that the document be read and adopted. When they refused, she took matters into her own hands: she purchased a mimeograph machine and made 200 copies of this twenty-four–page critique, a staggering 4800 sheets of paper. Simply owning such a machine would have been enough to earn imprisonment. She circulated these copies anonymously to church leaders: Dietrich Bonhoeffer and Karl Barth are known to have had copies in their possession. As clear as this critique was, and as righteous the cause, her Denkschrift fell on deaf ears.

When the pogrom known as "Kristallnacht" came in November 1938, she wrote her pastor, Helmut Gollwitzer, urging him to speak out against the violence. Gollwitzer did so, being one of only three or four pastors in all of Germany who preached against the violence in the weeks that followed. She retired from her teaching position in protest, again a subversive act, openly declaring that she could no longer teach her subjects of history and German language according to the Nazi program. Then she went on to perform her most subversive act of all: sheltering Jews in her apartment and in a vacation home north of Berlin.

Her story was unknown until 1998 when a friend first attributed the Denkschrift to her. This was confirmed in 2004 when the handwritten manuscript was discovered in a musty church basement in her hometown. Recently Yad Vashem, the Holocaust Museum in Jerusalem, recognized Schmitz as "Righteous Among the Nations," a designation reserved only for those who sacrificially rescued Jews during this most dark period of history.

Schmitz is the embodiment of the very best of kingdom community. She practiced enemy-love, allowing her eyes and ears to be opened through a friendship with someone her society had deemed evil. She practiced Matthew 25 vigilance and preparedness by gaining the best theological education available at the time and through regular prayer and worship. She took huge, selfless risks. She devoted herself to protecting the vulnerable. She seemed unaware that any recognition would ever come to her for her selfless deeds. Her faith was completely practical, although agonizingly difficult.

So if you were hoping for a chapter that would be a practical blueprint for a revitalized church for the twenty-first century and beyond, I am sorry to disappoint. But this age offers a new opportunity, perhaps like no other in all of history, to practice a biblical faith. What is needed is a new generation of leaders who will set their sights on the very highest calling: to be disciples of the Lord Jesus Christ. Churches are needed that will strive toward fidelity to Christ's most difficult teachings. "Are ye able?" says the Master…

SECTION II

Leading to Holistic Love of Marginalized Neighbors, Such as…

8

Those Trafficked and Commodified

Jennifer D. Crumpton

I received a jarring phone call back in the fall of 2004. The call opened my eyes to a surprising phenomenon. The voice of an old friend informed me that "a friend of his" had been perusing Craigslist—the well-known information-sharing Web site for people hunting furniture, roommates, jobs, and the like. He had seen me in an ad for a high-end escort service. I laughed impatiently. Obviously my friend was playing a sick joke on me. He was quite familiar with my outspoken stance against the exploitation of female bodies and psyches and against the casual denigration of human sexuality propagated by the sex industry profit machine. Besides, how would an ad for what amounted to prostitution make it onto Craigslist anyway?

Unconvinced, I logged on to Craigslist.com. My friend directed me past the Community section that connects neighborhood volunteers and parents seeking childcare, and on to the Adult Services section. Not long before, I had spent weeks on New York City's Craigslist site finding my apartment, but had managed to overlook the section I would never have guessed lurked there among the Vacation Rentals and the Lost & Found: unrestricted, pornographic ads selling sex. On that phone call, I was quickly learning that Craigslist's Adult Services section was all the rage in New York City, especially among associates of my friend on the phone, who were mainly well-paid Wall Streeters.

He guided me through endless postings for immediately available sex for sale, many with graphic headlines to appeal to various desires of "shoppers." Pictures of baby-faced, heavily made-up girls wearing little to no clothing accompanied most of the ads; many of them appeared adolescent. He pointed me to an ad for a service that offered "house calls." There among the "choices" was my smiling face. The image had obviously been cut out of a candid shot and awkwardly Photoshopped onto another body. My face,

66

visible to just past my chin, was looking one way; the unknown neck-down was turned the opposite direction. She displayed an outfit and a pose definitely not in my personal repertoire. I noticed that many of the photos seemed inauthentic, as if in all of their blazing over-exposure, someone was trying to cover something up. I was shocked by the bizarre invasion of my privacy and by the audacity of the person who felt justified in using unsuspecting women's likenesses for their unsavory profit without permission. I felt violated and disturbed. I contacted Craigslist's customer service, threatened to call authorities, and they removed the ad.

Fast forward six years. A familiar, disconcerting knot in my stomach forms as I listen to a story reported by Amber Lyon on CNN about the rampant sex trafficking of young girls across America on Craigslist. I was only vaguely aware of domestic sex trafficking—it was something that seemed to happen more in far-away places where societies perpetuate norms foreign to our American values of freedom, democracy, and personal autonomy. Indeed, it does: in Thailand, the total scope of the flesh industry (including generally accepted or legal activity) sees revenues between U.S. $18—21.6 billion a year, amounting to well over half of the 1995 budget of that country. In Japan, sex trade revenue equals approximately the amount of the Japanese defense budget, according to research by the Coalition Against Trafficking in Women (catwinternational.org) and ECPAT (End Child Prostitution, Child Pornography and Trafficking of Children for Sexual Purposes, ecpat.net), both international networks working to eradicate the problem.

As I further researched the Craigslist issue and began paying attention to an increasing circulation of media stories about illicit Internet incidents and sex ring stings around the country, the truth became undeniable: sexual slavery was happening in the land of the free. Not only was it happening, it was also rooting itself deeply into our national social ethos and economy. Overwhelmed at how many lives it touched, ruined, and even ended, I set out to understand the global problem, the domestic situation, and the role the Word of God can play in mobilizing Christians to combat such devastating oppression.

A World in Bondage: The Global View of Sex Trafficking

What exactly is trafficking? The United Nations Office on Drugs and Crime explains, "Human trafficking is the acquisition of people by improper means such as force, fraud or deception, with the aim of exploiting them." Article 3, paragraph (a) of the Protocol to Prevent, Suppress and Punish Trafficking in Persons defines it as "the recruitment, transportation, transfer, harbouring or receipt of persons, by means of the threat or use of force or other forms of coercion, of abduction, of fraud, of deception, of the abuse of power or of a position of vulnerability, or of the giving or receiving of payments or benefits to achieve the consent of a person having control over another person, for the purpose of exploitation. Exploitation shall include, at a minimum, the exploitation of the prostitution of others or other forms of sexual exploitation, forced labour or services, slavery or practices similar to slavery, servitude or the removal of organs."[1]

Globally, trafficking in persons is one of the fastest-growing criminal activities, second behind drug trafficking. Bridgette Carr, a professor at the University of Michigan Law School and national expert on human trafficking, says it is so profitable that experts and authorities are seeing some drug traffickers get out of drug trafficking and into human trafficking.[2] The United Nations estimates that anywhere from 700,000 to 4 million women and children are tricked, coerced, threatened, or kidnapped around the world for purposes of forced prostitution or other forms of commercial sexual exploitation, such as pornography, live sex shows, or nude dancing at strip clubs, among other types of sexual labor. The victims typically see little to no income, which is taken by the seller or pimp, on whom they become dependent for subsistence. The UN points out that "conditions in the current era of globalization, such as the growth of informal economies and economic discrepancies among nations, increasing flows of labour and commodities across international [zones], and transnational organized criminal networks are causing human trafficking to flourish on a global scale."

The Initiative Against Sexual Trafficking (IAST.net), a program of the Salvation Army, reports that day-to-day life for millions of vulnerable women and girls—not to mention boys and LGBT (lesbian, gay, bisexual, and transgendered) youth worldwide—consists of constant violence and fear, degrading sexual acts, and forced abortions. The attempt to survive under these conditions leads to drug and alcohol dependencies, sexually transmitted diseases, and acute physiological reactions as a result of the trauma. If the victims survive, says IAST, "the physical, psychological and spiritual impacts of these experiences on victims are devastating and enduring." The threats and resulting dependencies enable a cycle of exploitation that propels a thriving illegal industry of sex trafficking estimated to be a $7 billion dollar annual business worldwide.

American Girl: Stolen for Sex

This scenario is not just a foreign affair. Traffickers find a lucrative opportunity in the United States to sell sex with young girls, and they are responding to increasing market demand from American men. They stock up on their "products" using many different methods, often forming relationships and taking advantage of vulnerable kids who live in poverty and have little supervision, strained family situations, or low self-esteem. Other times, they simply take what they want. Fifteen-year old "Debbie" was a straight-A student, the middle child in a close-knit Air Force family in a quiet Arizona suburb:

> My friend Bianca called one night and wanted to stop by my house. I walked out into the driveway in my Sponge Bob pajamas when I saw her drive up. She was in the car with two older guys, Mark and Matthew. We talked for a few minutes. Before she left, I reached over to hug her goodbye. When I did, she unexpectedly pulled me into the car. Mark took off down the street and out of my neighborhood. They told Bianca to tie me up or they'd shoot her. As she tied my hands and put tape over my mouth and eyes, one of them told me if I did anything stupid, he'd kill me. Meanwhile, my mom, who was just inside the house with my siblings, didn't realize I had not come back inside yet.
>
> They drove me around for hours. and I got really exhausted and confused. They took me to an apartment. One of them put a gun to my head and he goes, "If I was to shoot you right now, where would you want to be shot—in your head, in your back, or in your chest?"
>
> Then I hear him start messing with his gun. He counted to three, and then he pulled the trigger. But I was still alive. I opened my eyes, and I just saw him laughing. They gave me something to drug me up.
>
> I heard someone else come in. He sounded older and said he'd really like to have a 15-year-old.
>
> Then he goes, "Bend her over. I want to see what I'm working with."
>
> That's when he started to rape me. Then I see more guys—four other guys had come into the room. They each took a turn. Later another guy drove me around and forced me to have sex with him in the car and in a park. He talked to me about prostitution.
>
> He took me back to his apartment and asked if I was hungry. When I said 'no,' he shoved a dog biscuit in my mouth. He forced me into a small dog crate and made me stay there for days. My body went numb.

Authorities call this the breaking down period, where the captors physically and psychologically gain complete control over the girl. Debbie's captors put an ad on Craigslist. Men began arriving at the apartment at all hours of the day and night, paying her captors hundreds of dollars to have sex with her. She had no other choice than to comply. She was threatened and brutalized by the captors and their friends who gang-raped her periodically. The captors forced her to have sex with at least fifty clients.

> I didn't know them, but most of the 'clients' were married, with kids. I asked every single one of them why they wanted me if they had a wife at home. They didn't answer. So, like, I felt so nasty. But I had to do it, because the men who kept me told me they would go after my family. They even threatened to throw battery acid on my 19-month-old niece. After they told me that, I didn't care what happened to me as long as my family stayed alive. That's pretty much what I had in my head—staying there to keep my family alive.

Police later revealed that Debbie had been held by her captors at gunpoint, beaten, forced to take part in degrading sex acts and prostitution, and kept in a dog kennel for more than forty days. While investigating the case, authorities had gathered tips that she was being kept in an apartment in a nearby city, but when they finally honed in and showed up at the apartment, they did not find the teen. Still suspicious, police later broke down the doors to the same apartment and figured out why they had previously not been able to locate Debbie—she had been bound and crunched into a drawer under a bed.

> I heard an officer calling my name but was too scared to answer. I didn't know what to say. I was just lying under the bed, stiff as a board, shaking. Then he opens the middle drawer. He was like, "Oh my God!"
> When they got me out of the drawer, I was sobbing. I gave the officer the biggest hug in the world.

Speaking about the case, Ernie Allen, Director of the National Center for Missing and Exploited Children, said, "These are human beings who are owned by someone else, who lack the ability to walk away, who lack the ability to make a decision in their own self-interest to do something else. If that's not slavery, I don't know what is."[3]

This is not some far-fetched story in a movie; it is very real. It is not an isolated case. Far from it, as a sampling of headlines attests:

"Birmingham man charged with attempting to lure 14-year-old into prostitution"

"Northern California teens sold for sex"

"Federal authorities from Memphis honored for breaking up child sex-trafficking ring"

"Fort Myers, FL, woman accused of using children as prostitutes"

"North Alabama man convicted in sex trafficking of an underage girl"

"Man gets 33 years for trafficking minor in Texas hotel"

"Georgia man arrested for engaging minors in sexual servitude"

"Somali sex trafficking ring in Tennessee"

"Mississippi man pleads guilty to sex trafficking"

"Sex Trafficking in the U.S. Called 'Epidemic.'"

As these recent headlines reveal, human beings are living in sexual slavery all around us—in cities and small towns alike. Forced sexual commerce finds an insatiable market in our very communities. Atlanta's Hartsfield-Jackson is one of the world's busiest airports, surrounded by the East Coast's and Southeast's highway thoroughfares. So those who study trafficking trends find no surprise that Hartsfield-Jackson serves as a primary hub for trafficking. For this reason, "A Future. Not a Past" established its first state-level anti-trafficking organization in Georgia. As a case study example, statistics in Georgia reported by the organization are as shocking as any of those reported in other parts of the world:

Seven thousand two hundred men account for 8,700 paid sex acts with adolescent females each month in the state of Georgia alone (about 300 each day).

More than 400 girls are being commercially sexually exploited each month.

About 10 percent of these men are actively, openly, and directly seeking to pay for sex with a female they know to be under the age of 18—the rest "end up" paying for sex with an adolescent female even though they did not ask that the young female be a teenager, per se.

Twenty-eight thousand men pay for sex with adolescent females each year in Georgia. Nearly 10,000 of these men purchase sex with adolescent females multiple times per year.

Men who buy sex from young females represent all adult ages and come from all over the metro area where the study posted ads. The age distribution of study participants was 34 percent under age 30, 44 percent age 30–39, and 22 percent age 40 or over.[4]

What mentality is at play when a grown man buys a young girl for sex like buying a hamburger for lunch? There is an unspoken, assumed "right" to satiate an appetite for any desire—seen to be a "need" that must be fulfilled. (Have you ever heard commonly accepted excuses such as, "It's a guy thing," "Men are just made this way," "Men have certain natural needs that must be met"?) This is only piqued and affirmed by legal activities such as streaming pornography online or on mobile phones, anytime, anywhere the mood hits. There is also a sense that young girls (or even grown women) do not qualify as human beings with feelings, needs, or rights. Girls are seen as means to an end, available on-demand for self-serving consumption and convenient disposal, for the exchange of minimal cash. Girls and women are simply aesthetic choices in size, shape, and features for the sake of men's sexual satisfaction. This idea is stealthily promoted in our culture via movies, television shows, magazines such as *Playboy* and *Maxim,* and Photoshopped advertising targeted at women themselves, twisting women's self-esteem and brainwashing us into playing the part for male culture. These societal conditions and many other factors contribute to the market run on commodified, on-demand sex for sale. And the numbers are rising daily.

In the United States, estimates show that up to 300,000 children and adolescent girls are the victims of domestic trafficking and commercial sexual exploitation every year.[5] In 2000 our federal government began to address the problem with legislation called the TVPA, or Trafficking Victims Protection Act, which provides a framework for criminalizing domestic human trafficking.[6] This allows federal agencies such as the Federal Bureau of Investigation (FBI) and the U.S. Department of Homeland Security's Immigration and Customs Enforcement (ICE) to investigate and handle trafficking cases. In 2003, the FBI realized the enormity of the problem and created the Crimes Against Children Unit's Innocence Lost National Initiative. According to data reported by the Assessment of U.S. Government Efforts to Combat Trafficking in Persons, 79 percent of people convicted of human trafficking during the years 2005–2007 were specifically convicted of sex trafficking (as opposed to other kinds of forced labor). Since 2003, the thirty-nine Innocence Lost Task Forces and associated working groups have recovered over 1,200 children from commercial sexual exploitation. Their website says, "The investigations and subsequent 625 convictions have resulted in lengthy sentences, including multiple 25-years-to-life sentences and the seizure of more than $3.1 million in assets."

Targeting the Most Vulnerable

The FBI chillingly notes that "at least 25 percent of adult prostitutes were enticed into the illegal activity as juveniles."[7] The average age of entry for female prostitutes in the United States is between twelve and fourteen years, according to a report by the University of Pennsylvania School of Social Work's Center for the Study of Youth Policy. This study breaks down the circumstances and factors identified in scholarly research that fuel sexual exploitation of minors, listed here in the order of frequency:

1. the use of prostitution by runaway and thrown-away children to provide for their subsistence needs;
2. the presence of pre-existing adult prostitution markets in the communities, especially where large numbers of street youth are concentrated;
3. a child's prior history of enduring sexual abuse and/or sexual assault;
4. poverty;
5. the presence of large numbers of transient males in communities— including military personnel, truckers, conventioneers, and sex tourists, among others;
6. for some girls, membership in gangs;
7. the example or promotion of juvenile prostitution by parents, older siblings, or boyfriends;
8. the recruitment of children by organized crime units for prostitution; and, increasingly,
9. illegal trafficking of children for sexual purposes to the U.S. from developing countries located in Asia, Africa, Central and South America, and Central and Eastern Europe.[8]

In addition to American girls who are exploited, about 14,500 to 17,500 girls from other countries are smuggled into the sex economy of the United States, according to the State Department—attesting to the profitable market that international traffickers find right here within our borders. In the borderless land of cyberspace, the exchanges are easier, quicker, and more accessible. In 2010, the number of registered social networking accounts outnumbered the world's population, hitting the ten billion mark.[9] The extensive, rapid growth of social media has enabled billions of people to create and share online content on a virtually unlimited scale hardly conceivable just a few years ago. The monumental, viral participation in these social networks is evidenced by the proliferation of data, opinions, personal stories made public, photos and videos, reviews of products or experiences, and news items that are exchanged on a minute-by-minute basis.[10]

Technology and the Body Commodity

This seamless economy of creating and sharing is used to exchange information, ideas, products, and connections that are both edifying and damaging to society. One of the most devastating reported crimes facilitated by social media is the purchasing of sex with female minors, specifically minors who are trapped against their will in the domestic sex trafficking industry. Social media and online transaction forums in the United States are simultaneously acting as tools for the exploitation of girls and as weapons for fighting against such crimes. Johns (a common term for the consumers of paid sex) are increasingly seeking out and finding underage girls for sale in the online social space. However, on the other hand, organizations ranging from grassroots to government-backed agencies are creating public awareness, educating at-risk girls, and conducting sting operations against trafficking rings using social media and online forums. Marty Parker, an FBI agent who works on human trafficking cases for the Oakland office, reported that men using online means to find underage prostitutes may try their best not to leave a trail for law enforcement, but they inadvertently do. "Just a pimp posting an ad for these girls on myredbook.com gives us their interstate nexus right there. We can then bring federal charges against him," Parker says. But that does not mean the perpetrators will actually be prosecuted, or even ultimately stopped. "We could [track them] every day if we had the manpower to do it," Parker says. "Unfortunately, there are too few people working in the FBI who work these cases."[11] Market forces are clearly more powerful than the backlash at this point in history.

Technology scholar Eran Fisher says that in the last forty years, society has experienced "two extraordinary transformations in advanced capitalism." One is post-Fordism and the subsequent rise of the new globalized economy; the other is the "emergence of network technology (or information and communication technology) and its integration into virtually every sphere of life." The new globalized economy, as noted earlier, provides more unregulated or undetected avenues to accommodate the trafficking business, and the latter phenomenon has created a technological revolution in commerce with its hallmark access and digital ease.[12] It is not hard to imagine why perpetrators of sex trafficking have honed in on social media technology—not only is it difficult to identify and track them in the "virtual world" of the online space, but it is also where their potential victims can be cultivated. According to a new study by the Pew Internet and American Life Project, in 2009, 73 percent of teenagers ages 12–17 subscribed to an online social networking site. The study also notes that teens who come from low-income families that earn less than $30,000 are more likely to log on to social networking sites daily than those who come from wealthier families and therefore have greater opportunities to participate in other extra-curricular activities.[13]

The Advanced Interactive Media Group, LLC, reports that online prostitution advertising generates approximately $33.6 million in annual revenue. The projected rate in late 2010 was originally $70 million, before Craigslist finally pulled its paid Adult Services ad section in the face of pressure from law enforcement, politicians, media, and anti-sex-trafficking groups who exposed the fact that the ads promoted sex with girls under eighteen.[14] *USA Today* recently reported about how sexual predators and traffickers are taking advantage of the soaring popularity of social media and mobile devices to victimize children. In the article, Ernie Allen, CEO of the National Center for Missing & Exploited Children, said that the widespread access and use of social networks, online interactive gaming, smart-phones, and webcams has translated into "more opportunities for potential offenders to engage with children" and also for pimps and sexually exploitative social media sites to make more money in a direct-to-consumer approach. The report said that CyberTipline, the U.S. national hotline for reporting the sexual exploitation of children, received 223,374 reports in 2010, nearly double the 2009 number.[15] With all of these social norms and new technologies stacked against us, how do we respond?

Finding Conviction and Courage in Christian Faith

The first thing that occurs to me when I hear these stories and statistics is Jesus' first announcement of his ministry. The Gospel of Luke says he stood up and read from the scroll in the synagogue and boldly proclaimed to the congregation, "Today this scripture is fulfilled in your hearing" (Lk. 4:21). He summarized his mission with a quote from Isaiah 61: "The Spirit of the Lord is on me, because he has anointed me to proclaim good news to the poor. He has sent me to proclaim freedom for the prisoners and recovery of sight for the blind, to set the oppressed free, to proclaim the year of the Lord's favor" (Lk. 4:18–19). If Jesus understood his ministry in this manner, how should we understand ours as Christ-followers? Christians have no more time to sit in the pews concerned with only their personal salvation, rules and regulations, and daily devotions.

Victims of human trafficking are silently screaming for release from captivity and freedom from abuse and oppression. We have a God-given duty to educate ourselves about the modern-day slavery occurring all around us and be vigilant in our communities. We must discard our scales of judgment and delegitimize legalistic interpretations of Scripture and denominational doctrine that crowd out radical love and mercy. Instead, we would do well to invest spiritual efforts in sensitizing ourselves to the systemic exploitation of the female body and personhood that is so widely ignored and simultaneously so widely accepted in our society today. Our praxis must quickly move away from resistance, blame, and exclusion to the active application of

God's Word—calling for protection for the vulnerable and liberation for the oppressed. The mass consumption of women's bodies does not just materialize without cause in an alternate universe of "bad" people. We must face the implications of our consumer-centric, marketing- and profit-driven popular culture, which is quietly undergirding and normalizing the sale of girls' and women's bodies as profitable commodities for immediate, unencumbered gratification. We must find the courage to speak out against all types of sexism and objectification, from overly sexualized toy dolls and Halloween costumes for young girls, to the mainstreaming of pornography and the commodification of sex, to the unrealistic portrayal of women's bodies and sexuality in advertising and entertainment, to the ever-looming gap in pay between men and women.

David Gushee and Glen Stassen outline an ethical paradigm that marks the hope of renewal for the world based on biblical standards.[16] Around the issue of sex trafficking, hope and renewal are dependent on drawing from some particular principles identified in that ethical paradigm: our focus on cooperatively ushering in the reign of God, our ability to consider and respect the perspective from the underside of society, our willingness to confront injustice, and our consistency in the practice of radical love. Constructing Christian thought, worship, and practice around these elements helps us learn to detect and act upon the will of God as articulated in the vision of Jesus: freedom for those imprisoned in a system of greed and corruption; recovery of sight and insight for those who have become deadened; the end of oppression; peaceful, healthy relations and equal access to prosperity in the year of the Lord's favor.

This is cooperative action to bring the reign of God (known also as the "kingdom of God") into our reality. Christ-followers believe that Jesus came announcing that the reign of God was at hand and that Jesus inaugurated the in-breaking of this reign into society with the inception of his ministry. In *Kingdom Ethics*, this belief is gleaned from passages such as Matthew 4, which says, "'...the people living in darkness have seen a great light; on those living in the land of the shadow of death a light has dawned.' From that time on Jesus began to preach, 'Repent, for the kingdom of heaven has come near'" (Mt. 4:17). The term "repent" has a meaning too often misunderstood. The Greek *metanoia* implies a change of perception after an event, the act of changing one's mind to accept a new reality. It has nothing to do with finger pointing or letting guilt immobilize us. Jesus didn't bring a new religion; he brought a new reality, one that required—and still requires—humanity to adjust to new standards and expectations for relationships and organized structures of daily living. This reality is constantly asserting itself—even in the face of opponents—over the course of human history. Those who perceive it know it sets people free from fear to become all God created us to be. Those who have tasted it crave it unrelentingly and will not stop until it is fully realized.

Mark 1 says, "as it is written in Isaiah the prophet: 'I will send my messenger ahead of you, who will prepare your way—a voice of one calling in the wilderness, 'Prepare the way for the Lord, make straight paths for him.'" (Mk. 1:3). In other words, the reality of God was ushered in with the preparations for the ministry of Jesus, and our continuing preparations and way-making for The Way are just as crucial today. The Word has written the arc of history in its trajectory toward increased compassion, interdependence, and desire for the common good. It is happening now. God's reign is coming to be even as we speak. The reign of God is dependent upon our active participation along with God in bringing this new reality to fruition in our own spheres of influence. This means that a major ethical imperative of a Christ-follower includes actively working to promote the reign of God on Earth. We can start by doing such work in our communities.

How do we know what we should be doing and working toward? Gushee and Stassen acknowledge "seven marks of God's reign" that can help us envision our long-term goal: God's deliverance, presence, justice, peace, healing, joy, and the restoration of outcasts into community.[17] Only a gut-level assessment of these indicators is required for a person to understand that God's reign cannot be recognized and fully claimed if the commercial sexual exploitation and slavery of human beings is taking place in our world. Freedom to live a fear-free childhood and to develop into God's vision for our unique purpose is a universal human right. We must understand action against sex trafficking as our calling in helping to bring God's reign, knowing that God's ultimate presence will finally eradicate such crimes.

In the spirit of Jesus' context as a marginalized Palestinian Jew in his first-century, Roman-occupied homeland, we must ask what the "good news" of the Gospel looks like from the perspective of those who most frequently endure oppression and affliction. For example, considering the issue of sex trafficking from the "underside" or less powerful position in society is what a program based in Harlem, New York, called GEMS (Girls' Education and Mentoring Services), is all about. Unlike in countries where sex tourism is part of the local culture, child and adolescent prostitution in the United States is often the product of poverty, lack of education and economic opportunities, rough or violent environments, substance abuse, physical or sexual abuse, or family dysfunction. GEMS Executive Director Rachel Lloyd notes that "over 70 percent [of victims of commercial sexual exploitation] have been in the child welfare system at some point. Such information indicates that something is going on in the home, whether it is abuse or neglect or alcoholism. Somewhere along the line the family got fractured, and the child is the one to suffer."[18]

Most of the young women in the GEMS rehabilitation program were manipulated into becoming prostitutes by pimps more than twice their age. These pimps preyed on girls they came across who were walking along the street alone, luring them by promising to take care of them, to become their boyfriends and love them, never mentioning their true intentions or that they were pimps. To a young girl in any of the circumstances I listed a moment ago, this sounds like her ticket to a better life. Jesus offered a real path to a better life, and that is why he came to announce the kingdom of God. In passages such as those found in Isaiah chapters 9, 35, and 60, it is promised that those suffering would find relief, and that "no longer will violence be heard in your land, nor ruin or destruction within your borders, but you will call your walls Salvation and your gates Praise" (Isa. 60:18)

A survivor of abuse and GEMS alumna, Dominique, says about her family: "We fought a lot in my house. Domestic violence like you wouldn't believe." She remembers that back when she ran away she hadn't gone more than a block before a pimp pulled up next to her. "[He said] 'I can really help you. I can really be like your father and a person you can love all in one. Like family.'" Dominique didn't need to think twice: "Family? OK! Family? Alright! I'm getting in the car!" Dominique is now an advocate for other girls like herself and on staff at GEMS, with her own apartment, and a loving husband and daughter.[19] It took an organization of people who were willing and able to see the issue from her perspective of vulnerability and understand her specific situation and needs to help her back on her feet. Even if it is not our own experience, we can also learn to be sensitive to the perspective of another and resist absolving ourselves from concern or involvement by way of judgment and legalistic scapegoating. Looking down from a far-removed perch, we too easily think that someone should be able to "pull themselves up by their bootstraps" when, in reality, we would all take our own set of risks out of our common core need for love and support.

The life of Jesus was characterized by his willingness to confront injustice. Confronting injustice in word and deed was a large part of Jesus' initiative to spread the ethics required to establish the reality of God. Confronting injustice is not always easy. Confronting injustice requires us to think critically about institutions and situations we live alongside in daily life and to say and do things against the grain of social norms. It can lead to rejection and isolation from certain people and social groups. In the name of Jesus' reign of confronting social injustice, we must prepare to make these sacrifices.

For instance, the greatest annual incident of domestic sex trafficking happens during one of our nation's most beloved sports events: the Super Bowl. During preparations for the 2011 Super Bowl at Cowboys Stadium in Arlington (in the Dallas-Ft. Worth area), Texas Attorney General Greg Abbott stated, "The Super Bowl is the greatest show on Earth, but it also has an ugly underbelly. It's commonly known as the single largest human trafficking incident in the United States."[20] Ernie Allen, President of the National Center for Missing and Exploited Children, told a *USA Today* reporter: "Tens of thousands of party-minded football enthusiasts descending into a Super Bowl host city make it an ideal setting for traffickers of underage prostitutes." He said that each year 100,000 to 300,000 American kids, some as young as twelve years old, are exploited in the domestic sex trade, and the pimps use the Super Bowl and other major events to make a huge profit selling sex with children and adolescents. "The traffickers try to seize that opportunity to do business," Allen noted.[21] In past years, incidents of domestic sex trafficking have spiked particularly during the Super Bowl, in the host city especially, but also in other cities around the country where fans are tuning in and partying.

Being the purveyor of such knowledge and statistics will not make any of us the life of the party; but educating our friends, family, and others about such alarming trends is our heritage of courageous confrontation. Jesus lived a life characterized by an imperative to recognize and face reality, to invest in the plight of others, and to address the suffering of the oppressed. He did not behave in a way that suggested waiting around for one day "bye and bye in the sky when no one will cry." He lived his purpose with equal concern and action in every situation and every moment of his daily living. During the feasts and festivals of his community, Jesus often was drawn away from the laughter, camaraderie, food, and wine to focus on injustices in the community, to tend to the healing of the afflicted, and to raise awareness and speak out against social norms, economic practices, and political power plays that hurt and enslaved vulnerable people. A celebration was not an excuse to check out and pretend as if the lighthearted tone of the event meant no systematic evil was being perpetuated in its midst.

We are called to do the same. It is not fun to think about or popular to talk about, but as Christ-followers we must encourage reflection on this issue. Even if it puts a damper on some of the things we enjoy most, we must accept our role as bold transformers of society. Gushee and Stassen break down the practices and teachings of Jesus into four key "transforming initiatives" of justice that will be valuable to us in our fight against sex trafficking: (1) naming the injustice of greed and pursuing deliverance into economic sufficiency/ fair economic practices, (2) naming the injustice of domination and pursuing deliverance through mutual servanthood, (3) naming the injustice of violence and pursuing deliverance through peace-making, and (4) naming the injustice of exclusion from community and pursuing deliverance into covenant relationship.[22] As we seek to follow Christ, we must be instigators who follow through on such transforming initiatives.

Injustice of Greed

The ability to confront injustice begins with being able to detect such injustices by recognizing them in busy, complicated, everyday life. Whether you are a parent, teacher, social service worker, law enforcement agent, neighbor, or someone who is on the same bus, in the same class, or otherwise in contact with a girl who might be in trouble—we must begin to see the problem, step up, and speak out. This requires us to trust our instincts; if something does not seem right, it probably is not. Personal indicators can include (but are not limited to):

1. inappropriate dress, including oversized clothing or overtly sexy clothing;
2. poor personal hygiene;
3. possession of large amounts of money;
4. rumors among students or friends regarding sexual activity, which the child may or may not deny;
5. behavior that is withdrawn, uncommunicative, angry, aggressive, clinically depressed, suicidal, and/or tearful; diagnosis of sexually transmitted disease(s);
6. older boyfriend(s) or an often-present male friend or relative;
7. older female friend(s).

Educational factors pointing to a girl in trouble may include:
1. not being on grade level;
2. being a special education student with personal indicators mentioned above;
3. low functioning and/or being developmentally delayed with personal indicators mentioned above;
4. having behavioral issues in school;

5. chronic absenteeism;
6. sleeping in class.

Family factors pointing to a girl in trouble may include:
1. runaway or throw-away child;
2. lack of adult supervision and support;
3. sexual abuse at home by family member or friend;
4. history with the Department of Family and Children Services;
5. parental substance abuse;
6. domestic violence;
7. living or hanging out in geographic areas known to be gathering places for prostitution.

Legal factors involved in a troubled girl's life may include:
1. a history in the Juvenile Court system, probably on repeated status offenses;
2. fake identification and/or fake dance permit;
3. substance abuse;
4. a history of recruiting others into prostitution;
5. the arrest of the child in or around an area known for prostitution, such as an adult entertainment venue, strip club, massage parlor, X-rated video shop and/or hotel.[23]

The organization "A Future. Not a Past." exhorts concerned citizens to advocate for solid state laws needed to provide protection for exploited kids and stricter penalties for the criminals who sell and buy them. AFNP encourages local communities to assess what policies and laws are currently in place by finding out whether their state has the following: felony status for pimping minors, laws against human trafficking, a law defining the commercial sexual exploitation of children as child abuse, budget directives specifically for services for victims and survivors to move from crisis to security, and a minimum age below which a child cannot be charged with prostitution.[24] We can also actively confront injustice by advocating for bipartisan federal legislation that seeks to provide crucial funding to develop and carry out collaborative efforts to combat the sex trafficking of minors in the United States. S. 2925, the "Trafficking Deterrence and Victims Support Act of 2009," was introduced in late 2009 by Senator Ron Wyden (D-OR) and H.R. 5575, "Domestic Minor Sex Trafficking Deterrence and Victims Support Act of 2010," was introduced on June 23, 2010 by Congresswoman Carolyn Maloney (D-NY) and Congressman Chris Smith (R-NJ).[25]

Finally, the greatest of these is love. Scripture impresses the importance of love in the teachings and actions of Jesus. Matthew 5 includes the parable of the good Samaritan (we all know how that passage instructs us to behave), while John's Gospel includes Jesus' new command: "Love one another. As I have loved you, so you must love one another. By this everyone will know that you are my disciples, if you love one another" (John 13:34–35). We are also familiar with the characteristics of love set out in 1 Corinthians 13: "Love does not delight in evil but rejoices with the truth. It always protects, always trusts, always hopes, always perseveres. Love never fails" (vv. 6–8a).

Gushee and Stassen advocate a practice of "delivering" love. This is "the embodied drama of acting to deliver another from distress and into community with freedom, justice, and responsibility for the future." They articulate this love as involving four movements that are applicable to our loving victims of commercial sexual exploitation: (1) seeing with compassion and entering into the situation of the person(s) in bondage; (2) doing deeds of deliverance; (3) inviting victims into community with freedom, justice, and responsibility; and (4) confronting not just perpetrators of this exploitation, but those others who would stigmatize the victims and exclude them from community.[26]

Because of the physically violent and psychologically abusive circumstances they endure, victims of sex trafficking are known to suffer from post-traumatic stress, sexually transmitted infections, substance abuse, and long-term health problems. Without access to a safe place, proper treatment, and guidance toward security and provisions, survivors are at risk of doing the unthinkable: returning to their abusers. Tasha Perdue of Ohio Trafficking in Persons has advised advocates and law enforcement in other regions that the abusers often either already are, or shortly become, "someone the victim trusts, and [the perpetrators] usually develop a relationship with them. It's a lot more damaging that way." Victims eventually begin to believe lies instilled in them by their traffickers, such as believing they are actually three or four years older, and hence "legal." Once they are rescued, Perdue says it often takes many rounds of interviewing to get the true story.[27] The principles of patience, endurance, faith, hope, and love found in our Scriptures provide a tool box that can be employed for the benefit of victims of commercial sexual exploitation.

Today, many faith communities are joining in the fight against sex trafficking and the venues that assist criminals. For example, currently many clergy groups and faith communities are speaking out against the popular general classifieds website Backpage.com, owned by Village Voice Media. At the time of publishing, Backpage remains the leading U.S. online publisher of prostitution ads and is the leading U.S. online publisher in the sex ad category. According to Women's Funding Network, it provides the nation's most frequently visited online marketplace for buying and selling trafficked girls. Backpage is the online classified advertising site for VVM's thirteen alternative weekly newspapers, the five weeklies published by Creative Loafing, and a number of other publications, mostly alternative weeklies.

In February 2011, the site generated $1.8 million from escort and body rub ads in that month alone. Village Voice Media, facing pressure from law enforcement officials and anti-sex trafficking groups, made minor changes to their adult advertising sections of Backpage but has taken no steps to actually protect girls from being trafficked through the paid ads for escort services and body rubs, which are both common euphemisms for prostitution and frequently used by traffickers and buyers to exploit girls.[28] In the U.S., publishers of online advertising posted directly by advertisers are protected by the Communications Decency Act if they have not been reviewed before they appear online—even if they promote prostitution or include, for example, illegal references to discrimination in housing.[29] Religious groups and leaders are coming together with petitions and other action, calling for the complete removal of the Adult ad section.

The implications of the activity on Backpage.com's Adult site are exemplified in a story uncovered by Youth Radio (affiliated with National Public Radio). Youth Radio reports that trafficked girls have described photo studios in Oakland, California, where girls pose in sets that appear like bedrooms. "Studios provide lingerie, wigs and makeup. For an extra fee, some studios will upload the X-rated photos and post online ads on behalf of the pimp. By posting the ads on sites based in other cities, pimps line up customers across the country and send the trafficked youth on 'sex tours.'" Youth Radio investigated and found out firsthand how easy it is for a minor to tap into these resources. A reporter called a photo studio in East Oakland, pretending to be a young girl wanting to get into the prostitution business. She was then connected with a man who offered to manage her online marketing—with payments made via PayPal. "She asked him if it mattered that she was only seventeen. He said, 'I wouldn't even mention it.' He said he would post ads to several of the popular online classifieds, including Village Voice Media's Backpage.com, where he had a 'pretty good hookup' that allowed him to buy sponsored banner ads."[30]

Looking back to 2004, I will never forget the unnerving experience of seeing my disembodied face in an ad that sold women and girls on Craigslist. That was just my likeness being abused, and I—by the grace of God—had the power and agency to demand it be removed. Every day, young girls are being trapped and forced into actually going through with the acts promised to buyers targeted by those ads, strategically crafted by the callous people who sell them. Those faces could be the actual girl next to you on the bus, sitting next to you in class, in the seat beside you at the movies, or attending community or church events alongside you. She is too frightened or embarrassed to speak up. These are our sisters, our daughters, and, most importantly, God's children, and their faces desperately need our voices.

9

Those Suffering from Preventable Diseases

Andi Thomas Sullivan

Because the previous contributors to this volume have provided valuable insights into the broader vision of kingdom Christianity, I want to focus on one aspect of love of neighbor, namely caring for those suffering from preventable diseases. Preventable diseases are those diseases that can be prevented or treated by vaccinations, medications, sanitation, or basic nutrition. They generally afflict the segment of the world's population that is poor and marginalized.

"I was sick and you took care of me."

"If a brother or sister is naked and lacks daily food, and one of you says to them, 'Go in peace; keep warm and eat your fill,' and yet you do not supply their bodily needs, what is the good of that? So faith by itself, if it has no works, is dead" (Jas. 2:14–17, NRSV). Christians agree that faith needs to be demonstrated through action. Moving from this theoretical agreement to concrete action is how Christians can become a sustained moral presence in our world. "For in Christ Jesus neither circumcision nor uncircumcision counts for anything; the only thing that counts is faith working *through love*" (Gal. 5:6, NRSV).

For me, loving my neighbor means living out Jesus' words: "I was sick and you took care of me" (Mt. 25:36, NRSV). According to the New Testament, Jesus spent most of his time teaching, feeding, and healing. That combination of activities spoke to the basic needs of people to be healthy both physically and spiritually. For centuries, Christian ministers and missionaries have continued to do those same things at home and around the world. Yet despite great advances in medicine, agriculture, and philosophy, people in even greater numbers still have those same needs.

For the most part, the need has not changed since Emmanuel walked this earth. What has changed is that for the first time in human existence, we now have the technology to prevent many diseases that ravage hundreds of millions of lives. Guinea worm is a parasitic infection contracted when people drink stagnant water and ingest Guinea worm larvae. The disease is excruciatingly painful, and incapacitates its victims for long periods of time, preventing them from working, farming, or attending school.

Today Guinea worm is entirely preventable. Stopping the Guinea worm and other water-borne illnesses can be done by preventing people from drinking infected water and educating them on using cloth filters to strain out the fleas that carry the larvae. In 1986, 3.5 million cases of the disease were diagnosed in Africa and Asia. By 2010, largely due to the efforts of the Carter Center and its partners, fewer than 1,800 cases were reported worldwide. Similarly, in children across the Two-thirds World, worms contribute to widespread anemia and malnutrition. One study in Kenya found that children given inexpensive de-worming pills at school for two years attended school longer, and 20 percent earned more as young adults than children given de-worming pills for just one year.[1] Another study has found that if every mother took iodine capsules during pregnancy, this would lead to a "7.5 percent increase in total educational attainment of children in Central and Southern Africa."[2]

Christians today must reclaim the call of the Incarnate God to cure, heal, and protect those most at risk of contracting the most common preventable diseases. As a young twenty-first century Christian, I am interested in how I can live my faith *now*. That is the story of "His Nets."

I am the child of Baptist missionaries. My parents instilled in me and my sisters a deep desire to spread God's love in the world and an appreciation for initiative and action. When I enrolled in college in the fall of 2003, I was excited about the possibilities for my future. What amazing class would train me to make a difference in the world? What major would best guide me in my life journey? As I settled into a routine, I realized that I could easily become trapped in my little world of challenging classes and extracurricular activities. In the meantime, people all around the globe would be dying as a result of hunger, disease, and war. I knew that nothing could make me wait until the summer of 2007 to start making a difference. Filled with both energy and frustration, I called my father. We made a date to sit down at Christmas break and talk about ideas and strategies.

One afternoon during the holidays we sat around the kitchen table talking about the problems of the world, a broad and far-reaching topic.

We finally settled on the subject of malaria, a disease that kills hundreds of thousands of people annually, most of whom are children under the age of five. No universal malaria vaccine exists. Drugs are expensive and must be taken on a regular schedule. Our family had experienced the dangers of malaria before I was even born. As a child, my oldest sister contracted a severe form of the disease and nearly died. My parents had the means to treat her, and she is now a healthy mother of four. But the majority of the world does not have the same resources my family had to counter the malaria.

After some exploration, my father and I discovered that while money was being poured into malaria research—beneficial in the long run but having no immediate impact—no organization was distributing on a global level the most cost-effective method of preventing malaria: insecticide-treated bednets. We discovered this oversight and saw it as an opportunity. More brainstorming and planning ensued. We found that bednets cost only $6.00 each. One net can protect an entire family from malaria. In the early months of 2005, we established a nonprofit organization called His Nets and held our first board meeting. That summer, we did our first net distribution in Ghana. I participated in my first distribution trip in 2006. During that trip, I kept a journal, recording the events and my response to the sights and sounds we encountered.

As we bumped along to our first distribution site in the two vans weighed down with huge bundles of nets, I saw some people walking. Actually, I just saw the color of their dresses. As we got closer I realized that hundreds and hundreds of women and children had gathered near the small health clinic. Music was playing in the distance. Under the bright sun, some women were selling creamy brown goat's milk in clear bags. You had to bite the corner off the bag and suck the liquid out. One woman was selling boiled eggs from a basket that was balanced perfectly on her head. Other women were carrying bread wrapped in newspaper. The red dirt made the bottoms of everyone's feet a strange color. The crowd was packed in. Mothers wiped the sweat off their babies' faces. One woman slapped a fly off of my arm. The children gaped at us. The brave ones held my hand and tried to get me to dance. The atmosphere was one of celebration. Some women had walked as far as thirty-seven miles to receive the life-saving nets for their families. We started distributing nets. I locked eyes with a woman who had strapped her baby to her back with a bright green wrap. She looked tired and hot. As I handed her a net, her face broke into a huge smile. She knew that this net could protect her children from the ravages of malaria. As I took part in my first net distribution that day, I realized how God could use one tiny idea and turn it into an amazing life-saving operation. We ran out of nets that day. While many women went home with a net, others went home without one. There was still work to be done![3]

Why Bednets?

So why are insecticide-treated bednets so vitally important to the well-being of our world? To answer this question, we must understand the persistent and global threat of malaria.

Malaria has plagued humans for centuries. Ancient Assyrian, Chinese, and Indian texts refer to seasonal fevers that afflicted masses of people. In the fifth century B.C.E., Hippocrates became the first person to chart in detail the effects of malaria and the complications of the disease.[4] The biblical texts also provide hints of the presence of the disease during Jesus' lifetime. In the Gospel of Matthew, we are told, "When Jesus came into Peter's house, he saw Peter's mother-in-law lying in bed with a fever. He touched her hand and the fever left her, and she got up and began to wait on him" (Mt. 8:14–15). The fever Peter's mother-in-law experienced was probably the result of malaria. The disease has long been with us. Attempts at combating the disease have also long been with us. From as early as the 1600s, European popes and kings were calling for a cure to the deadly disease.[5]

Even now, in the twenty-first century, malaria kills between one and three million people each year. In Africa, a child dies every thirty seconds of malaria. The disease has been eradicated from the West, but is still rampant in Two-thirds World countries, concentrated in tropical areas where lack of drainage creates pools of stagnant water.[6] Female anopheles mosquitoes carrying microscopic parasites transmit malaria. When a parasite-carrying mosquito bites a person, the mosquito transfers some of the parasite into the bloodstream. This injected parasite will eventually travel to the body's red blood cells, attacking them until they rupture. When the red blood cells burst, they release toxins into the body that cause the common symptoms of malaria: fever, chills, and vomiting. A person bitten by enough infected mosquitoes will eventually die. Pregnant women and children under the age of five are the most at risk of contracting malaria. The situation of pregnant women is compounded by the fact that they pass along the infection to the fetus, which results in low birth weight and impaired growth and development in the child after birth. The infection also lowers the child's immune system, and, thus, he or she is more susceptible to dying from malaria.

The impact of malaria spreads quickly beyond individual infections. One infected person can infect up to one hundred other people through additional mosquito bites. In countries heavily afflicted with malaria, the disease can decrease the nation's GDP by 1.3 percent and can be a deterrent to international trade and foreign investment. In those same countries, malaria is responsible for 60 percent of outpatient visits and 30–50 percent of hospital admissions.[7]

Malaria disproportionately affects the poor. Because they cannot afford treatment or do not have access to healthcare services, poor families become trapped in a cycle of poverty. The same can be said for all preventable diseases: they disproportionately affect the poor who cannot afford basic healthcare, clean water, or a balanced diet.

His Nets: Beginnings

In 2005 when my father and I founded His Nets, we began by establishing a board of directors. We have intentionally expanded it each year. The board of directors has a president and meets twice annually. Throughout the year, the board corresponds through e-mail, communicating about distribution opportunities and voting on new projects. In 2009, the board hired my father, Charles "T" Thomas, as part-time director of His Nets. He actively promotes the organization, oversees the day-to-day logistics of net distributions, and provides a monthly report to the board of directors.

Several things had to take place to grow His Nets into a functional 501(c)3 organization. First, the board had to establish the need for bednets and formulate a plan to meet the need. Establishing the need was easy. Malaria is concentrated in humid regions all around the equator, and approximately 500 million people are infected with the disease each year. To meet the need, the board determined to distribute the highest-quality, longest-lasting insecticide-treated bednets and to provide them at no cost. Based on this plan, the board contracted with a company that agreed to sell nets at a huge discount—for $6.00 a piece or less depending on location and the quantity purchased. The board also determined that all money donated to His Nets would go directly to purchasing and distributing nets.

Second, the His Nets board wanted to cooperate with already existing organizations to avoid duplicating efforts or wasting resources. We have cooperated with the missions organization Global Women as part of its public health initiative of collecting birthing kits to send to women in Hyderabad, India. His Nets partnered in this project and provided bednets so that each mother and newborn could be protected. A rotary club in Maywood, New Jersey, wanted to be involved in combating malaria, and His Nets connected the club with a primary school in Kenya, where the nets purchased by Maywood citizens were distributed. As part of Mercer University's Mercer on Mission program, college students traveled to the Lake Baringo area of Kenya and distributed 6,000 nets. His Nets has also partnered with the United Nations High Commission for Refugees and dozens of local churches, schools, and universities.

His Nets seeks to involve people from around the world in the net distribution programs. The board will continue to partner with any community-based organization or religious denomination that wants to be of assistance in preventing malaria. Some organizations sponsor the distribution of nets to a whole village or sponsor an entire His Nets project in a particular country. Sponsoring organizations might provide all the nets for the project, or provide the travel costs of the His Nets distribution team, or sometimes provide both the nets *and* cover the travel costs. Sometimes organizations participate in the project by accompanying the His Nets team on the net distribution project. Regardless of the degree of participation, His Nets provides the technical advice, assistance, logistics, and leadership for the completion of a net distribution project.

His Nets: Financing

His Nets relies on private donations to finance the purchase of nets. The organization is supported by individual donors, churches of many denominational affiliations, rotary clubs, schools, and universities. His Nets has been the recipient of two in-kind grants from the United Kingdom-based Against Malaria, which has funded projects in Ghana and Kenya. His Nets has also received a grant from the Christian Life Commission of the Baptist General Convention of Texas. The work of His Nets has received support and recognition from the state of Oklahoma and Baptist World Alliance (BWA). One of its primary partners for the work is the All-Africa Baptist Fellowship (AABF), the African branch of the BWA based in Kumasi, Ghana.

Financial support has come to His Nets sometimes in unusual and creative ways. In 2008, the Upward Basketball and Cheerleading program at St. Matthews Baptist Church in Louisville, Kentucky, celebrated its tenth year. In appreciation, the league leaders decided to raise money to help others. In December, they gave each basketball player and cheerleader in the league a coin bank with the His Nets logo on it. The children were charged with going home and filling up their banks with change. In February, they returned their overflowing banks at the Awards Nights program. The offering that night totaled $5,886, with more than $3,000 of it in coins! Some children were so excited about His Nets that they took the project back to their schools and raised more money. In the end, the offering ended up providing more than 1,000 nets to people in need.

In 2008, Nadia, a sophomore at St. Mary's Hall in San Antonio, Texas, used her speaking skills and some resources downloaded from the His Nets website to launch a fundraising campaign. Through a bake sale and with the assistance of the school's Red Cross Club, Nadia helped raise $1,080 for net distributions. In Kentucky, three boys had a birthday party and asked their friends not to buy gifts. They asked them instead to bring the money they would have spent on a present and pool it together to purchase nets. Hundreds of dollars were collected and sent to His Nets.

His Nets: Partners

As a nonprofit, nongovernmental organization, His Nets is developing several unique approaches to delivering international public health preventive services through the active participation of members of local communities. The community focus of His Nets involves independent, local organizations—including churches—whose members demonstrate their belief in humanitarian assistance by supporting His Nets programs. By relying primarily on donor contributions and maximizing voluntary assistance in both the United States and targeted African and Asian communities, His Nets can efficiently provide high quality, long-lasting, insecticidal bed nets to families in great need.

All bednets are distributed without cost to the receiving families, with priority distribution to pregnant women and families with children under five years of age. His Nets distributes nets through the network of existing in-country health services, including governmental health departments, hospitals, clinics, and in-country His Nets volunteer partner organizations. In-country partner organizations are an essential key to successful net distribution projects.

One in-country organization vital to the work is the AABF, whose member churches are located in all African countries. Because many of the African national Baptist organizations sponsor ongoing preventive health clinics and community medical services, we have discovered a readily available source of talent and services at the local level. Through its affiliation with the BWA, the AABF also has built-in connections to many Baptist churches in the United States. The common link of mutual membership in the BWA between all involved organizations ensures trust and common humanitarian interests. His Nets has also participated in net distribution projects with mission personnel of the Cooperative Baptist Fellowship in Africa, Haiti, and Southeast Asia.

One example from this partnership is seen in our connection with First Baptist Church, Garland, Texas. In October of 2007, a five-member team from that church collaborated with His Nets and an Angolan national Baptist association. The team traveled to Angola to provide 2,000 nets to an extremely needy neighborhood in Luanda. The Garland church and His Nets together purchased the nets; His Nets leaders provided technical advice and traveled with the team to make the net delivery; and the Angolan Baptists had a team of public health "trainers" that accompanied the Garland team and provided instruction of net installation and use. A clinic managed by the Angolan Baptists was used as a distribution station. Interpretation (English-Portuguese) was provided by the Garland Team leader and a public health nurse-educator, who was sponsored by the British Missionary Association (BMA) and stationed in Luanda. The initial contact between His Nets and the Angolan Baptist association was made via the AABF-BWA. Hence, five organizations were participating partners in this particular net distribution in Angola, with each partner organization providing what was necessary to succeed. Practically all other His Nets distribution projects to date have experienced similar partnering connections.

In January and February 2009, His Nets partnered with Milledge Avenue Baptist Church in Athens, Georgia, and the Commission Baptist Church in Monrovia, Liberia, to distribute bednets in Liberia. Comfort L. Ylonh, mother of five, wrote the following in appreciation: "The fourteen years of war has brought untold suffering to many to the extent that many cannot afford a fitting meal daily let alone some basic necessities of life… We could see smiles on the faces of many when the distribution [of nets] was carried out… The distribution brought relief to many who could not afford medical treatment or malaria treatment… May God Almighty bless you as you continue to be a blessing to the needy."[8] In December 2010, Christian and Muslim volunteers conducted a weeklong distribution trip in Tanzania, working together to distribute 2,500 nets in the area surrounding Dar es Salaam. Malaria does not have a religious preference.

His Nets: Volunteers

Although the costs for the U.S. volunteers to travel to Africa has never been a part of the His Nets annual budget, such costs are substantial and often sacrificial on an individual basis. American volunteers who travel to malaria-ridden countries at their own expense to assist in net distributions are a vital part of His Nets. These volunteers return to their home churches with visions of the next distribution project and are enthusiastic community supporters of His Nets. They have been exposed to the reality of malaria and have worked with their African AABF/BWA partners to prevent malaria in their world. Community groups and churches can actively work together to achieve a common goal, even when they are located halfway around the earth.

Even government leadership has become involved in the missional vision of His Nets. Oklahoma Governor Brad Henry and Kim, his wife, participated in a His Nets distribution project in Ghana in 2007. This experience prompted Henry to declare April 25 as Oklahoma Malaria Awareness Day—making it the first and so far only state to have a day of awareness.

Individual volunteers also have contributed to the work of His Nets. Don Lassiter, a recognized public health expert, became an early and loyal supporter of the organization. Before his untimely death in December 2009, he volunteered hundreds of hours to His Nets by writing the weekly e-newsletter, researching grant opportunities, and keeping up-to-date on the latest malaria news.

His Nets: Why It Works

As of December 2011, His Nets has completed seventy-nine projects and distributed over 100,000 nets in twenty different countries throughout the world. Perhaps the real success of His Nets is its simplicity. One $6.00 net saves two lives. It is such a simple formula. This formula highlights the fact that in the face of a devastating disease such as malaria, one person can make a difference. Providing $6.00 and saving two lives is so much more effective than saying, "Malaria, isn't it awful!" The future is bright for His Nets. It has no big corporate or wealthy sponsors. It will continue to depend on individual donations to resource this work. It will also continue to offer a customized approach to helping people, civic groups, classes, and other organizations "Fight Malaria One Net at a Time!"

Neighbors are more than the people next door. We are a part of a larger community, and our neighbors are our fellow humans. Christians cannot plead ignorance to the plight of our more distant neighbors. Globalization has increased our exposure to world events and also our potential impact on our global neighbors. Following Jesus' mandate to love our neighbor is a question of stewardship. The biblical directive is not to bury our money in the caves of consumption, self-preservation, and greed, but to share (Mt. 25:14–30). Meeting the needs of those suffering from preventable diseases is a simple way to live out Christ's example.

An earlier version of this chapter named "A Twenty-First Century Mission Endeavor Called His Nets" was previously published in On Mission with God, *edited by Pamela R. Durso with William O'Brien (Atlanta, Georgia: Baptist History and Heritage Society, 2011).*

10

Our Muslim Neighbors

Rick Love

Sixty-one people gathered at the Mile High Vineyard in Arvada, Colorado, to attend a "Love Your Neighbor Dinner."[1] Almost half of those attending were Muslims from the Abu Bakr Mosque in Denver. We gathered to share, to talk, and to break down barriers...by breaking bread together.

I opened this event by describing the massive peacemaking effort initiated by Muslims, known as the "Common Word." According to Muslim leaders all over the world, a "common word" exists between Christians and Muslims: We are to love the one true God and our neighbor as ourselves.[2] What a great starting point for peacemaking!

Imam Karim and Pastor Jay Pathak then spoke for fifteen minutes each on love of neighbor from an Islamic and a Christian perspective. Next, we had a time of Q&A with Imam Karim, Pastor Jay, and myself. One of the questions stuck out to me. Ahmad asked: "Do all Christians around the world really believe that love of God and neighbor is that important?"

I thought Ahmad's question was merely theological. He wanted to make nice to talk about important sounding topics that never impact real lives. After the Q&A Ahmad came up to me and wanted to talk more. So we went through the buffet line, talking and filling our plates with tasty Middle Eastern cuisine. When we sat down, he leaned toward me and got serious.

"Rick," he said. "I asked that question for practical reasons. My family has been warmly welcomed in our neighborhood. Our neighbors treat us well. What bothers me is that one of our neighbors is known for being a Christian, yet he is the least friendly of all of our neighbors. That's why I asked the question. My Christian neighbor does not love us. The nonbelieving neighbors make us feel more welcome."

Wow! What was this "Christian" neighbor thinking? What kept him from obeying Jesus' command to love his neighbor?

The Challenge of Islamophobia for the Church

Christian-Muslim relations comprise one of the momentous challenges of the twenty-first century. From the Christian point of view, three major causes contribute to a growing Islamophobia in the United States. First, *global trends* such as terrorism, increased persecution of Christians worldwide, and Muslims' strong reactions against Westernization and American foreign policy; second, Christian theology that favors Israel and a belief that Islamic theology promotes *jihad*; third, negative stereotyping of Muslims usually caused by a complete lack of personal relationship with Muslims.

So many Christians have this fear of Muslims—usually Muslims they have never met. This fear has caused the church to shrink back from the fundamental biblical command to love. Instead of loving Muslims, we perpetuate prejudices. We are promised a love that drives out fear (1 Jn. 4:18; 2 Tim. 1:7), but we experience a fear that drives out love.

How do we overcome our fears? How can we combat Islamophobia?

The media has bombarded us with sound bites and stereotypes. Sometimes we are told that Islam is a religion of peace. Yet the more disturbing and frequent picture painted in our society depicts militant Islam.[3] We need an accurate and discerning view of Muslims.[4]

We realize that Christians vary immensely from one another in many ways, yet many of us still tend to assume all Muslims are alike. We perceive them as either terrorists or backers of persecution of Christians. We feel that they all hate us. Much of what we hear about Islam leads Westerners to conclude that Islam represents "the evil empire" of today.

I have been working with Muslims for over thirty years. I have had the privilege of walking the streets of over twenty Muslim countries—spanning the Muslim world from Morocco to Malaysia. I have enjoyed coffee with rich Arab Muslims in the Gulf States and tea with poor African and Asian Muslims. I have had meals with high-level religious and political leaders, discussing the great theological issues of life. I have also sat many times on mats on the floors of huts joking and enjoying the simple things of life (like friendship!) with my hosts. When I lived in Indonesia, I would often join the men in my village at the mosque during times of community deliberation or whenever we had to vote on something.

People in the U.S. usually think that Muslim women are oppressed. My answer: It depends on what country, what ethnic group, and what form of Islam is affirmed.

We need simply to turn to politics to recognize the diversity of roles and privileges women have in Muslim countries. The largest Muslim country in the world, Indonesia, had a female President, Megawati Sukarno. I have had the great honor of meeting the late Benazir Bhutto, who served as Prime Minister of Pakistan, at the National Prayer Breakfast in Washington, D.C. As Madeleine Albright notes, "The countries with the largest number of Muslims—Indonesia, India, Pakistan, Bangladesh, and Turkey—have each elected a female head of government; this is a distinction that neither any Arab state nor the United States can claim."[5] So let's be careful about saying women are oppressed in Islam.

The Muslim world is radically diverse. In some fifty-two Muslim-majority nations over 1.5 billion Muslims reside, comprising over two thousand different ethnic groups, with large minorities in another forty countries. There are huge differences and varied expressions of Islam. Ultra-conservative Islamic states such as Saudi Arabia and Iran contrast sharply with secularized ones such as Turkey and Indonesia. When people think of Muslims, they usually think of Arabs. Yet less than 25 percent of the Muslims in the world are Arabs. The vast majority of Muslims live in Asia.

The Islamic world contains rich theological and ideological diversity as well. Islam has two major sects: Sunni, comprising 85 percent of the Muslim world, and Shia, comprising 15 percent, with eight recognized schools of Islamic jurisprudence.[6] Fundamentalism is on the rise, but at the same time a large number of Muslims are calling for reform and speaking out against extremism.[7] The Royal Aal al-Bayt Institute for Islamic Thought in Jordan leads the way in this important quest.[8]

Sufis are the mystics of Islam but do not represent a separate sect. Some Muslims affirm the rigorous, external path of Shariah law;[9] and some Sufis seek the internal, mystical path of love. Some researchers estimate that as many as 50 percent of the world's Muslims may be Sufis in the widest sense of the term.[10] The impact of Sufism on other forms of Islam can be compared to the charismatic movement's permeation of evangelicalism. The mystical Sufi emphasis on the love of God tends to cause Sufis to be more open to others' views of God than other forms of Islam (e.g., the *Salafis* of Saudi Arabia).[11] It also makes them more positive toward peacemaking and more resistant to Islamism and terrorism.[12] Stephen Schwartz argues that Sufis provide a potential medium for interreligious conciliation and global harmony: "Sufi pluralism and tendencies toward an exalted spirituality, love of Jesus, and resistance to Shariah-centered literalism all represent alternatives to the stagnation imposed in Islam by radical ideology. Sufism is…an indispensable element in any real solution to conflict between Islam and the West."[13]

The chart below describes the spectrum of Muslims in the world today:

| Secularist | Modernist | Traditionalist | Fundamentalist | Terrorist |

Secularists reject Islam as a guiding force for their lives, whereas Modernists have a "West is best" approach to Islam. They want to change and adapt Islam to the modern world. Traditionalists view Islam as a treasure that must be wisely and flexibly applied to the modern world.[14] Fundamentalists are literalists who strive to obey the Qu'ran and the Hadith, while ignoring or rejecting many of the classical traditions of Islam. They seek to model their lives after Muhammad and his earliest disciples.

Terrorists are militant Muslims who espouse violence to impose their expression of Islam on others. They declare Muslims who think otherwise as apostates ("*takfir*"). Therefore, they believe less-strict Muslims and all non-Muslims need to be coerced to submit to their truth, even if violence is needed to accomplish their mission. The result is that thousands upon thousands of people have been killed in the name of Islam. But it is important to note that more Muslims have been killed in terrorist attacks than Westerners.

Traditionalists comprise approximately 90 percent of the Muslim world, while Modernists and Fundamentalists comprise slightly less than 10 percent. Some estimate there are only 150,000 Terrorists in the world today, less than one hundredth of 1 percent of all Muslims.[15] Therefore the percentage of Muslims who are prepared to hurt people for their cause is roughly the same as the percentage of Ku Klux Klan members among American Christians in the first half of the twentieth century.

So Islam is not monolithic. When people make broad pronouncements about Islam you need to ask: Which Islam? What country? What school of theology?

The vast majority of Muslims are just like you and me. They want to live in peace. They want good jobs and good educations for their children. They want to be treated with dignity and respect.

But let's suppose for a moment my evaluation of Islam is wrong. (It isn't! But just suppose…). So what?

We may (and even will) differ in our understanding of Islam. But we can all agree about what Jesus teaches. Jesus commands us to love our neighbors *and* enemies.

Muslims: The New "Samaritans"?

The relationship between Christians and Muslims today parallels the racial and religious tensions between Jews and Samaritans in New

Testament times. Both Jews and Samaritans were monotheists. Both Jews and Samaritans worshiped the God of Abraham. Yet the Samaritans were seen as heretics—syncretistic in faith, ethnically inferior, excluded from the true worship of God.

The animosity and hostility between these two communities is explicitly mentioned twice in the Gospels: (1) "The Samaritan woman said to him, 'You are a Jew and I am a Samaritan woman. How can you ask me for a drink?' (For Jews do not associate with Samaritans)" (Jn. 4:9). (2) "but the people there did not welcome him, because he was heading for Jerusalem. When the disciples James and John saw this, they asked, 'Lord, do you want us to call fire down from heaven to destroy them?' But Jesus turned and rebuked them" (Lk. 9:53—55). The similarities are stunning. James and John's hostile response to the Samaritans does not reflect the Spirit of Jesus. It sounds hauntingly similar to how some Christians respond to Muslims today.

The biblical description of Samaritans provides us with insights for our interaction with Muslims. The Gospels record three stories about Samaritans. Jesus told the parable of the Good Samaritan (Lk. 10:29–37) to show that love for one's neighbor reaches out beyond race and religion. The hero of the story was a Samaritan! (A "good" Samaritan would have been an oxymoron for a Jew.) In another incident, Jesus healed ten lepers, but only the Samaritan showed gratefulness (Lk. 17:11–19). Then, with the spiritually inquisitive Samaritan woman, our Lord reached out across the barriers of race, religion, and gender to communicate the words of life to her. Through this woman he then ushered other Samaritan "rejects" into his kingdom (Jn. 4:1-43).

Surely Jesus and the authors of the Gospels didn't believe that all Samaritans were compassionate like the Good Samaritan, grateful like the healed leper, or spiritually receptive like the Samaritan woman. Why then did they make the Samaritans the "good guys"—the "heroes" of their stories? As he does throughout the Gospel, Jesus wanted to challenge Jewish prejudices and break down the wall of hostility that had been built between the two communities.

Muslims are the new "Samaritans." So how would our Master, Jesus Christ, have us respond to today's "Samaritans"?

Let's check out Jesus' personal interaction with the Samaritan woman in John chapter 4. Does Jesus reflect the animosity or hostility typical of Jewish-Samaritan interaction? No! Jesus takes the initiative to engage the Samaritan woman. He begins his discussion with the Samaritan as a bridge builder. He overcomes religious, racial, gender, educational, and even moral barriers to connect with this woman, to meet her where she was. No condemnation. No finger wagging. No debate. Bridges of love.

But Jesus doesn't ignore the hard issues. He begins with dialogue, but addresses doctrine. He clearly states: "salvation is from the Jews" (Jn. 4:22). But please note. He doesn't say she has to be a Jew to be saved. Instead he talks about the new thing God is doing. Now is the time to worship God "in the Spirit and in truth" (v. 23). Jesus invites her to this new thing.

Notice the Samaritan woman's progressive understanding of who Jesus is. In many ways her experience becomes paradigmatic of what happens to monotheists who become followers of Jesus. First she sees Jesus as a Jew. Then a prophet. Next the messiah. Finally the Savior of the world. She was suspicious of the Jew, respectful of the prophet, longing for the messiah, and finally adoring the Savior.

That's Jesus one-on-one with the Muslims of his day. Now how does his teaching about Samaritans guide us regarding our relationships with Muslims?

A fresh look at Jesus' teaching about the Good Samaritan in context should make us tremble. In Luke's gospel a lawyer tests Jesus by asking: What must I do to inherit eternal life? Jesus' answer: Obey the command to love God and neighbor and you will live (Lk. 10:25–28). Not exactly the typical evangelical answer to that question. Jesus says our eternal destiny is linked with obedience to those two great commands!

The Gospel of Mark seems to confirm this. Jesus says no other commandments are greater than love of God and of neighbor. When a religious leader affirms these truths (Mk. 12:28–34), Jesus says, "You are not far from the kingdom of God" (v. 34). Note that he doesn't say, "You have *entered* the kingdom." Understanding the greatness of these commands merely puts you *near* the kingdom.

Evangelicals talk a lot about a "personal relationship with God." In fact, we've really got this right. For example, the command to love God with all our heart, soul, mind, and strength is in the "singular" in Greek—*you personally* are called to this loving relationship with God. There is a unique focus on the individual. This is profoundly significant since the vast majority of commands in the New Testament are in the "plural"—*you, the community of faith*.

Evangelicals fail in not emphasizing the relationship between love of God and love of neighbor. Jesus purposely put these two commands together. In other words, love of God must lead to love of neighbor. Don't talk about your love for God unless you show it to your neighbor. This is the point of the Good Samaritan.

Jesus taught the parable of the Good Samaritan (Lk. 10:29–37) to show that love for one's neighbor reaches out *beyond race and religion, even to the enemy*. If we dared obey the words of Jesus, we would experience a revolution in our attitudes and relationships with Muslims (and all other people looked down upon by society or evangelicals—"illegal immigrants" and the "gay community," for example...).

How did Jesus define *neighbor*? Anyone in need, even if of a different—or even despised—religion, nationality, or race. The Samaritan felt compassion and showed mercy. What did Jesus conclude? *"Go and do likewise."*

Jesus is calling the Jews to imitate the "bad guy," the Samaritan. If Jesus were teaching this to Christians today, he would probably make a Muslim the hero.

Let me tell you a modern story about a Muslim Good Samaritan. A decade ago our Indonesian Christian friend James and his young wife, Ida, got caught in anti-Christian riots on the island of Lombok. Fleeing their rented room, they hid in nearby fields for three days and nights, too frightened to emerge in search of food and shelter.

The riots followed a Muslim-led rally calling for racial harmony and an end to sectarian strife on the island. Furious protests broke out instead. Muslim youth demanded revenge for a reported massacre of Muslims by Christians on a neighboring island. While thugs burned eleven churches, killed one Christian, and looted Chinese stores, other Muslims quietly and heroically acted to save the lives of Christians. James and Ida were among those rescued.

A Muslim family found them and invited them to their home to wait out the rioting. When they heard that local police were offering shelter to Christians at police stations, the Muslim family hid James and Ida in their car and drove them to the nearest station. Afterward, they went to the place where James and Ida had been staying and collected their things for storage.

Not long after, James and Ida were transported back to Java, their island of origin, with nothing but the clothes on their back. The Muslim family who rescued them shipped their belongings to them—including a motorcycle—free of charge. Each year that family makes the costly trek to Java to visit James and Ida. A friendship was born in a frenzy of hate, a friendship that still lasts today.

Jesus described one other practical way his followers can demonstrate his love toward Samaritans: "But you will receive power when the Holy Spirit comes on you; and you will be my witnesses in Jerusalem, and in all Judea and Samaria, and to the ends of the earth" (Acts 1:8,). No one is beyond the reach of Christ's love or omitted in his commission. The God who is "not willing that any should perish" (2 Peter 3:9, KJV) compels us to be sure everyone on earth has an awareness of Jesus' liberating love! Even Samaritans. Even Muslims.

Loving Our Muslim Neighbor Without an Agenda

When people want to join my organization, Peace Catalyst International (PCI), we ask them about why they want to join a peacemaking organization. People who want to join PCI are typically people who like Muslims and who want to reach out to them. Because of this, we are serious about helping them determine if PCI fits, or if what they really want is a mission agency. What is their motive for joining PCI? It is easy for Christians to love their neighbors or do peacemaking in order to bear witness. We don't want people joining PCI with that kind of attitude. God commands us to love God and neighbor. Period.

During a PCI leadership team meeting recently, we confessed that our past approach to sharing our faith was not focused on love or friendship. Even with the best intentions, our approach to bearing witness was really "project evangelism"—we saw people as targets and projects. Of course, in theory we were committed to friendship evangelism. Still, we acknowledged what Christopher Heuertz and Christine D. Pohl say so well:

> "Friendship evangelism" is another evangelistic approach very vulnerable to misuse and misinterpretation. Befriending someone merely so you can tell them the gospel is a form of manipulation and a violation of trust. Augustine argued that loving the neighbor meant wanting what was best for them, which is to know and love God. So desiring this for a friend is a very good thing. But it must involve more than words and strategy; it involves fidelity within the friendship itself.[16]

We in PCI are trying to understand and practice what it means to have "fidelity within the friendship," as these authors state. God's command to love our neighbor governs his command to share our faith. We need to love our neighbor with no strings attached—whether they want to hear the Gospel or not. We please God when we love our neighbor without any other agenda.

Why don't we take the command to love our neighbor more seriously? Why do we value doctrine over ethics, creeds over deeds? Why do followers of Jesus put a much greater emphasis on right belief about Christ (orthodoxy) than they do Christlike living (orthopraxy)?

I would like to conclude with what Jesus' little brother, James, says about the importance of obedience. I could imagine James saying something like this about loving our Muslim neighbors:

"What good is it, [Christian neighbor to Muslims,] if you say you have faith but do not have works? Can faith save you?" (Jas. 2:14 paraphrased).

"Show me your faith apart from your works, [Christian neighbor to Muslims,] and I by my works will show you my faith" (Jas. 2:18 paraphrased).

"But be doers of the word, [Christian neighbor to Muslims,] and not merely hearers who deceive themselves" (Jas. 1:22 paraphrased).

11

People of All Races

Lisa Sharon Harper

I sat in a circle of emerging evangelical leaders when someone raised the question: "Is America a post-racial society?" They were not asking if race still exists in the United States. It does. That is clear. Rather they were asking if race is a relevant topic for the church to focus on anymore. Is it still an issue or is talk of race and racial reconciliation "so 1990s"?

So 1990s

Throughout the 1990s the issues of race and racism seemed to hover over the American consciousness like a blanket of smog over America's most polluted cities. All through the '90s national events pushed the issue to the fore. The videotaped police beating of Rodney King and the acquittals of all of the implicated officers triggered the 1992 riot that burned parts of Los Angeles to the ground. Within 36 hours of the court's announcement, Atlanta, Chicago, Philadelphia, and New York City were battling to contain their own raging eruptions.

Only three years later, the nation sat transfixed for more than nine months by one of the first reality television courtroom dramas, telecast by Court TV and other networks. America's historical and current-day racial biases took center stage in *The State of California v. O.J. Simpson*. The verdict in Judge Lance Ito's courtroom was telecast on split screens across the country: white viewers on one side, black viewers on the other. Their disparate reactions to the announcement of Simpson's acquittal exposed the vast divide between white and black experiences of justice in America. Blacks cheered; whites raged.

Evangelicals dove headlong into the business of "racial reconciliation" in the mid-1990s through movements such as Promise Keepers (PK). Founded in 1990, PK had taken up the mantle of Billy Sunday's "by men, for men" Men and Religion Forward Movement (1911–1912). Through stadium revivals in cities across the U.S., PK promoted the 7 Promises of a Promise Keeper. PK founder Bill McCartney, an award-winning football coach from the University of Colorado, looked out over the large crowd at PK's initial rally in 1991 and realized the crowd was almost all white. The realization of racial disunity in the church led McCartney to declare racial reconciliation a mandate of the movement the following year. The value is promoted through PK's 6th Promise: "A Promise Keeper is committed to reaching beyond any racial and denominational barriers to demonstrate the power of biblical unity."[1] In 1996 PK focused its year of stadium revivals on Promise #6. The following year PK event attendance dropped by more than 50 percent.[2] The organization had focused on "unity," which in evangelical-speak means "diversity"—the presence of every racial group before the throne in the kingdom of God.

However, PK did not deal with the intercultural power dynamics that inevitably arise once all are present. PK did not deal with present-day systems and societal structures and how the politics of white evangelicals affect the earthly lives and livelihoods of their kingdom brothers and sisters of darker hues. PK did not lay a foundation for how to understand or engage systemic sin. As a result, everyone was eventually disillusioned. Blacks who attended the rallies were met with scores of white men who wanted to befriend them, only to find out these white "brothers" weren't interested in learning about the structural issues facing black communities. Rather, white Promise Keepers just wanted to have lunch with and "get to know" their brothers of the darker hue.

Divided by Faith

According to Michael Emerson and Christian Smith, authors of *Divided by Faith: Evangelical Religion and the Problem of Race in America*, a seminal sociological study, PK's individual-focused, relationally framed, anti-structural tactics were true to evangelical form.

Emerson and Smith utilized the theory of cultural toolkits, originally developed by sociologist Ann Swidler, to understand white and black evangelicals. According to Swidler, people groups develop cultural tools to interpret the world around them. These tools are limited by the group's experience and, in turn, limit the group's capacity to accurately interpret the world, integrate information, and adapt to change. Having conducted more than 2000 phone interviews with evangelicals across the nation and hundreds of face-to-face interviews, Emerson and Smith identified a marked difference in the cultural toolsets of white and black evangelicals.[3]

Both black and white evangelical worldviews are deeply influenced by the evangelical faith's requirement of individual agency. For evangelicals, salvation is an individual's choice—not a community's or a family's choice and not bestowed upon an individual at birth by virtue of culture or heritage. One chooses to believe in Jesus, or not. One chooses relationship with God through Jesus or not. One chooses repentance or not. This focus on individual agency, also known as rugged individualism, provides a main frame through which evangelicals interpret the world. The frame leads to two basic assumptions: (1) individuals have ultimate agency over their destiny and, thus, they have ultimate responsibility for what happens to them in life; and (2) what matters are the decisions made by individuals—not communities, societies, or governments.

Both black and white evangelical worldviews are permeated by the evangelical relational framework of salvation. For evangelicals, salvation is not ultimately about a list of practices, precepts, or principles one has to profess to enter heaven. Salvation is ultimately about relationship with God through Jesus Christ. In other words, evangelical faith is not ultimately about ethics; it is about relationship. This relational lens leads to a laser-like focus on relationships as the vehicle for redemption. Questions of public and private ethics matter only as much as they enhance or break relationships between individuals.

Emerson and Smith's last major finding uncovered the great gulf between black and white American worldviews. While black evangelicals' experience of oppressive structures and systems makes them keenly aware of the presence and consequence of systems and structures on individuals and whole people groups, white evangelicals demonstrated a forceful revolt against the idea that structures and systems matter to anyone at all.[4]

Thus, according to Emerson and Smith, individualism, relationalism, and anti-structuralism are the three basic cultural tools that white evangelicals tend to have at their disposal to interpret and respond to the world around them. This does not have to be a permanent reality, according to the authors. The exchange of the tool of anti-structuralism for the tool of structuralism simply requires white evangelicals to invest time immersed in communities where pervasive, repeated exposure to systems, structures, and institutions impacts the whole community. This seems a simple enough path, and it is. Yet, rarely do white evangelicals follow this path. They tend to live, work, learn, and worship within the most self-segregated corners of American society.[5]

America's Racialized Roots

So, when the young—mostly white—evangelical leaders I sat with recently wondered out loud if America is a post-racial society, I understood their reference point. They were probably thinking: "Most Christians today harbor no ill will toward people of other races. So, why is this relevant?" They were probably thinking: "Most of my friends voted for Barack Obama for President in 2008. So, how could race still be relevant?" They were probably thinking: "I have several black friends. It's not relevant to me." They might even have thought: "Race isn't the only marker of suffering. I'm white, and I've suffered. Why doesn't that matter?"

Each of these reference points are arrived at using the white evangelical cultural tool kit identified by Emerson and Smith. They were focused on individual feelings, thoughts, or relationships. The historic and current day racialization of American institutions and systems as well as their implications for the present-day plight of ethnic minority communities was probably not in their purview. So, my response focused on racialized structural sin, America's lack of repentance, and its implications on contemporary society and the church.

Prior to 1640, no definitive legislative or judicial policy defined the status of Africans in America.[6] Thus, in the earliest years of colonial America servitude was not necessarily race-based. Nor was it necessarily in perpetuity (forever). The 1655 court case of Elizabeth Key, who won her case and thus her freedom, reveals enslaved blacks were presumably able to work for their freedom after a proscribed length of time, like white indentured servants.[7] Yet, evidence indicates records for white and black "servants" were kept differently. Listings of white indentured servants included the year their servitude began—essential information to figure the end of a servant's term of bondage. Black "servants" had no such indicator.[8]

The Key case also offered evidence slaves could earn their freedom by converting to Christianity. One of the three pillars of Key's successful case was that she had converted to Christianity. Under English law Christians could not be enslaved.[9] In 1640 three escaped indentured servants were brought before a Virginia court. As penalty for their escape, the court extended the two white servants' terms by four years. As penalty for the black man's escape, the court extended his term to encompass his entire natural life. While the court justified its ruling based on the black man's status as a non-Christian, it was the color of his skin, not his faith status, that was immutable. This 1640 ruling planted the seed of race-based slavery in America.[10]

Then within one generation, in 1662, the Virginia legislative body passed a law using the doctrine of *partus*. Until then, one's status as a freeborn English subject was granted based on the legal free status of the father. Borrowed from Roman civil law, *partus* held that the status of a child followed the status of the mother. This policy presented slaveholders who raped enslaved women with a convenient way to confine the evidence of their sin to the slave quarters while absolving them of any legal responsibility to acknowledge or free their children. Likewise, *partus* ensured slaveholders' free-labor force, extending race-based slavery beyond the term of an individual's life to encompass all future generations of the mother's line. Even if all traces of African heritage disappeared from the matrilineal line over time, children born to enslaved mothers would be considered black and would also be subjugated in perpetuity.[11]

The 1662 Virginia law created a new kind of permanent underclass in the New World—the black slave—to support its new kind of permanent nobility—the white American. Though the abolitionist movement and the Civil War put an end to the most extreme outcomes of the New World's caste system, it by no means put an end to it altogether.

The forebears of the United States mirrored Great Britain's social order, with its aristocracy and servant classes where privilege or subjugation was inherited by birthright or circumstance, with one crucial difference. In England, everyone was white, so blood lineage, rather than race, was the delineator.

The founders' Declaration of Independence: "We hold these truths to be self-evident, that all men are created equal, that they are endowed by their Creator with certain unalienable Rights, that among these are Life, Liberty and the pursuit of Happiness" signals that in this hallowed New World, every man is equal to a king. In America every man is free and equal and able to reap the benefit from the land, its resources, and its representative democracy. *Every* man, that is, except those who were not white.

Just seven years after the end of the Revolutionary War, our forebears felt the need to clarify who could enjoy the ultimate privileges and protections of U.S. citizenship. Through the Naturalization Act of 1790, they made it clear. The privilege of citizenship was reserved for "free white" people. One might argue that the qualifier for naturalization was not necessarily color, but rather the resident's free status. One would be wrong. In 1790, at the time of the first United States Census, there were approximately 59,511 free black persons in the United States.[12] They were not eligible for naturalization.

Thus, woven through the fabric and patterns of America's early years, "race" as we know it was invented and levied to establish and protect an economic and political system that granted white people extreme privilege— and all others, extreme degradation.

The Racialized Roots of Party Politics

The Democratic Party ascended to be America's chief viable party after the war of 1812. As such, it was the party that maintained the fledgling nation's economic stability. It did so largely dependent on the Southern, slave-based economy. In the years leading up to the Civil War, anti-slavery Democrats defected from their party and joined other small parties to form the Republican Party. Abraham Lincoln was the Republican Party's choice for president in 1860, and they won.

In the days of secession, the South broke off completely to form the Confederate States of America. In response, regardless of party affiliation, most Northerners rallied to the aid of their Republican president to preserve the Union. After the Civil War, the 1866 Congressional elections gave enough power to so-called "Radical Republicans" in Congress that they overrode Democratic President Andrew Johnson's vetoes and enacted the Reconstruction period. During this period the Republican Congress passed the Thirteenth Amendment, which officially ended legalized slavery in the United States; the Fourteenth Amendment, which extended citizenship to all people born in the U.S. or naturalized here; and the Fifteenth Amendment, which guaranteed all citizens the right to vote. The "Radical Republicans" also deployed the army to protect Southern black voting rights.

Democratic President Andrew Johnson ignored the Confiscation Acts passed by Congress in 1861 and 1862. These acts declared that upon winning the war, the North would redistribute all Southern land to the freedmen. Instead, Johnson pardoned Confederate landowners and returned their land to them. Resentful of the Republican-led Civil War victory and the party's process of "radical" change during the Reconstruction Era, the Democratic Party became the choice of the Southern elite. Reconstruction lasted from 1865–1877.[13]

Republican General Ulysses S. Grant became the eighteenth President of the United States in the middle of the Reconstruction era. One of his great contributions was the creation of the Department of Justice, an agency created to protect the rights of all Americans. The department paid special attention to the freedmen during the period of Reconstruction that saw the rise of Southern vigilante lynching and the establishment of the Ku Klux Klan.

During the period of Reconstruction, approximately 1500 African Americans were elected or appointed to public office! They were U.S. Senators and Representatives, State Senators and Assemblymen, mayors, judges, and Lieutenant Governors, among many other public posts.

Reconstruction ended in 1877, with a back room deal to settle the disputed election of 1876. In exchange for Southern Democrats' recognition of Republican Rutherford B. Hayes as president, the Republican-controlled Congress would have to withdraw all troops from the South and end its policies of Reconstruction. It did, and they did.[14]

The result was nearly ninety years of personal, communal, and systemic horror for black families across the South. Separate water fountains, bathrooms, and swimming pools humiliated black souls. Separate schools subjugated black minds. Bombed churches broke the backs of black communities. Jim Crow laws blocked black bodies from entering voting booths. Lynching sprees between 1882 and 1964 erased 3,445 images of God reflected in the faces of black men, women, and children from American soil.[15]

In response to the vicious consequences of the unofficial policy called the Compromise of 1877, nearly 7 million African-Americans migrated north to wherever the nearest trains would take them. From 1910 to 1970, black Southerners sought peace and family and a chance to live in cities such as Washington, Philadelphia, New York, Boston, Chicago, Detroit, and Los Angeles.[16]

In the midst of the great mid-century migration of blacks from South to North, another twentieth-century migration—a political one—took place among the Southern Democrats. In the 1940s' crooning era of Billie Holiday's "God Bless the Child," Nat King Cole's "Take the 'A' Train," and Lena Horne's "Stormy Weather," Southern Democrats fought in the U.S. Congress to preserve their right to lynch and charge poll taxes throughout the South.[17]

At the 1948 Democratic Convention President Harry Truman tried to assuage the Northern Democrats who wanted a strong progressive civil rights party platform, while at the same time he catered to the Southern Democrats who mimicked the Confederate mantra that federal intervention in the Southern "way of life" (Jim Crow segregation) would impinge upon states' rights. To appease the Southern faction, Truman cut a deal with Mississippi Senator John Rankin to keep the civil rights plank of the DNC platform vague enough to be ineffective. Then Minneapolis Mayor Hubert Humphrey took the stage to speak on behalf of the Minority Report on Civil Rights.[18] Humphrey said:

> It seems to me that the Democratic Party needs to make definite pledges of the kind suggested in the Minority Report to maintain the trust and the confidence placed in it by the people of all races in all sections of this country… There's no room for double standards in American politics!… For those who say that we are rushing this issue of civil rights, I say to them "We are 172 years late!" For those who say this civil rights program is an infringement on states' rights, I say this: "The time has arrived in America for the Democratic Party

to get out of the shadows of states' rights and to walk forthrightly into the bright sunshine of human rights!"[19]

The Democratic National Committee voted to adopt the pro-civil rights plank for the 1948 election season. They agreed to push for federal legislation to outlaw lynching, school segregation, and employment discrimination.

Thirty-five delegates from Mississippi and Alabama staged a walkout of the Convention. The Dixiecrat Party (*aka* The States' Rights Democratic Party) was formed, and South Carolina Governor Strom Thurmond was nominated as the Party's presidential candidate. The Dixiecrat Party, whose platform opposed racial integration and called for the preservation of Jim Crow laws and white supremacy,[20] was short-lived. Within two years most Dixiecrats were absorbed back into the Democratic Party. Then came the ultimate deal-breaker: Democratic President Lyndon B. Johnson pushed through the Civil Rights Act of 1964 and Voting Rights Act of 1965. Dixiecrats deserted the Democratic Party en masse. Welcomed by the Republican Party, they have resided there ever since.

The same year as Lyndon B. Johnson's passage of the Civil Rights Act, he declared "unconditional war on poverty" in the United States. Throughout 1964 anti-poverty programs such as food stamps, work study, Head Start, Medicare, Medicaid, and Social Security rolled out one after another, each adding a brick to the foundation of Johnson's "Great Society."[21] As a result of both rapid economic growth and concerted government efforts, within nine years the poverty rate in the U.S. dropped from 19 percent in 1964 to 11.1 percent in 1973—its lowest point before or since the rollout of the legislation.[22]

Since the mid-1970s, though, America has largely dropped its commitment to its short-lived war on poverty and its commitment to racial equity in tandem. According to Sheldon Danziger, professor of public policy at the University of Michigan, Americans responded to the recession of the late 1970s by calling for cuts in programs that benefited the poor, particularly African American poor communities, and to redirect public monies to support the white middle class in its time of need.[23] As a result, poverty rates rose sharply between 1975 and 1983 and settled between 11 and 15.2 percent until 2010, when the U.S. poverty rate jumped to 16 percent for the first time since 1965.[24] Government officials say the 2011 rate would have risen to 18 percent had it not been for the earned income tax credit for people with low to moderate income.[25]

The national numbers are grim, but African American and Latino communities have always served as the canary in America's proverbial coal mine. Due to institutional barriers to progress, these communities have always been most sensitive to shifts in economic policy. The poverty level for African Americans in 1959, the earliest date available, was 55.1 percent. By 1974, the rate had fallen nearly 25 points to 30.3 percent. Like the rest of the population, the rate rose sharply from 1975 to 1983 and settled between 35 and 33 percent through the George H. W. Bush presidency.[26]

President Bill Clinton catalyzed the first significant drop in the African American poverty level since Lyndon B. Johnson when he poured monies back into Great Society programs such as Head Start, children's health care programs provided through WIC (aid to Women with Infants and Children), and Medicaid. In 2000 African Americans reached their lowest poverty level ever in the U.S., at 22.5 percent.[27]

In the ten years since 2000, the African American poverty rate has risen again, in tandem with President George W. Bush-era economic policies, which called for tax cuts for the wealthiest Americans while simultaneously cutting key services for America's most vulnerable. Since 2000 the African American poverty rate climbed steadily again, reaching 25.4 percent in 2010. [28] Experts say the rate would have been much higher had it not been for safety net programs such as Food Stamps that kept many from falling into destitution.

For perspective, we need only to view the poverty rate of white Americans when separated from the rest. The first numbers available are for 1973, nine years after the declaration of the War on Poverty. The poverty rate for white Americans was 7.5 percent. White poverty rose to its zenith at 10.8 percent in 1983 under Reagan, and fell to its nadir at 7.4 percent in 2000 as a result of President Clinton's policies.[29]

What is the lesson? When America took steps of active repentance for inequitable political and economic structures, all Americans were blessed. When America sought to bless a few at the expense of the least, suffering observed no racial boundaries.

Repentance

Why have I spent so much time analyzing America's political and economic landscape in a chapter focused on the relevance of race? Political and fiscal structures have been the primary means by which people of color have been subjugated in the United States. This intersection is where the rubber meets the road in the American struggle to become a post-racial society.

The genesis of the United States is permeated with the creation of systems, institutions, laws, and social structures created to ennoble the status of people of European descent while subjugating people of color to a permanent status of serfdom, particularly African Americans and Native Americans. Thus, the struggles for political and fiscal fairness are at the heart of the quest toward the reconciliation of American institutions to all people made in the image of God.

Many times over the nearly 400 years of racialization in America, God has raised up prophets to call the nation to repentance for its institutional racial sin. In fact, American evangelicals as a religious movement were born in the context of such a moment. Evangelist Charles Finney invented the altar call for a twofold purpose: (1) to give people the opportunity to demonstrate their individual agency to follow Jesus, and (2) to give those same converts the chance to repent of the ways they had not been following Jesus. In his day, the primary public call to repentance was to renounce the institution of slavery. On the altar lay sign-up sheets for the abolitionist movement. God also called Sojourner Truth, Harriet Beecher Stowe, Phoebe Palmer, and others for such a time as theirs.

In the days of Jim Crow, God raised up Ida B. Wells to tell the stories of the lynchings, Hubert Humphrey to sound the call for political repentance, Rosa Parks to say "No" to subjugation any longer, Fanny Lou Hamer to move the feet of thousands with theologically rich walking songs, Dr. Martin Luther King to sound the cry for national repentance, and Lyndon B. Johnson to enact it.

In current times, as the nation recovers from the worst recession since the Great Depression, the Occupy Wall Street movement has sounded a clarion call for America to re-examine the inequitable outcomes of President Ronald Reagan's fiscal policies. Framed in the language of equity, the Occupy movement is calling for a leveling of the playing field between the disadvantaged 99 percent and the new American aristocracy dubbed "the 1 percent."

At each turn, with each prophetic window in American history, evangelical followers of Jesus have had to make a choice. Would they step through the window and join with the prophets in God's clarion call to "Let my people go!" or would they stand silent or, worse, join the perpetrators?

Evangelicals look back on the abolitionist movement with pride today. Our forebears heeded the call, and God moved mountains! We were not so faithful during the era of Jim Crow. In fact, the evangelical church took point on the segregationist side of the struggle. We largely sat out the civil rights movement and missed the call to wage war on poverty. Rather, we moved out of urban centers to our *de facto* segregated suburban communities, built *de facto* segregated "Christian" schools, and founded a new kind of fiefdom in the form of *de facto* segregated megachurches. It is no wonder, then, with our current level of isolation from people of color and the poor, that we were and are the primary purveyors of the glories of Reaganomics—the very system that not only ended America's war on poverty, but waged a war of omission on the poor, especially poor people of color.

It is not enough for evangelicals to have an African American, Latino, or Native American friend or two, though that is an important step on the road to the kingdom vision. It is not enough for evangelicals to seek representative "diversity" or "unity" in our churches and institutions, though that is a kingdom desire. It is not enough for evangelicals to confront our own personal racial and ethnic partiality, though that is one of the most fearsome endeavors in our world. Our call as followers of Jesus is to live the great commandment: "Love God with all your heart, mind, soul, and strength, and love your neighbor as you love yourself."

If I love people with my right hand and slap them with my left, have I loved them? No. We are called to love our neighbor with both hands, both feet, our whole hearts, and our whole minds. That love must extend through our personal confessions and acts of love, through our interpersonal relationships, in and through our communities, in and through the systems that we create and govern, and, yes, even through our votes.

As I said to that group of young evangelical leaders: until the United States and the church take bold action to dismantle and re-form our nation's racialized political structures and its economic policies that have racialized outcomes, then race will remain a relevant focus of analysis and repentance in society and in the church.

12

Women

Jennifer D. Crumpton

During August 2008 I sweltered in my hometown of Birmingham, Alabama. Back from New York, I was visiting my family in my last few free days before embarking on an odd twist in my eleven-year career as a Fortune 500 advertising executive: seminary. The opportunity to study and work toward a career in the realm of what truly inspired me had appeared before me like a divinely inspired spring in the desert. Not immediately sure what a Master of Divinity degree would mean for a woman raised in the Southern Baptist context, I was sure of one thing: God had found me in a dry land and was leading me to restoring waters. The days before graduate school started were to be spent reading and praying, transitioning into the mind-frame of a new purpose, listening for God's continuing guidance.

During the visit, I heard that a prominent evangelical megachurch in a wealthy suburb of Birmingham had recently brought on a (then) 29-year-old pastor. This was notable. Though I had disassociated from the Southern Baptist scene long before, I interpreted this new youthful leadership as a sign of hope for the evangelical reputation. Maybe this Gen-Xer would shake up the traditional church format with a fresh worldview. Maybe the Bible Belt could don a new buckle.

I visited the church that Sunday, ready to find inspiration in the crowded, cavernous auditorium. The congregation was nominating elders and deacons. During the sermon the young pastor launched in an unexpected direction, declaring his conviction that women are not allowed by God to serve in such leadership positions in the church. He presented an apologetic, weak-voiced argument based on 1 Timothy 3:1–13. He declared the Scripture excludes women from being deacons or elders simply by way of the ancient innate social assumptions and unending masculine pronouns it employs. Never

114

mind that this would be expected of most any first-century document of the Roman diaspora. But this was 2008. Some of the well-off women who tithed to this church were probably high-level corporate executives, small business owners, and community leaders. Yet they were listening to a young preacher fresh out of New Orleans Baptist Seminary tell them God did not accept or bless their leadership skills in the "upper management" of the church. "Sorry, ladies," he said in so many words... "You are not as holy as men."

I looked around at the crowd of hundreds to see if anyone else looked confused, but all eyes were on the spot-lit stage. Surely I was not the only one shocked and disappointed that a voice of my own generation was indulging in an idolatrous act of Scripture-worship, bowing to the ghosts of centuries-old, patriarchal political and social structures that were historically captured in the Bible. The pastor added his own extrabiblical addendum that children's care and education, clerical work, or social planning were areas God would surely be pleased to see a lady lead. Since he still was not laughing, I finally realized it was no joke. I personally could not help but chuckle aloud at the irony. A young, motivated, arguably post-evangelical woman visits sweet home Alabama for pre-seminary preparation and gets put back in her place. Forget a new buckle, the belt had actually tightened up a couple notches. I could hardly breathe in that enormous, technologically well-appointed, stadium-seated glass house of worship. Equally disconcerting was the fact that I could recall a couple of evangelical church plants I had attended in New York City that also still restricted the roles of women, but without blatantly saying so.

Then the young pastor zeroed in on 1 Timothy 2:11–15, where women of the day are expected to "learn in quietness and full submission" (v. 11). Not a far reach for first-century women, who were often considered little more than property or slaves, save some exceptional women who held family wealth or experienced other rare opportunities. Just to be allowed to listen in quietly and learn something was a big step up in those days. The author, said in the text to be Paul, goes on to make a statement of personal opinion: "I do not permit a woman to teach or to assume authority over a man; she must be quiet. For Adam was formed first, then Eve. And Adam was not the one deceived; it was the woman who was deceived and became a sinner. But women will be saved through childbearing—if they continue in faith, love and holiness with propriety" (vv. 12–15).

To my ears, this extreme view might as well have come from Charlie Sheen standing at the pulpit talking about goddesses, tiger blood, and winning. Today, Paul's "order of appearance" jargon seems a ludicrous argument to attribute to the mind of God. The mythical blame game cannot serve as a mature assessment to be readily embraced by a modern world with the benefit of long experience with the equal intellectual abilities and proven leadership skills of women, especially in light of the many downfalls of men in power.

Furthermore, to continually dangle the illusive "apple" over the head of the illusive "Eve" is not only highly suspect in its truthfulness, but it willfully disempowers the forgiving, renewing nature of God that the universal church claims. It is plausible that 2000 years ago, the author's mind would not have been able to fathom the equality of humanity and the capacity of purpose innate in the female.

It is not understandable, however, that 2000 years later, a young, educated man would be incapable of making this crucial distinction and would continue propagating such a damning, death-dealing idea about gender in the name of religion.

Even more dangerous about the pastor's teachings on women is the portrait of God that it paints. Many other sectors of society recognize the contributions women make as they teach, speak, and lead. This young pastor suggests, however, that God—our very creator—does not think women are capable, reliable, or worthy of knowing God well enough to teach Scripture and model faith. How are women supposed to feel about a God who, when interpreted irresponsibly by men in positions of power, tells us in bitingly pointed language that we are not worthy, not fit for certain ways of relating to God and to others? Incapable as we are, we must be quiet and just believe whatever men tell us is true about the world and the Divine?

Even the most devout conservative women, if they dig down deep and momentarily block out other voices long enough to hear their own (yes, God does actually speak directly to women), are made to feel insecure, doubtful, disappointed, even self-loathing and worthless...hopeless. This situation does not sound like God's presence is in it, does it?

Interestingly, the young Birmingham pastor found it acceptable to rework the author's rule in 1 Timothy 2:15 that women are saved by childbearing, opting to override that "fact" in the Scripture with the conflicting idea that women are instead saved by the death of Christ just as men are, a typical modern Christian exhortation. This seems an apt admission that all of the author's statements in 1 Timothy and beyond are not universally sound, his ancient assumptions are not eternally correct, his wishes should not always be our command.

Why hold so stubbornly to some tenets of the passage and not to others? How does it logically work to say Paul/the author is inalterably right on some crucial things and completely wrong on others, all within a few sentences? If Scripture is going to have any type of real "authority," especially as it pertains to human rights and dignity, it cannot be a pick-and-choose deal where some parts must be unequivocally true and strictly carried out today lest we be in "sin," while other parts that do not serve an individual's or community's purposes are readily revisable.

This duplicity in interpretation is one reason modern readers cry out for a rethinking of the ways we arrive at our interpretations of the Bible. The Bible was never meant to be a rule book. It is not a closed document that dictates social practice and hierarchical structures for all places and all times. By its very nature the Bible is a compilation of ancient stories told by many different, often dissonant, voices about the trajectory of humanity in its relationship with God, in its exploration, in its missteps, in its process of figuring how to live into what it means to be people of God. Attempting to actually implement the whole of Scripture as a rule book without inserting our lessons learned and newest wisdoms would render us a violent, primitive tribal society, carrying out injustices toward women and other oppressed people in ways not unlike societies the United States chooses to oppose vehemently today.

The Bible is known as the "living Word" because of the way people testify to its speaking to human beings throughout our history of change and growth, mistakes and victories, fights and reconciliations, atrocities and healings—all the things that signify a person, society, or text is alive, breathing, and reaching out to meet the divine. Anyone who has read the Bible all the way through from cover to cover knows the Bible is not fixed and static. Just when you think you have a handle on where it's coming from and where it's going, the story takes an unexpected turn, just like real life. Otherwise, it could not still hold potential to speak to us today and 2000 more years from now.

A Bible interpreted to kill the spirit, the hope, the dreams, and the natural potential of any one group of people—especially one that constitutes more than half of the world's population—is a dead Bible. Women are particularly vulnerable victims to this misjudgment because of the time and culture in which the Bible was written, a culture that manifests itself in a range of violent and costly ways, even today. Biblical authority does not come from forcing people to live out Scripture's record to the letter today. Biblical authority comes from its unprecedented, instructive view of the arc of human history: its misery, its mistakes, its malleability, and how it eventually begins to bend toward justice, freedom, and a kind of pure love that unleashes the dignity, self-worth, and potential of every human being and all members of creation.

That sermon in Birmingham changed the way I went into seminary. I was listening that Sunday for God's voice and guidance—and for a moment my heart sank, thinking, "This is what God wanted me to hear? That I cannot be the leader I know I am called to be?" The situation was almost hilarious. You might think it burned enough to seal the deal—that any sentimentality or lingering value I held for the evangelicalism of my youth had been scorched. Actually, it lit another kind of fire inside. After a day of prayer, reflecting, and discussing that fateful sermon with others, I realized that God had used the young pastor to show me my purpose, to incite a righteous rage against injustice and oppression, to open my eyes to the lies that can be disguised as the will of God and accordingly enforced to our collective detriment. Instead of turning away from the ruthless sexism being played out in the churches of my childhood faith, I decided to take back my tradition.

I began to wonder, what does it really mean to be "evangelical" anyway? Diverse and politicized as the meaning is today, at its core it connotes a foundational relationship to the "evangel." This term comes from the Greek word *evangelion*, meaning "the good news," commonly called "the Gospel." This good news proclaimed by Jesus was a declaration that God had come for humanity—all of us. The Gospel of Mark tells us: "Jesus went into Galilee, proclaiming the good news of God. 'The time has come,' he said. 'The kingdom of God has come near. Repent and believe the good news!'"(Mk. 1:14–15).

If we really examine the evangel without all the manmade creeds and liturgies heaped up on it, we realize that God came to us in the human form of Jesus not to put a magic spell on us and get us to fall into line with old ways, traditions, and rules, but to model The Way that offers new life at its fullest to all. He exhorted people with great urgency to "repent and believe the good news."

The term "repent" also has a meaning too often misunderstood. The Greek *metanoia* implies a change of perception after an event, the act of changing one's mind to accept a new reality, one far different from the old assumptions and ways of doing things. It has nothing to do with guilt, finger pointing, suppression, oppression, or reverting to old customs or superstitions. These terms actually call evangelicals and all Christians to seek to engage in the reality of God, and that includes the reality that God created women in God's own image.

Creation and Other Stories

The text of Genesis is widely considered by experts to be a theological document, meaning the narrative purpose is more concerned with introducing us to the nature of God and illustrating how God deals with humankind, rather than recounting any historical events.[1] The text initially reveals God as one who is all-powerful, all-knowing, all-creative, not prone to mistakes or second guessing. One primary element in Genesis is the introduction of monotheism over the popular polytheism of the predominant cultures of the time. When the young Birmingham preacher bought into and based his worldview on 1 Timothy's story that God made Adam first and then Eve—and furthermore the misguided assumption that the story therefore implies the woman is secondary and lesser than the man—he ignored the fact that two starkly different creation stories appear in the Bible. The first account (Gen. 1:26–31), describes God creating both male and female human beings alike at the very same time, both very clearly in the image of God, and both placed in an equal position of creativity, productivity, and rulership. Then chapter 2 recreates the entire scenario, seemingly reversing the primal equality chapter 1 has affirmed. Chapter 3 goes on to tell a story in which Eve falls prey to sin and tempts Adam to go along with her.

We do not need to delve into scholarly theories about the conflation and redaction of texts to realize the delicate task that interpreting Scripture presents, especially as it pertains to telling half of society that they are secondary to, and less than, the other half, based on a particular reading of Genesis 2. Anyone who looks closely at the stories in Genesis 2—3 will have to make a decision about the nature of Scripture, its purpose, and its repurposing in the New Testament letter of 1 Timothy. In the latter, the author seeks to stake his claim to how the first-century church should be run and who should have what positions of authority. How are we to choose which view to promote, if we are looking at Scripture as a rule to be continuously re-enacted in perpetuity? Knowing what we experience daily among men and women in modern time—they are equally capable, equally intelligent, equally reliable, and equally made in the image of God—we must abandon the notion of oppressing and punishing women based on the premise of "who was created first" and "who fell prey to sin."

Finding the Femmevangelical

The letters to Timothy were written well after the death of Jesus, when church leaders of the time were debating and competing, trying to figure out what a "Christian" religion would look like in the context of their social, political, and economic structures. Jesus' true purpose was not to institute a new religion. He came to set people free from the oppressive forces of the day: primarily the brutal political system of the Roman Empire, which taxed people so heavily that they could barely survive, and whose government gratuitously used the death penalty—crucifixion—to scare people into submission. The Gospel accounts offer a series of vignettes from various points of view depicting Jesus speaking out against burdensome and violent imperial rule, and spending a lot of his free time with those considered "secondary" and even "tertiary" in that society.

It is well-known that women have little to hold to in Scripture by way of role models or positive accounts of the female experience. I believe this is less an effect of God's inspiration and more a lack of human imagination (not to mention literary fashions of the day). For instance, it is rarely acknowledged that the Gospel of Mark has at least two endings, and interestingly the difference hinges on the role women are "allowed" (by ancient Judeo-Roman culture's writers) to play in witnessing and announcing the resurrection of Jesus. In the last chapter of Mark, Mary Magdalene, Mary "mother of James" and Salome go to the tomb of the crucified Jesus to anoint his body, but instead a figure in white tells them Jesus has risen from the dead and gone ahead to Galilee, where they will see him. The earliest ancient manuscripts end Mark's story by saying, "Trembling and bewildered, the women went out and fled from the tomb. They said nothing to anyone, because they were afraid" (Mk. 16:8).

Later scribes added in the popular tale that the risen Jesus appeared first to Mary Magdalene, who was in fact not a prostitute, but actually a brave and beloved disciple. (This is the second ending you will find in your Bible today.) She was entrusted by Jesus to not only witness and believe this shocking new reality, but also to take the news that he was alive to the rest of the disciples. In this story, Jesus chose a woman to reveal his resurrection to the world, and to prepare the disciples for his subsequent appearances. In what Christians may consider the most important moment of history, there was no boundary, no glass ceiling between God and woman. In fact, there was trust, collaboration, and holy anointing for this woman to act on behalf of God.

In the version of the resurrection story found in John 20, Mary Magdalene again has the primary role in announcing the appearance of the risen Jesus. Mary arrives at the tomb while it is still dark, sees that the body of Jesus is gone, and notifies Peter and the "other disciple," who then go to the tomb, see that it is true, and go back to where they are staying. But Mary does not turn away. Once she is alone, Jesus appears to her. He calls her by name: "Mary." He then tells her to go and tell his brothers that he is ascending to "my God and your God." He waited for her—her specifically and her alone. Mary is literally the recipient of the initial Easter epiphany about the nature of Christ, upon which the faith of the Johannine community of Christ-followers was based.

Even less obvious stories, such as that of the servant-surrogate Hagar in Genesis 16, serve to remind me of the important role of underdog women in the story of God and humanity. Here it is found in the shortsightedness of "Father" Abraham when he fails to trust God's own birth plan for the forthcoming people of God. When the pregnant slave Hagar runs away from Sarah and Abraham's harsh treatment into the desert, God finds her by a spring and promises her a future. Then she becomes the only biblical character to actually name God: El Roi, the God who sees me.

Likewise, I can trust that my value and position in my faith tradition has little to do with ancient hierarchies and everything to do with the God who sees me. This is good news. We do not have to run from a deadening evangel, but can find life at its fullest in a new reality. Like Mary Magdalene, Jesus calls us by name, as women, to serve his God and our God. This is God coming for us specifically as females, females created equally in the image of God, calling us to lay claim to our important role in the inbreaking of God's kingdom into the world—no matter what our religious titles or denominational associations. Like Mary, we cannot turn away.

Refusing the Ruse

Our world honors incredible leaders, such as Leymah Gbowee, the Lutheran peace activist who organized women to help end the violent civil war in Liberia, and Ellen Johnson Sirleaf, the first female president in Africa, with the 2011 Nobel Peace Prize. Such worldly recognitions makes the church sound more and more ridiculous in its claim that only men are capable of doing the type of work it takes to lead the church. The American evangelical church is one of the last frontiers where a handful of men can deny women access to our own, full God-given potential. What are the actual effects of telling women they are secondary, that they are responsible for introducing sin into the world, and that God rendered them incapable of fulfilling certain roles in society?

Evangelical Christians have some of the loudest voices in the market-place when it comes to criticizing media, entertainment, music, advertising, "Hollywood's" rampant exploitation of sexuality and violence, and "secular society's" lack of morals related to appropriate, healthy human behavior. Yet consider this: Jennifer Siebel Newsom's documentary film "Miss Representation" reveals that women hold only 3 percent of "clout positions" in the telecommunications, entertainment, publishing, and advertising industries. Women make up just 16 percent of all writers, producers, directors, cinematographers, and editors in our country. Men wield largely unquestioned power as they create all of the elements that form our collective national consciousness and, hence, our lack of ethical moorings. How different would things look, what different perspectives would we be exposed to, if women were in power, or even if they just had equal access in these influential industries?

Newsom's film also points out that women make up 51 percent of the U.S. population, yet comprise only 17 percent of Congress. The U.S. ranks ninetieth in the world in terms of the participation of women in national legislatures. Cuba, China, Iraq, and Afghanistan have more women in government positions than do we. The common refrain leading up to the 2012 election is that America is falling behind, unable to keep up with emerging economies, the novel ideas being birthed and skills being honed in other places around the world. Maybe, as Newsom's film notes, that is because we only choose our leadership from a limited pool of a mere 6 percent of our population: white, male, European (until Obama), married heterosexuals with professional-level degrees and high-end pedigrees of exclusive wealth. If we really want to see things change, consider the film's opening quote from Alice Walker: "The most common way people give up their power is by thinking they don't have any." Evangelicals can no longer afford to be a force in society that makes women feel they have no power to make a difference, when, like Leymah Gbowee, we have unique abilities to bring peace, reconciliation, empowerment, and new methods of promoting child welfare, health, and prosperity.

What about the ramifications on a global scale? As one of the most powerful, influential nations in the world, where many women are considered to have an enviable quality of life and some of the best opportunities for equality, growth, education, economic independence, and ability to make social change for the common good, the evangelical church sends an irresponsibly dangerous signal to the rest of the world—that women actually are inherently inferior and subservient to men. This practice serves to endorse implicitly conditions in less economically stable, less industrialized, and less "progressive" areas that continue to restrict women's political participation and socio-economic rights, neglect protection from sexual violence, and sustain educational and vocational discrimination.

The traditional evangelical suppression of women espoused by the Birmingham pastor makes a mockery of the brutal daily living conditions of women in other parts of the world, especially where it is nearly impossible for women to support themselves, where therefore they have no choice but to be dependent on those men in power who may exploit them. The UN Commission on the Status of Women can attest that subsistence, violence and war, lack of educational opportunities and decent employment prospects, poverty, rape, sexual abuse and mutilation, lack of health care, harsh labor conditions, and political and social intimidation are the reality of the majority of women on our planet. The CIA can report that 80 percent of the millions of international human trafficking victims in the world are women, and 50 percent of them female minors. Obviously the U.S. is not exempt from these phenomena, but there is no shortage of irony in the fact that one of the most privileged societies would perpetuate demonizing women and putting them in a limited place. The message is that women do not yet enjoy true respect, consideration, or equality even under the best circumstances.

As Hillary Clinton exhorted at the Fourth World Conference on Women in Beijing in 1995: "As long as discrimination and inequities remain so commonplace everywhere in the world, as long as girls and women are valued less, fed less, fed last, overworked, underpaid, not schooled, subjected to violence in and outside their homes—the potential of the human family to create a peaceful, prosperous world will not be realized." In other words—in the language of Isaiah 61 and Jesus' very inception of his own ministry—God's will cannot be done, the imprisoned cannot be released, the oppressed cannot be liberated, the voiceless cannot be heard, and the diminished cannot be redeemed. The impending reality of the Lord's favor cannot be expressed or experienced.

Jesus modeled an imperative to call the powerful, the elite, and those with great influence to reconsider their responsibilities for improving reality for all people. In the Gospels, he called tax collectors who benefited from loyalty to powerful Roman forces to recognize and renounce the life-stealing burden that unfair taxation put on the poor for the sake of the rich rulers. He stopped a self-righteous mob from stoning a woman accused of some form of adultery, reminding the crowd of their own complicity in her oppression, and beseeching the woman to walk away with a vision of a new reality for herself in relation to society and to God.

Today, evangelicals and all Christians must emulate this imperative to create equality and justice in the world. We each have our own unique sphere of influence and the personal responsibility to make it happen. The dualism created when we excuse misogynistic beliefs and practices in the Christian realm implicitly excuses and exacerbates the oppression of the vulnerable within our own borders and around the world. I would argue that the patriarchal language and stories of the Bible generally offer no better protocol for societies or hope for women than the language and stories perpetuated in our exploitative culture of entertainment and news media today (which probably says more about the backward state of modernity than the troubles of ancient mores—we've had a couple of millennia to change, after all).

But given the Bible's formidable religious authority, its results have been and continue to be much more damaging than that of popular culture. This is why Jesus' choice to invoke Isaiah 61 to announce his ministry's purpose is so crucial: "[The Lord] has sent me to proclaim freedom for the prisoners and recovery of sight for the blind, to set the oppressed free, to proclaim the year of the Lord's favor" (Luke 4:18–19). It invokes a living, organically growing promise that transcends time, texts, cultures, demoralizing social milieus, and human shortcomings.

We can still believe the promises of Scripture when we focus on the actionable ethos of Jesus, unbinding him from the old dualism created by the ancient language and customs of the literary contexts that surrounded him. Ancient hope is found in modern life when we allow Jesus to be the embodied expression of God's ultimate will for humanity: that societies promote the well-being and the realization of the full potential of all people. We can—and must—hold every false motivation and demeaning narrative in our modern environment up to the revealing light of Christ, which helps us recover our vision. Only then can we help free the prisoners and liberate the oppressed. By refusing to perpetuate the young Birmingham pastor's interpretation of Scripture in evangelical circles and beyond, we can live that promise even today. That's precisely why, as a young, motivated, arguably post-evangelical woman, I became a pastor myself.

13

Children

Laura Rector

In the 1989 cult classic, *Bill and Ted's Excellent Adventure,* the two teenage characters stop briefly in the future, where they find that civilization looks to them for wisdom. They advise their followers, "Be excellent to one another!" before ending with, "Party on, dudes!" Perhaps the first bit of advice is really just a secular way of encapsulating the Christian command to "love one another." Certainly as we approach ideas about a kingdom vision for public life, we need to heed Bill and Ted's advice to "be excellent to one another" if we ever hope to achieve Jesus' higher standard to "love one another" (Jn. 13:34).[1] This seems even more crucial when we add children into the midst of public discussions. Our littlest people are capable of producing strong emotional reactions in the hearts of the bigger people who love them. Because of that capability, we also run the risk of reducing children to mere emotional tools in the rhetoric of our political stalemates while doing little that actually helps them. To move forward, we must do much more than agree that children are important *in theory.* We must also support children *in practice.* To do less than that falls short of following the way of Jesus.

My assignment in this chapter is to address the topic of "children," but children are more than just one item on an agenda. In fact, every other chapter of this book should be read with children in mind. Creation care, for example, calls us to understand that nearly 90 percent of the world's children live in the developing world[2] and that the poor are impacted the most by climate change.[3] War forces us to see that children fought as soldiers in at least nineteen countries and territories between 2004 and 2007[4] and that even more have had lives displaced and disrupted by such violence. As we ponder both gender and abortion, we remember that an estimated 60 million girls have been lost due to gender-selected abortion.[5]

In this chapter, we will ask what the kingdom of God looks like when we remember that Jesus pointed to a child and said the kingdom belonged to "such as these" (Mk. 10:14)—and how that should affect American Christians' public engagement. We will find repeatedly that in large part our answers include putting children into the midst of *all* our public discussions, including the chapters that come before and after this one.

Our task, then, is a difficult one. We do not have a magical time machine to help us with our project as Bill and Ted did. Instead, we have something better—the words of Jesus himself as recorded in the Gospel of Mark.

Children and Jesus

Mark's text is the crucial Gospel used by theologians to understand "child theology." Joyce Ann Mercer sums up the reasons for this very well:

> Mark's gospel comes to the foreground primarily because of the place of children in the story. Children in Mark's narrative mirror the journey of Jesus. They embody the *reign of God* in human history. Through stories of Jesus' engagement with children who struggle with illness and spirit possession, Mark communicates what is meant to be part of the reign of God. As Mark's text portrays Jesus blessing children whose low social position places them in sharp contrast to the desired places of honor and power sought by Jesus' adult male disciples, Mark offers his view of what it means to follow Jesus.[6]

In particular, Mark 9—10, with an even more specific emphasis on Mark 10:13–16, contains the section of Mark most emphasized by theologians interested in children. As we think of a kingdom vision of children, we will start with this passage:

> People were bringing little children to Jesus to have him touch them, but the disciples rebuked them. When Jesus saw this, he was indignant. He said to them, "Let the little children come to me, and do not hinder them, for the kingdom of God belongs to such as these. Truly I tell you, anyone who will not receive the kingdom of God like a little child will never enter it." And he took the children in his arms, placed his hands on them and blessed them. (Mk. 10:13–16)

W.A. Strange and others were right to point out that Mark describes children's entrance into the kingdom.[7] Strange points out that the Israelites' faith tradition welcomed children. They built their own synagogue schools for male children.[8] They saw children as the future of Israel,[9] and that meant that children learned faith from their early days:

Children were participants in the home-based worship of Judaism, as well as being encouraged to observe the Temple-based rites. At Passover, the children were to ask the important questions which elicited, year by year, the explanation for the Passover ritual (Exod 12:26f.). A gradual course of initiation is suggested by the following saying, which comes from a period later than the first century, but no doubt reflects a sentiment which had guided Jewish parents for a long time: "A minor who knows how to shake a *lulav* [palm branch] is obliged to observe the laws of the *lulav*; a minor who knows how to wrap himself in the *tallit* [prayer shawl] is obliged to observe the law of the *zizit* [threads on the corners of the *tallit*]" (Tosefta, Hagigah 1.2).[10]

Ancient *Jewish* society at the time of Jesus had a much more inclusive view of children than either the Greeks or the Romans.[11] *Jewish* children occupied a central part of the Covenant. They were promised to Abraham, a sign of God's blessing, and the means through which Israel would see God keep his promises to them. The overall status of children depended on their religious significance for the future, not because they were valued simply as children, however.[12]

Why then would the disciples expect Jesus to be dismissive toward children? Some argue that the children in the story were considered a bother, just as they would have been to any Jewish man.[13] Strange has noted that rabbis educated children and that Jewish culture generally welcomed children,[14] but then points out the vulnerability of children elsewhere.[15] Most likely children got a mixed reception, welcomed by some and turned away by others, depending on context, as well as Jewish assimilation to Greek and Roman culture.[16] Perhaps something particular characterized this group of children. Hans-Ruedi Weber says that the children were brought to Jesus to be touched. "In the four gospels, almost all of the 30 occurrences of the verb 'to touch' are found in stories where Jesus heals lepers, the blind, or the sick."[17] As Ched Meyers points out: "Indeed, from the narrative world of Mark we have cause to suspect that all is not well for the child in first-century Palestinian society. For where do we meet children in the Gospel? In every case, it is in situations of sickness and oppression: the synagogue ruler's daughter (5:21ff), the Syrophoenician's daughter (7:24ff.), the deaf and dumb son (9:14ff.)."[18]

Is it possible that the children were sick? That would hardly make sense in light of Jesus healing other children without recorded interference from the disciples, although it would not be the first time that the disciples did not comprehend Jesus' kingdom actions. Another suggested reason is that Jesus was seen as a rabbi and that this would not be normal behavior for a rabbi.[19] William Barclay painted the disciples in more sympathetic light. He points out that Jesus was already on his way to Jerusalem for the last time and so the disciples wanted to spare Jesus further concern.[20] Joyce Ann Mercer presents her interpretation in less romanticized terms. Like Meyers, she interprets Jesus' action as both political and an act involving real children. She rightly puts Jesus in his context, associating his action with Jewish hospitality and God's provision for the vulnerable in the Old Testament.[21]

If this last scenario is the case, we dare not see the children in Jesus' experience as merely political object lessons. Jesus treated the children like the other people he encountered. They were loved for themselves,[22] not simply as a useful illustration for a political agenda. Clearly, whatever the case, they were being marginalized. This was cause for indignation by Jesus on their behalf (Mk. 10:14). The kingdom of God was a kingdom of deliverance, though, and this included delivering children from very real circumstances that made them vulnerable. Jesus included yet another group into his kingdom alongside tax collectors and sinners.[23] Whatever the status of these particular children may have been, Jesus' point is clear: in his kingdom of upside-down social relationships, children have a special place and become models for adults.[24]

Fulfillment of Isaiah's Prophecy

Strange points out that "Jesus called on those who heard him to enter the kingdom of God"[25] and that the entrance of children into such a kingdom "highlights that entry into the kingdom is not by way of merit, privilege and status."[26] Glen Stassen notes that Jesus understood this kingdom ministry in light of Isaiah.[27] In Mark 10:13–16, Jesus also fulfills a prophecy of Isaiah:

> He said and did things no rabbi ever would. He "let the children come" to him and gave them his personal and undivided attention. Acting as God's Messiah he demonstrated that his kingdom and covenant extended to them, even while they were still children: "the kingdom of heaven belongs to such". That is, the new covenant, by which a person has direct access to God, not mediated through parents, can include children. This is why he went further and embraced them. He did this as Messiah, for of him it was prophesied that he "gathered the lambs into his arms and carries them close to his heart" (Isa. 40:11). Here is the Promised Shepherd of Israel carrying out his mission.[28]

When Jesus welcomed the children, he fulfilled what the prophet Isaiah said about him.[29]

Connecting These Children to the Sermon on the Mount

This background, along with parts of Markan material, lends itself to the suggestion that this material should be connected to the Sermon on the Mount if we hope to achieve a practical vision of children in the reign of God. Consider this evidence:

As stated previously, Jesus interpreted his ministry in light of the prophet Isaiah's words. Mark 10:13–16 contains connotations of Isaiah 40:11. Likewise, scholars have argued that Jesus understood the kingdom of God proclaimed in the Sermon on the Mount in light of Isaiah.[30]

The major passages on children speak of children's entrance into the kingdom of heaven, as well as their symbolic worth for the discipleship of all believers. These passages also recognize the vulnerability of children. The Beatitudes speak specifically about the "kingdom of heaven" (Mt. 5:3) and use "child" language to speak of the vulnerable (e.g., "those who inherit" and "sons of God" imply a parent-child relationship). Both are needed to give content to Jesus' teaching on the kingdom.

Mark mixes material about children and the family with echoes of the Sermon on the Mount. This suggests a connection between the materials in some tradition of the early Church. For example, Mark sandwiches the Sermon on the Mount material about divorce (Mk. 10:1–12) between teachings about harming children (Mark 9:42) and the story of Jesus welcoming children (Mk. 10:13–16). One almost could argue that he has not changed themes, only focus. The emphasis is protection for both women and children. David Gushee points out that the divorce teaching emphasizes the permanence of the family structure.[31] There are also parallels between Mark 9:43–50 and the Sermon on the Mount with hyperbole about maiming body parts, as well as a discussion of "saltiness" (Mt. 5:13, 27–30).

When we see that the most famous biblical passage about children is mixed in with the bulk of Jesus' teaching found in the Sermon on the Mount, we see that children should be a central part of our thoughts about the kingdom, rather than marginal "add-ons" to an agenda or emotional tools in political rhetoric. When Jesus brought people who happened to be children into his kingdom, what did that mean for children? Were they mere recipients of the kingdom, or did they become participants in the kingdom?

Certainly, when we also look at traditional interpretations of Matthew 18 and Mark 10, we see that part of this kingdom ministry included Jesus defending children. Children were treated as objects of protection, and so our public engagement must also include such protection. That sets up children as both subjects participating in the kingdom and objects protected by the kingdom.

Strange points out that Jesus normally did not speak directly to children in Scripture.[32] This seems a technical matter, however, if we start to read in the margins and between the lines of the text. Children were present in the crowds when Jesus spoke to them (Mt. 14:21). Jesus used the fish and loaves of at least one boy (Jn. 6:9). He pulled a child out of one audience and made him the example of what it was like to be a participant in the kingdom (Mt. 18:2). Jesus welcomed children when others expected him to disparage them. The most that can be implied by Strange's observation is that children did not have the same moral responsibilities as adults, not that Jesus failed to see them as participants in the kingdom of God.

Jesus also interacted as a child. He was a child participant in worship, reading the scroll of Isaiah in the temple (Lk. 2:41ff.). He was also a child at risk. He faced execution, and his entrance into the world meant the execution of other innocent children like him—an act that receives no approval in Scripture. He knew what it meant to live in humble circumstances, to experience tragedy as a child, flee danger, and need adult protection.[33] Jesus not only interacted with children, but also lived through the vulnerability of childhood.

The message of the kingdom was not for an adult-only audience. In a world where children are at risk from the womb on through development, we must remember that a kingdom agenda must be God's word for all people, not simply adults. What might this look like in terms of public policy? What would it mean to follow Jesus and put children in our midst?

Certainly, it means that we must think about how each of the public issues discussed in this book affects children. Traditionally, evangelicals have for the most part focused on children in discussions of abortion. Indeed, welcoming children means we must protect vulnerable children in the womb—and this should mean moving past current stalemates that have done little in actuality to reduce abortion or to protect them by also protecting their caregivers.[34] It also means having an ethic of life and theology of childhood that say children must be protected not only in the womb, but also from poverty, a lack of medical resources, environmental costs, violence, a failing school system, and other ways they are put at risk.

We should remember that Jesus encapsulated his teachings on the permanence of the family with the "child" passages in Mark. Currently, half of American children will experience their parents' divorce(s) in their lifetimes.[35] If scholars tell us that the kingdom of God is marked by peace, deliverance, righteousness/justice, joy, God's presence, healing, and the return from exile,[36] sociologists tell us that divorce is the antithesis to this in every way for children whose parents divorce, often even in so-called "good divorces." Instead of peace, for example, children face an increase of violence in their homes around the time of parents' divorces,[37] increased physical abuse in single-parent households,[38] and are at greater risk for sexual abuse.[39] At minimum, they face lives of inner tension, no matter how amicable the parents are toward one another.[40] Instead of justice, children face the economic consequences of single-parent households. Ron Sider tells us, "Marital status is a better predictor of who will become poor than education, race, neighborhood, or family background."[41] Likewise, instead of joy, children of divorce lose a basic structure that cultivates their sense of safety and trust.[42] They also are more likely to experience more depression and mental health problems.[43] It can be shown that divorce violates each of the other marks of God's reign as well.

Promoting family permanence with the goal of child protection also affects issues beyond divorce. Family problems contribute to children living in the streets,[44] child exploitation, and child soldiery.[45] Current immigration policies often separate families through deportation.[46] Likewise, we should be very concerned about holding prisoners indefinitely without a fair trial and in effect separating children from family members, unless it can be proven there is a valid reason for such separation.[47] We should be wary of the disruption of family life caused by war as well as its other effects on children.[48] We should be very concerned about children raising children in the AIDS crisis which has left 12 million children without parents in sub-Saharan Africa, as well as 2 million children with AIDS as of 2007.[49] We need to put children in our midst as we think about both foreign and domestic policies that affect them.

Finally, putting children in our midst also means recognizing that children are participants in God's kingdom. Does this mean that children vote and do everything that adults can do? No, but it does mean that we should encourage participation in keeping with their development. Fear of such participation has factored amongst reasons that the U.S. is the only UN member nation besides Somalia that has failed to ratify an international human rights document called the UN Convention on the Rights of the Child.[50] With nearly 90 percent of the world's children living in the Two-Thirds World,[51] we must find ways to be part of the global conversation, even as we seek to better integrate children into domestic policies.

Conclusion

Until Christ's return and the day comes when "[t]here will be no more death or mourning or crying or pain, for the old order of things has passed away" (Rev. 21:4), or, in the words of Bill and Ted, we get to "party on, dudes," a Christian engagement for the common good must focus on children as much as adults, recognizing their potential for kingdom participation as well as their unique vulnerabilities. The current political landscape in America often asks us to pit different groups of children against one another—the unborn against children in poverty, for example. It also rarely allows room for children's participation. Yet, a kingdom vision means that we cannot choose sides between unborn children and children in poverty, American children and children overseas; nor can we ignore children and still live out the ethics of Jesus holistically. Just as Jesus declared his kingdom belonged to "such as these," we must declare that our earthly communities, too, belong to the world's smallest and most vulnerable citizens.

14

The Dying

Scott Claybrook

The Ever-Present Past

With typical teenage abandon, I bounded down the stairs two at a time. My eighteenth birthday loomed two weeks away. I was wheeling toward the kitchen to find something for lunch. Turning the corner, I froze. My father, a habitually stoic man, stood in the middle of the kitchen crestfallen, holding my mother as she sobbed. I stopped. We stared.

My father looked at me, helpless. My mother caught her breath and began to recount the phone conversation she had just finished with her doctor. Her precautionary tests came with terrible news: colon cancer. It was bad and spreading. She was forty-five. I was seventeen.

For the next six years my mother became a professional patient. She underwent colon surgery, brain surgery, twenty-seven rounds of chemotherapy, experimental treatments, and radiation. She would die at the age of fifty-one.

Throughout those six years, however, my mother never lost her faith—quite the opposite actually. In the midst of her sickness she began to find new pieces and greater depths to her faith in Christ; so too did those around her. A child of the church, she loved it dearly. As her disease worsened, she continued to work part-time in our local church's office. She loved the people and the work. It gave her something to do, something to work on, something to contribute. Even though my mother loved this local church dearly, the church struggled at times to love her back. They stumbled, and they fumbled. The church my mother loved so dearly was unprepared to walk with her toward death.

My mother's six-year battle represents an emerging norm in Christian ministry, that of the prolonged illness and protracted death. Even with terminal illnesses, people now live longer and die slower. As ministers and Christians, how we care for the dying, both in their lives and in their deaths, will help to define the Christian witness of the twenty-first century. The New Evangelical Partnership is fundamentally committed to stand "*against* needless human suffering due to a lack of health care and *for* human health." It is time evangelicals reexamine (or examine for the first time) their stance on disease, death, and dying.

I write this introduction one year to the day after her death. I realize that our past experiences with death never really leave us; they remain ever-present. What we experience personally and think existentially about death continually shapes our response to those dying around us. The following pages, written from personal experience and ministerial reflection, attempt to point the way forward in living alongside those with terminal illnesses. Though I speak from experience with the terminally ill, the following can be applied and discussed in the more general areas of disease, death, and dying. So I now offer the following to you as a reflection on my own ever-present past.

Care in Life

For most of her illness, mother never *appeared* to be sick. She preferred it that way. She suffered silently and preferred it that way as well. When others began to dwell on her illness, she would be forced to do so too. Friendship, family, and work became powerful agents of peaceful distraction throughout her illness.

This silent suffering, however, caused problems of its own. Because she spoke so little of her illness and rarely publicly acknowledged any of its painful realities, people sometimes forgot she was sick. The worst moment of such forgetfulness came in the fall of 2009. That fall, roughly five years into her illness, my mother's cancer had spread throughout her body, including to her brain. She underwent specialized brain surgery and targeted radiation. We knew that these treatments were measures aimed only at "quality of life." The hope of a "cure" had long since disappeared.

Once doctors found the tumor, we made rapid preparations for brain surgery. The entire process, from diagnosis to surgery, took only a few weeks. The surgery was significant, and the risks great. In the flurry of anxiety and activity, however, my mother noted the absence of a particularly important person in the process: a pastor.

At the time, she was working as a part-time office manager in the congregation where our family had been members for nearly fourteen years. Throughout the weeks leading up to the surgery, not one of the several dozen ministers of the church ever approached my mother. They forgot, but she did not. The effect was devastating.

The ministers realized their mistake only after some of our family brought it to their attention. Embarrassed, two ministers came and stayed with our family at the hospital throughout the day. Still the fallout from this event was significant. It started a process of hurt and distrust between my family and the church that never fully healed. My mother did not need or want someone to be at the hospital all day. It made little difference to her. What she craved was to be affirmed as a member of the congregation, to be remembered.

Thomas Reynolds sees the basic question of human existence as "whether there is welcome at the heart of things."[1] He suggests that individuals crave a fundamental orientation in their lives, a "starting point" rooted in a community conditioned through a commonly shared narrative.[2] Everyone desires a center of safety, a home. The body of Christ becomes this "home" for Christians. Through the common narrative of Scripture and tradition, Christians craft an identity of belonging and purpose. As my mother's illness progressed and its eventual end became inevitable, her personal narrative began to sharply diverge from the common narrative of her local church. People no longer knew how to speak with her.

My mother's part-time work in the local congregation gave her purpose and identity. She loved the people and the place so much that she continued working there for years after qualifying for federal disability assistance. Yet in her final months, the church was no longer a place of welcome. She stopped making the effort to go, she said, because her presence (and illness) made people uncomfortable. As the cancer spread, her friends and pastors lacked the tools to synthesize their community "alive in Christ" with the dying life of their friend and parishioner.

In the end, the church did all it knew how. It bombarded her and our family with well-meaning "ministry." For weeks and months, people provided meals for our family and offered unceasing prayers on our behalf. Yet this deluge of good intentions had unintended consequences. It forced my mother to *consume* the care of so many others, and, in the process, she somehow lost the ability to *contribute* anything in return. Those meals and prayers made a great difference to all of us, but they did not meet the underlying need. She simply desired to be a member of the congregation, to contribute to the story of the community, to be valued as someone with something to offer.

Caring for the dying in life necessarily involves balancing the care and the contribution of the individual. Congregations need to imagine ways in which they can both *give* and *receive* from those dying in their midst. Individuals facing terminal illnesses often possess a rare kind of faith and self-awareness. These individuals and their personal narratives need to become parts of the larger communal experience.

Finally, congregations must resist the temptation to confuse someone's disease with that person's identity. Too often, the terminally ill become known as "the one with cancer" or "the one with ALS." Congregations must remember that there is more to a person than the illness. Communities should present individuals the opportunity to decide for themselves whether or not they will live and give from a place grounded in their illness.

Care in Death

Many terminally ill patients consciously decide to stop fighting their illness at some point. Often, they strive to meet a milestone such as seeing a child graduate or holding a new grandchild. Once this goal is reached, however, their resistance to death weakens and their condition often rapidly deteriorates. This pattern was true of my mother as well.

The doctor's decision to proceed with brain surgery in the fall of 2009 truly underscored just how serious my mother's condition had become. The risks involved for someone in my mother's health were great. Without the surgery she would die within months. These treatments, however, were measures aimed only at improving her "quality of life." The following spring, we knew that she was finally beginning to die.

She had been dying for five years, of course. Now it finally seemed like a possibility, an inescapable reality. The cancer was now in her lymph nodes, adrenal gland, lungs, hip, liver, and leg. Doctors could no longer predict the spread of the disease. She had outlived all their expectations. And yet she seemed to still be living, to still be fighting, for something.

That spring I proposed to my girlfriend, and we decided to set our wedding only three months later, for my mother's sake. My mother's health was getting noticeably worse. Thankfully, she made it to the wedding, and with help was able to walk down the aisle and participate in the service. She was able to be my mother one more time.

By the time we returned from our honeymoon, she was done fighting. Hospice was called, and final preparations were made. My mother then went about the painfully slow work of dying.

Much of contemporary Christian thought looks at death as the enemy of human wholeness, the negative of humanity's positive potential. Writing in *Kingdom Ethics,* David Gushee and Glen Stassen explore this view of death where illness and death are "enemies that may be fought using the best of our divinely given human intelligence and creativity."[3] A similar mindset led my mother to fight and endure years of treatment and pain only to eventually stop after her youngest child (me) was finally married. This mindset comes from Jesus' unending mission of healing (and resurrection) throughout the Gospel accounts. Similarly, the Supreme Court sees a compelling state interest in preserving *all* life, an interest likely grounded in America's Judeo-Christian heritage.[4] The majority of Christians would therefore consider death a bitter conclusion to avoid, yet not a hopeless one; however, I am unsure.

I am inclined to view death as an act of healing, an extension rather than an enemy of the medical profession. While many see death as the enemy of wholeness, I believe Christians can actually envision it as the gateway to wholeness. Our lives on Earth groan under the burden of sin's separation. By sin, I again follow Tom Reynolds' work on welcome that suggests sin comes in "turning away from an original relationship with the divine Creator upon which all other relationships are founded."[5] Sin begins with human anxiety over welcome/acceptance; humans develop a mistrust of God's welcome; finally, they refuse God's offer of relationship.[6] In turn, we sin against one another as we "desire to manage and guarantee welcome," crafting a false sense of welcome by means of manipulation and exclusion.[7] In order to offer atonement/salvation to creation, Christ endured his own breaking of relationship with God and humanity through death; however, he healed and reconstituted this broken relationship by way of resurrection.

Three weeks before my mother's death, as her body began to weaken, she held my hand and said, "Scott, I know you want us to have as much time together as we can, but I'm ready to go. I'm ready to see Jesus. I need you to let me go. I'm ready. I'm ready." For her, death was not only a conclusion to six years of pain, but it was a much more important conclusion to a lifetime of incomplete relationship. Death represented a pathway to healing wholeness with Christ. In the end, her cancer presented a significant barrier to her death as it made her last weeks ones of hellacious, physical pain running rampant and a new brain tumor causing severe confusion, agitation, and fear. Even as she refused food and water (with the exception of taking medication), it still took her 51-year-old body weeks to die. As I sat watching her slowly walk toward death, I wondered, would not hastening this death serve as a merciful act of care? I believe it might have; however, conventional Christianity would disagree.

Let me be clear. I am suggesting that any new movement of evangelical Christianity, particularly one committed to stand "*against* needless human suffering due to a lack of health care and *for* human health," must reexamine the role and function of death within its theology. Within its praxis, new evangelicals must consciously examine their stance toward physician-assisted suicide and euthanasia.

Traditionally, according to Paul Ramsey, assisted suicide and euthanasia involves choosing one's own death, "which in Christian thought human beings are not permitted to do because it involves 'throw[ing] the gift [of life] back in the face of the giver' (146)."[8] Such a broad statement, however, now sounds to me ignorant and offensive. Choosing suicide or euthanasia *in the face of terminal illness* is no more throwing the gift of life in the face of the Creator than the absence of healing is God throwing God's omnipotence (or impotence) in the face of creation.

Life is a gift; however, so too is death. Some may consider assisted suicide and euthanasia the ultimate sin, the pinnacle moment of "turning away from relationship with God." In reality, however, assisted suicide and euthanasia may be the ultimate act of devotion, embracing the promise of restored relationship to God (atonement) in the face of undeniable death. Ramsey fails to imagine the pursuit of death actually being the pursuit of God. Likewise, traditional Christianity would dispute claims that death, induced or otherwise, can serve as a healing measure: "The role of the healthcare professional is to cure if possible, to care always, and never to harm or to hasten death."[9]

Such a stance dovetails into a second topic for consideration: Does assisted suicide/euthanasia constitute a "foreign" form of death or a consequence of an underlying illness? Implicit in the anti-euthanasia argument is a privileging of letting death take its natural course. I grew up in a similar tradition that claimed suicide was an unholy usurpation of God's sole authority/power to give and take life. While many do not make this argument explicitly, their stance suggests a preference for death to come on its own rather than by any hastening attempt. Such posture insinuates that God's will—an admittedly slippery term—rests behind natural causes of death.

By privileging natural death, we (often unknowingly) suggest God prefers, condones, or even sends death by way of disease and decay (old age). Therefore, hastening death constitutes an evil, lesser form of death. I disagree with such assumptions.

Death through cancer or old age comes just as "unnaturally" as does death through suicide. Death of all types represents an affront to God's intention for creation. Nevertheless, through Christ's resurrection God redeems the unintended act of death to become an eternal-life-giving, rather than life-ending, experience. For this reason, Revelation 21:3–4 speaks of God's new creation, where "God himself will be with them and be their

God. He will wipe every tear from their eyes. There will be no more death or mourning or crying or pain, for the old order of things has passed away." The relationship to God now restored, the value of death becomes superfluous; death passes away. Death is a foreign, though redeemed, occurrence in human life. Therefore, resisting assisted suicide in the face of terminal illness on the grounds of privileging the underlying disease—so that someone may die from "natural causes'—seems disingenuous. When death becomes inevitable, why resist putting an end to the suffering?

Still, many resist the option of assisted suicide or euthanasia. Many turn to the advances of palliative care as an appropriate pain management alternative to hastening death. Even Supreme Court Justices Sandra Day O'Connor and Stephen Breyer take up this argument in their decisions against physician-assisted suicide.[10] While accurate in citing advances in palliative care, such belief in palliative care is overconfident.

In August 2010, three months before my mother died, a local hospice began providing extensive care. My mother was on oxygen, pain medication, anti-nausea medication, and a myriad of other drugs aimed at controlling her blood pressure, thyroid levels, and other bodily rhythms. Over the next two months, as cancer further spread throughout her body (including her spine and brain), she became confined to a hospital recliner in our home. Despite heavy doses of morphine and other medication, the pain was never fully contained. In addition to her bodily aches, my mother suffered immense emotional trauma. Weeks before her death, she became incontinent while still mentally alert. Embarrassed and ashamed, I remember sitting with her as she cried and told me how the night before she accidentally wet herself, her clothes, and the chair. Days later she requested a catheter.

While advances in palliative care continue, too often people overestimate the ability of medication, familial support, and spiritual guidance in meeting the needs of dying patients. As my mother's condition worsened, she began confusing family members, experiencing prolonged nightmares, and growing increasingly agitated. Her fear and distress constituted an emotional pain no medication could assuage. Near the end, she was unable to think or communicate reasonably. Death, or "seeing Jesus" as she would say, became her only desire. My mother's Christian convictions catalyzed, not mitigated, her wish for death.

Of course, the debate over assisted suicide and euthanasia reaches far beyond my story. The history of euthanasia and assisted suicide involves more despair than hope. The horrors of the Nazi euthanasia program remain ever-present in this debate.[11] A concern for rightly protecting the vulnerable from involuntary euthanasia motivated many of the Supreme Court's decisions and still dominates much of the discourse today. Admittedly, the potential for losing control over assisted suicide and euthanasia remains great. What constitutes a "mentally competent" wish? Who determines, regulates, and enacts euthanasia procedures? What are the moral and emotional consequences of assenting to the euthanasia of a loved one? These concerns deserve great attention. Therefore, I do not presume to suggest a sweeping advocacy for assisted suicide and euthanasia. On the other hand, I resist any similarly sweeping attempts to downplay its potential healing effects. In this coming age of prolonged illness and protracted death, concern for the health and integrity of the individual must engage again the possible role of death as healer.

Invitation to Conversation

I do not presume to offer a systematic public policy of assisted suicide and euthanasia. Nevertheless, as the Church enters a new era of public advocacy and personal ministry, the need quickly emerges for Christians to determine their view on death. Many will follow Paul in 1 Corinthians 15:20–28 and elevate death to the greatest of enemies, a phantasmal force against which Christians wage war. Another way, however, exists.

The writings of Paul also contain a positive construction of death, one in which "living is Christ and dying is gain" (Phil. 1:21ff, NRSV). In his letter to the Philippians, Paul holds in great tension his *life* of work for Christ and his desire for *death* to be with Christ. Such tension shows an appropriate balance for the Christian life. Christians cannot advocate a life of escapism, one promoting suicide just to attain a restored relationship with Christ. On the contrary, Christians can begin such a relationship with Christ now. This relationship constitutes a responsibility to carry on the ministry of Christ on earth, a ministry that necessarily includes the care of souls and bodies. For Paul, Christians become the embodiment of Christ's care and concern for the world (Eph. 1:22–23; 5:23; Col. 1:18–20). This does not, however, mean Christians should lose sight of the fact that death is *gain*.

As the body of Christ, the Church cannot annihilate the positive and negative attributes of death. When a loved one dies, the death severs that intimate relationship. Christians must not forget that life is a blessing and a gift, something to hold on to as long as possible. Nevertheless, death does not demand despair. It also serves to craft a renewed relationship between the individual and Christ, a "new life" so to speak.

Uncritical rejections of assisted suicide and euthanasia for the terminally ill fail to accurately comprehend the multilayered experience of pain and suffering as one with a terminal illness begins the walk toward death. Any stance on this topic, whether in support or opposition, needs to honor the struggle of individuals by engaging the conversation with openness and understanding. The Church would do well to articulate a vision of death and resurrection that honors the pain of death without surrendering to despair.

Finally, the Church must strive to articulate the life-giving aspects of death. Those left behind can celebrate the much-deserved end of pain and suffering. Likewise, we can rejoice in the restored relationship of a loved one to Christ. While devastating in so many respects, my mother's death offered an end to suffering, and peace to her and to us.

In the era ahead, the Church should begin to conceive of how the death of a loved one brings hope and healing for a family previously preoccupied with a loved one's imminent departure. Family members often experience a profound sense of relief and freedom following the end of a lengthy disease. These feelings, however, often generate guilt in those still living. The Church might assuage this guilt by stressing the connection between their relief and freedom and the relief and freedom the recently departed now experience in Christ.

Ultimately, the Church needs to treat questions of assisted suicide and euthanasia with dignity. It should honor the conventional desire to protect the vulnerable from economic, political, and societal pressures to end their lives. In honoring this commitment to the protection and value of all life, new evangelicals must consider whether or not aiding someone in their death is an act of protecting their dignity and valuing their humanity. New evangelicals must ask, does the illegality of euthanasia and physician-assisted suicide stand as a lack of healthcare that perpetuates needless human suffering?

15

The Global Poor

Adam Phillips

We were hurtling through the busy downtown streets of Freetown in a beat-up—let's call it "red"—Peugeot 205 converted taxi cab. I call it "red" because I'm not certain if that was the new wash of paint on the Peugeot or if it was a long-lost ancestral color, having been scratched and nicked and painted over many times since. At any rate, red was the most prevalent color on the cab, and that's how I'm telling the story.

CAR Magazine named the Peugeot 205 "car of the year" in 1990, but this current specimen was not going to win any kind of award any time soon. Typical of most taxi cabs I've encountered in West Africa, the automobile drove perfectly fine, but the interior was utterly destroyed: ripped seats duct-taped together, musty, rain-saturated interior, and a cabbie who had definitely not showered in weeks. Actually, come to think of it, the cab reminded me of a taxi I grabbed once in Brooklyn, but that is another story for another day.

It was August 2007. I was in Sierra Leone to observe the nation's second presidential and parliamentary elections after the brutal decade-long civil war (1991–2002). The country was high with expectation and knitted together with a fragile hope. In 2002, elections were conducted merely four months after hostilities had ceased and were administered largely by the United Nations Mission in Sierra Leone (UNAMSIL). The 2007 elections may have been the second since the civil war, but in many ways they felt like the first—and nobody knew what Election Day might hold. I was co-leading a group of students alongside my friend Jason Fileta with Micah Challenge. We were young, pretty brave, naïve, and full of excitement—we were election monitors!

A field of seven candidates (all with their own respective platforms, colors, and even soccer teams) was vying for the highest office in the land, but really only two were contenders: Ernest Bai Koroma of the All People's Congress (APC) and Solomon Berewa of the incumbent Sierra Leone People's Party (SLPP). All over the capital the dominant colors of APC's red or SLPP's green hung in storefronts, restaurants, street corners, and taxi cabs, indicating support. This particular taxi did not have any colors hanging from the rear-view mirror, so I thought to engage the driver in conversation about the elections.

"What are you thinking, sir? How do you think the elections will go?" He replied with some respectful chit-chat about both parties and warned me not to forget the third-strongest party candidate, Charles Margai and his orange-clad People's Movement for Democratic Change (PMDC). Then, just past the fishing-village-turned-slum, Kroo Bay, he changed the topic, back to the campaign just under way in the United States.

"You tell me, sir, who do *you* think will win in the States? Do you think it will be Hillary? Obama? Or your war hero Mr. McCain?" A bit astonished (again, I was naïve) I mumbled, "Err I dunno." The cabbie then went on to break down who he thought would win, given the state of global affairs, the need for strong leadership amidst conflict in the Middle East, as well as a determined public policy back home—*in lucid, politically savvy detail.* "I hope Hillary will win for you guys. She is very strong, and I like her platform. Obama is too untested and, while I respect Mr. McCain, I think you guys are ready for a change."

Clearly, I wasn't the only one monitoring another country's elections.

The Global Poor as Part of Us

If we are going to address the global poor in any way, we need to reconsider who they are: they are part of us, not merely a *them.* We need to reflect critically and hopefully about the church, the world, and the global poor. Perhaps it is time to wipe away old notions and naiveties to imagine a more beautiful and global church for the common good. We cannot simply look at the global poor as objects of our affection, charity, and prayers. They are partners in seeking first the kingdom of God. When we look at any notion of a new evangelical partnership for the common good and any mission for addressing the plight of the global poor, we must shed old understandings of mission, evangelism, and relief and replace them with a focused global partnership for the common good.

I write as a 32-year-old white heterosexual privileged evangelical male living in an American urban context. You pull open my dresser drawer, and you will see countless social justice T-shirts and wristbands for various causes. Check my e-mail inbox, and you'll see daily petitions for various campaigns. I am of the generation that grew up with a few U2 albums and a World Vision kid on the fridge, looking at the world with purpose and hope, thinking we could change it a bit—not only for that kid on the refrigerator door whom we sponsored for a few bucks a month, but for ourselves, as well.

My perspective, as a pastor working these last few years in an advocacy and campaigning organization, lends itself to focus primarily on what is currently going on in sub-Saharan Africa and how we, in the United States, can get involved to fight extreme global poverty. As I reflect here on a potential new evangelical approach to the global poor, I recognize it is still too easy to remain too limited in view. Our world gives us so much to reflect on throughout the entirety of the Global South, including Latin America, Asia, and the Middle East. I *do* think, however, that any discussion on the global poor and the church, given recent trends, must begin in Africa, where a "Bottom Billion"[1] of our sisters and brothers live amidst dire circumstances.

So, with that said, let's consider a new way to live evangelically for the common good.

Life Together: The Body of Christ Is Global

"If one part suffers, every part suffers with it; if one part is honored, every part rejoices with it" (1 Cor. 12:26).

We are a global church. Philip Jenkins clearly makes his case for this claim. His argument? The global church's center of gravity would shift from the cathedrals and castles of Europe, beyond the expansive frontier of the American West, and find its heart in the Global South. Jenkins presciently writes, "If we want to visualize a 'typical' contemporary Christian, we should think of a woman living in a village in Nigeria or in a Brazilian favela."[2] Guess what? Jenkins' analysis is coming to pass.

The Pew Forum on Religion and Public Life validated this description in a recent report on global Christianity. With comprehensive research in 200 countries, the Pew Center determined that nearly a third of the world's population (2.19 billion) is made up of Christians of all ages spread out all over the world. More striking than this, however, is the scattering of global Christians, "so far-flung, in fact, that no single continent or region can indisputably claim to be the center of global Christianity."[3] No longer a Eurocentric religion, one third of the global Christian population lives in the Americas (North and South), one-fourth in sub-Saharan Africa, one-fourth in Europe, one-eighth in Asia, and a dwindling less than one percent in the Middle East and North Africa. Predominantly, the church is from the Global South (1.3 billion strong compared to the Global North's 860 million).

These numbers become startling when you consider that the church was born on the fringe of a European empire in the deserts and burgeoning cities of the Middle East and Mediterranean. The more mind-blowing consideration is not the changes from the first century of the church, but the exponential change in the last century. In 1910, over two-thirds of the church was European, with a quarter of the church in the Americas. Sub-Saharan Africa made up just over 1 percent of the church, with Asia and the Pacific islands making up 4.5 percent. This is a tectonic shift in identity, and the church in the United States needs to awaken to this reality.

In my denomination, the Evangelical Covenant Church, we have seen rapid change in very recent history. As a global family of free-church denominations, the old Svenska Missions-förbundet ("Swedish Mission Covenant") of our foremothers and fathers has given rise to exponential growth and to many Evangelical Covenant Churches throughout Latin America, Southeast Asia, and sub-Saharan Africa. The largest national body of the Evangelical Covenant is no longer in Sweden or North America, but in the Democratic Republic of Congo. That reality should convince us to pause and consider how we go about doing church—more as one extended, global family. So, to echo Jenkins' observations, the typical "Covenanter," as my friend and colleague in ministry Rev. Amy Rohler has observed, is a woman living in rural Congo—and she may read the Bible a little differently than her Covenant brother with Scandinavian roots in suburban Minneapolis, Minnesota!

The center of gravity of the global church is not just in the Global South. It has a more recent missionary impulse to come evangelize the United States and Europe. The Redeemed Christian Church of God, with roots in Nigeria, is only one of many emerging Christian groups sending missionaries northward and westward. Andrew Rice details this in a 2009 *New York Times* magazine piece: in Kiev, a 30,000+ predominantly white congregation is led by a Nigerian pastor, while megachurches in London are expanding under African leadership.[4] American cities such as New York and Houston are seeing nascent congregations forming as well. The church in Europe and America is African, too.

What does this entail for us today? We need to start living globally. Not just "thinking globally, acting locally," but more like "rooted locally, prayerfully and actively global." That's a mouthful, but maybe it is time to move beyond slogans and pithy sayings and think and act more thickly as the church in the world, the body of Christ extended globally. I think the ministry of the apostle Paul is helpful here.

Paul is often tossed aside, especially by our more progressive sisters and brothers in the States, for the more radical teachings of Jesus and the prophets of the Hebrew Bible. However, Paul's understanding of the role of citizenship *is* quite radical and subversive. We need to reclaim it as a way to think about our public discipleship today. Paul was not looking to overthrow the kingdoms and empires of his day. He was, ultimately, savvy with his own citizenship in this world and leveraged it to move throughout the Roman Empire to build the church and take up collections for the needs of the poor.

Paul writes to a church in Corinth that found itself at the crossroads of Roman roads and emerging global markets. Corinth was literally a city of the future, anticipating trade hubs and global cities such as Hong Kong, Dubai, New York, and London. As a bridge city in the Mediterranean between Europe and the Middle East, it was a swirling hotbed of pluralism. Cultures clashed, and ethnic identities were challenged and confused as the church in Corinth began to grow. Would it be Jewish or something different? Debates and competing interests from the various cultures collided. Paul inserted himself into the conversation to remind the church broken and scattered across the city of Corinth that they were, in fact, one body with many members in the risen Christ.

If one member of the body suffered, they all suffered. In turn, if one rejoiced, they all rejoiced. The church was about unity and not division, solidarity and not competition. Whether you were with Chloe's people, Apollos, Peter, or Paul, what mattered most was that you were identified solely as one body with Christ. There was no "them," only "us." Essential to this radical unity of "us" was the reality of the resurrection of Christ.

The resurrection was a very real moment of history that has radical implications for daily living in the present. The hope of the resurrection broke down all barriers and infused everyone with eyes to see and ears to hear with the reality of a common purpose for all: total flourishing and salvation. "Everything" was subject to the risen Christ, Paul reminded the church at Corinth (1 Cor. 15:27). Now was time for everyone to repent and "be steadfast, immovable, [and] always excelling in the work of the Lord" (1 Cor. 15:58, NRSV). To remind them that this kingdom work was rooted in the here and now, Paul concludes his letter to the Corinthians by reminding them to take action for the poor and "collect for the saints" in need as he had reminded Christians elsewhere.

Paul's work and witness reminds us, today, that the church is not only one body, but found in local places and bound with one common purpose. I'm convinced that purpose is the common good.

The Body of Christ Is Living with AIDS

In 2002, 50,000 Africans were able to access life-saving HIV/AIDS therapies called anti-retrovirals (ARV). Today over 5 million Africans are living with HIV, having access to these ARVs through U.S. federal funds. President George W. Bush led this effort through programs such as his President's Emergency Plan for AIDS Relief (PEPFAR) and the multilateral Global Fund to fight AIDS, TB, and malaria. These programs remain one of the biggest accomplishments in global health in human history, and hardly anyone knows about it.

Let's be clear—President George W. Bush's work here is a shining light for global healthcare and achievement of the UN Millennium Development Goals. Because of his leadership and the advocacy of countless citizens, including people such as Pastor Rick Warren and his wife, Kay, we are seeing the endless cycle of AIDS deaths beginning to turn around. We are now able to see "the beginning of the end of AIDS" because of programs such as PEPFAR and the Global Fund. On World AIDS Day 2011, President Barack Obama committed the U.S. to treating an additional 2 million people by 2013.

I remember when PEPFAR was announced. I was sitting down to dinner with my newly wed wife. I was a first-year seminary student at North Park. We listened to the State of the Union address. America had been in a costly war in Afghanistan and was on the brink of invading Iraq. In church basements and even on cable news, debates sprung up about peace and security, just war and visions of peace. We turned on the TV that night anxious about the times we were living in. It was a terrible time. As the President spoke to the joint session of Congress, half of the room repeatedly stood and cheered, while the other half sat on their hands. The country remained divided from the 2000 presidential election, and tensions remained high after September 11, 2001. Any sense of unity that that day had brought seemed lost. We could not see a lot to hope for.

Late in the speech came Bush's historic leap of faith to beat back the AIDS pandemic in Africa. Those words jolted me from my seat:

> AIDS can be prevented. Anti-retroviral drugs can extend life for many years. And the cost of those drugs has dropped from $12,000 a year to under $300 a year, which places a tremendous possibility within our grasp. Ladies and gentlemen, seldom has history offered a greater opportunity to do so much for so many. We have confronted, and will continue to confront, HIV/AIDS in our own country.

And to meet a severe and urgent crisis abroad, tonight I propose the Emergency Plan for AIDS Relief, a work of mercy beyond all current international efforts to help the people of Africa. This comprehensive plan will prevent 7 million new AIDS infections, treat at least 2 million people with life-extending drugs and provide humane care for millions of people suffering from AIDS and for children orphaned by AIDS. I ask the Congress to commit $15 billion over the next five years, including nearly $10 billion in new money, to turn the tide against AIDS in the most afflicted nations of Africa and the Caribbean.

In the seminary coffee lounge the next morning people talked about two things: Bush's justification for invading Iraq and his line about "the wonder-working power of the American people," borrowed by his speechwriter Michael Gerson, from the old hymn "Wonder Working Power in the Blood of the Lamb." When I brought it up, no one remembered his commitment to fight AIDS in Africa. Today, some ten years later, people are only beginning to realize what sort of "Lazarus effect" for the sick, the widow, and the orphan has been achieved.

President Bush deserves credit for his bold and courageous leadership in the fight against HIV/AIDS as well as malaria and TB. Like William Wilberforce before him—remembered for legislating the end of British slavery—a movement below and around the legislation had been advocating for social justice. In Bush's case a global movement advocated for social justice for nearly fifteen years, organized around what has since been called the Millennium Development Goals. These goals included working to halve global poverty by 2015, beat back preventable, treatable diseases, ensure environmental sustainability, and foster global partnerships for development, amongst others. A hundred eighty-nine countries at the United Nations agreed on the MDGs. The Irish rock star Bono described this action as a "millennial new year's resolution." Millions of citizens around the world supported the resolution and its goals.

Evangelical churches, mission agencies, and relief and development organizations launched the Micah Challenge to seek these Millennium Development Goals, which my friend Joel Edwards describes as "covenants with the poor." Central to achieving the MDGs is a commitment by the church globally to seek "integral mission" by bearing witness evangelically (speaking the good news of Christ) while also living out biblically the kingdom of God in social action. Integral mission in the twenty-first century means not only holding evangelism and social action in tandem, but also an undergirding for the church to bear witness holistically as one global body with many members.

Joel Edwards notes that our "biblical witness is not called to tip-toe through the twenty-first century. It is meant to transform society. [We] will do so by presenting Christ credibly to the culture. For evangelicals this means reclaiming the idea that we are good news, called to a long-term vision for spiritual and social change."[5] For a new generation of global evangelicals, seeking the MDGs by 2015 is one integral part of what it means to live biblically.

Advocacy is central to the equation of millions of lives being saved. Without advocacy for smart policies like PEPFAR and the Global Fund that get at the root causes of poverty and disease, efforts by individuals, churches, and institutions are simply charity and not justice. To truly achieve social justice and seek the common good, advocacy is a necessary instrument of a holistic missional Christian life lived for the kingdom of God. Each of us has a role to play in building for the kingdom of God, and the government has a distinct role and responsibility to this end. It's a twenty-first-century way to exercise our earthly and national citizenship today, as Paul lived out his in the first century.

Beating back AIDS and achieving the Millennium Development Goals are part and parcel of a life lived faithfully for God and our neighbor today. Some fires need to be put out first if we are to seek the flourishing of families and communities. Fighting AIDS and malaria, seeking global health for our most vulnerable sisters and brothers, is essential to integral mission—social justice and evangelism are intertwined for the redemption of all.

Jesus and Justice

I once attended a seminary event in which the host introduced the keynote speaker as someone he admired because the speaker "knew Jesus and knew justice." Because these words just so quickly and easily rolled off the tongue of the host, I heard the statement that the speaker "knew Jesus and knew 'Justice'" as if they were two separate people.

Huh?

I thought to myself, who is this "Justice"? Was "Justice" the half-brother of Jesus? Was he that guy that who lived in his parents' basement, wore cargo pants and campaign T-shirts, attended rallies and demonstrations, but was often absent from church? Justice probably found more spiritual significance in attending a Radiohead concert than a mid-week Bible study, right? Yeah, he was that guy we went to college with who drank a little too much coffee in the morning and a little too much draft beer at night, rambling on and on about conspiracy theories, corporations, and the evils of the military industrial complex. Yeah, I know that guy.

But I also know Jesus, and he didn't spend all of his time in mid-week Bible studies, either.

For too long, the evangelical church in North America has treated Jesus as if he did not have much to do with social justice. For too long, evangelicals have bifurcated the spiritual teachings of Jesus, his miracles and healings, from the bold portrayal of him as one who would literally turn the world upside down. Our Bible teachers, for whatever reason, taught us a bifurcated Gospel.

We were taught that the One born to Mary, the one she sang her Magnificat about (Lk. 1:46–55), came to "spiritually" fill the hungry and "spiritually" overthrow the rulers of this world. We were taught that the radical teachings of the Sermon on the Mount were more about "spiritual" poverty and "spiritual" meekness than about real, physically embodied material reality. We were told that the turning over of the tables in the temple was not really about the moneychangers taking advantage of the poor. We were even told to switch out our prayers regarding "our debts" for "our sins."

Thankfully, evangelicals have been dismantling these false teachings over the past ten years. But it is taking some time, and some unlearning. Groups such as World Vision and International Justice Mission are leading the way, not only introducing American evangelicals to new ways to care for and sponsor children, but to new ways to systematically undo the oppression of extreme poverty as well as prosecute sex trafficking. Movements such as Advent Conspiracy are leading the way in reclaiming a holy season focused on God's inbreaking kingdom amidst the consumer-saturated false worship of Christmas. Christian artists such as Jars of Clay, Third Day, Switchfoot, Sara Groves, and David Crowder Band regularly incorporate causes into their tours, urging their fans to take action beyond their inspirational music.

"Do you intend to use your beautiful voice to praise the Lord or to change the world?"… *'We humbly suggest you can do both.'"* —Amazing Grace

The 2006 film *Amazing Grace* offered a new way for evangelicals in the Global North to be engaged in the public square by looking back at the public ministry of British abolitionist William Wilberforce, a member of Parliament from 1780–1825. The film depicts two conversations with which Wilberforce had to wrestle. I believe these conversations must animate the church today. In one scene, his dear childhood friend and newly elevated Prime Minister, William Pitt, confronts the recently converted, wallowing Wilberforce with a challenge: "Do you intend to use your beautiful voice to praise the Lord or to change the world?"

In a subsequent scene, Wilberforce is hosting a dinner of some strangers who turn out to be anti-slavery activists. In what is likely an amalgamation of many conversations, the persistent Hannah Moore, Olaudah Equiano, and Thomas Clarkson run what the twentieth-century rabble-rouser Saul Alinsky would have called "an action." They interrupt the dinner with stories of injustices and sketches demonstrating slave-trade torture devices, all to force a reaction from Wilberforce and enlist him in the movement. Equiano, played by Senegalese artist, activist, and devout Muslim Youssou N'Dour, even shows Wilberforce his scars from the slave master's whip and cattle brand, thus bringing an unceremonious end to dinner. Clarkson and Moore then declare, "Mr. Wilberforce, we understand you are having problems deciding whether to do the work of God or the work of a political activist… We humbly suggest you can do both."

William Wilberforce would heed the charge and do both. Leading the legislative charge from within Parliament to undo the global British Slave Trade, he tirelessly campaigned for twenty-six years for the end of the slave trade, helping pass the Slave Act of 1807. The full end to British slavery would come through the Slavery Abolition Act of 1833—passed by the House of Lords a month after Wilberforce's death. Wilberforce is a model evangelical political witness for life lived out in the public square.

Not everyone is called to work from within the structures of political power. The roles of Hannah Moore, Olaudah Equiano, and Thomas Clarkson must serve to inspire a new generation of evangelicals as well. Without the movement's outside pressure, the inside influence of Wilberforce never would have happened. Clarkson was a preacher's kid who followed his calling into political activism over parish ministry. Equiano was a famous public speaker and writer who may have even "remixed" his own personal narrative a bit for the cause. The poet-playwright-philanthropist Hannah Moore was a sole, strong woman among the male-dominated Clapham sect.

A motley crew, indeed—but as we've seen from modern-day civil rights and anti-poverty movements, it takes all kinds. *Bury the Chains: Prophets and Rebels in the Fight to Free an Empire's Slaves,* by Adam Hocshchild, tells the abolition movement's story in more vivid detail and should be a small group discussion book in every church.[6] As a new generation of prophets and rebels emerge today, it is good to be able to tell the stories of those long since past because we stand on the shoulders of faithful giants such as Equiano, Moore, Clarkson, and Wilberforce.

Zambia

Thank goodness we have current-day models of public disciples. Thank goodness they do not exist only in the history books and that we can point to people in our own day who are using their beautiful voices to praise the Lord *and* change the world.

With those stirring conversations in Freetown buzzing in my head all the way back to Chicago on the flight home, I was thankful to be joined by some of our sisters and brothers in the broader Micah Challenge movement across Africa to engage voters and candidates in the U.S. Presidential election throughout 2007–2008. Partnering with the ONE Campaign, we literally went out, two-by-two, one American and one Zambian, like some postmodern-day public witnesses for Jesus and justice. Off we went, engaging candidates and voters in town hall meetings, church basements, and rallies in the early primary states and battleground states of the U.S.

Two of our comrades from Micah Challenge Zambia were able to join us: Pastor Lawrence Temwfe of the Jubilee Center and Bishop Paul Mususu of Zambia's Evangelical Fellowship, a leader in the Pentecostal wing of the church. I have some vivid memories of walking with Lawrence on the Las Vegas strip heading to an Obama rally, and with Bishop chatting up Sarah Palin on the rope line in Columbus, Ohio. These guys were not only passionate rabble-rousers for Jesus and justice, but also characters. Lawrence somehow survived on four hours of sleep each night and dressed way hipper than me in his sport coat, jeans, and black T-shirt. Bishop Mususu really loved Starbucks coffee and became rapidly addicted to "buffalo sauce" once he discovered it somewhere in the Midwest.

Both Lawrence and Bishop Mususu totally got the notion that Jesus was all about justice and that advocacy and elections were part of the equation for seeking the common good. They killed it at every town hall, church basement, and campus event we did: describing not the bloated bellies, flies in the eyes images of African children in need, but also a vibrant people looking to partner with their sisters and brothers in the U.S. to build a better future.

Bishop Mususu and Lawrence got this notion of public discipleship and political engagement because they had long been doing it back home in Zambia. Much later, Bishop Mususu shared with me the role of the church in preventing the nation's former President Frederick Chiluba from seeking a third term in office back in 2001. He relayed how the evangelical church, working ecumenically with mainline Protestants and Catholics, served to apply pressure and prevent the president from seeking an unprecedented (and unconstitutional) third term.[7]

What was critical for the evangelicals at the time was to have faith, be bold, and "not be afraid—but to come out and be public about their pressure on their government," Mususu said. To have public events and rallies in Zambia, a costly permit is often required—paid to the police, who often prevent these sort of gatherings from even starting or even skim a little off the top for themselves. The churches got around this by holding what they called "Prayer and Reflection" meetings where they gathered around the Scriptures, using Romans 13 (on authorities, taxes, and respect/honor) to reflect together as one community on the issues of the day. The gatherings included not only church folk and others, but also local officials and members of parliament!

These Prayer and Reflection meetings spread "like wildfire" across the country. While evening meetings were taking place, the evangelicals also mobilized a campaign to secure signatures from members of parliament to seek Chiluba's impeachment if he tried to go any further in his efforts for a third term. President Chiluba tried to go around these churches by appealing to other faith leaders, but Mususu and others in the Evangelical Alliance had also garnered support from the mainline Protestant members of the Council of Churches, as well as the Catholic Church, to stand in solidarity with their efforts. A united, ecumenical front, led by the Evangelical Alliance and sustained by grassroots pressure, pushed back Chiluba's attempts to seek a third term, and he eventually stood down.

The church was not simply a spiritual place for prayer and reflection—it was an organizing body for collective public and political action, Bishop Mususu concluded. As he told me the story, I scribbled on my coffee cup: "Yes, the church is supposed to be salt and light, but it is the government that is collecting our tax and making foolish decisions and policies. We can't allow these things to go unchallenged. We need to address needs along the way with mercy, but our task as the church is to not simply pick up babies downstream that have been tossed in the river. We must go upstream and confront these challenges where they start, and that is why we as a church need to advocate and confront unjust laws."

Lawrence Temwfe, who continues to do amazing holistic mission and local development out of the Jubilee Centre in the Copper-Belt region of the country, also spearheaded political action during the rewriting of Zambia's Constitution. Political authorities in the capital of Lusaka were inviting local pastors and church leaders to take part in the Constitutional convention, offering stipends and financial support to those who took part. Realizing that "stipends" and "support" could soon turn into "graft" and "corruption," Lawrence and others pushed back and said, essentially, "We will come to the Convention, but we will not accept your money." So, the church leaders took weeks out of their busy schedules, held a fund-raising drive for support, and with significant financial burden on the churches, arrived at the proceedings, able to influence the process while staying above reproach, not accepting any financial gains from the government or political parties. Talk about costly prophetic, nonpartisan witness!

So often in the U.S. we talk about advocating our own elected leaders and holding them accountable. It's important to know that churches and leaders in other countries around the world are doing their part to hold officials accountable in a spirit of good governance. We stand as members of a global body of Christ—each having a role to play and gifts therein. Bishop Mususu and Lawrence's stories are evidence that African leaders are doing their part in mobilizing for the common good, and it remains an inspiration for us do our part as well.

Concluding Thoughts amidst Another Election

Here's the bottom line. We need to think differently about Africa and the world's poorest places. It's time to look beyond antiquated notions of "us" sending stuff and going to help fix things over "there." There is no "them." In the resurrected Christ, there is only "us." And that has some serious ramifications for how we live today.

Things have changed. A decade ago, the weekly international politics and business magazine *The Economist* dubbed Africa "the hopeless continent." You could say they repented of that misnomer in a December 3, 2011, cover story illustrating the continent as "Africa Rising."[8] True, there remain nearly a bottom-billion people below the poverty line where disease and hunger are a daily matter of concern. But hope remains: "From Ghana in the west to Mozambique in the south, Africa's economies are consistently growing faster than those of almost any other region of the world."[9] Parts of Ethiopia, which suffered such devastating famine in the 1980s, have weathered the drought. Christians in the Global North need to celebrate the fact that a dozen African countries have seen their economies expand by more than 6 percent for six or more years straight. In the U.S., we're lucky to see economic growth rates at 3–4 percent a year. Christians in the Global North need to celebrate the fact that modern science, agriculture, and the work of remarkable secular and faith based NGOs have partnered to beat back hunger and disease. The church in the Global North should be in awe of a place like Ethiopia, in many ways a cradle of our global church, where the economy has grown by 7.5 percent "without a drop of oil to export."[10]

Why? Because expanding economies matter for human flourishing; growing economies matter for the common good—or as we once described it, "the common wealth." For the common good, we need to reconsider our approach and grasp of global economics. In the North, for so long, the thinking has been, "Let's send money and resources and people to people in need." Yes, foreign assistance matters. Poverty-focused development assistance matters. Foreign missions and compassion and relief efforts matter—in short term needs, and long term horizons. But trade and partnership for development matter, too, for people to reach their full potential in Christ.

We need to reimagine Africa's potential as *our* potential. We need to move beyond the paradigm of "us" and "them." As the church, we need to fully imagine and live simply as "us." That change of paradigm will certainly include the tension of growing pains. We need to celebrate the redemptive arts and culture that come from the Global South. We should marvel at the ability to hold global sporting events like the World Cup in South Africa and celebrate such massive achievements—they reflect growth and economic progress. We also need to ask questions about the poor, our sisters and brothers who are being overshadowed in such places by magnificent stadiums and hotels. We cannot forget them. We must be resolved in our approach to seeking the common good: resolute to suffer as one suffers, rejoice as one rejoices.

This requires living in tension, and the tension at times may be unbearable. That's what it means to live in the light of the resurrection, in the "not quite yet" realized kingdom of God. Today, some of us are very, very rich, and some of us are very, very poor. Some observe that the hole in the middle is getting larger every day, despite the growth I described earlier. I agree with World Vision's Rich Stearns that the biggest challenge facing us today is the gap between the rich and poor and addressing "the hole in the gospel" of our lives that we profess.[11] We need to remember the whole Gospel.

To truly realize our potential, not simply as a global body of believers, but as a global community seeking the common good, we need to account for economics and elections. Any new kind of evangelical partnership for the common good must recollect the biblical matter of economics, in which all in the household are lavished upon with equal concern. Any new kind of evangelical partnership for the common good must also recollect a biblical matter of governing leadership, too, most specifically the role of government. As we approach another general election in 2012 (I swear they seem to be coming up on us faster these days), it's important to remember that we are not simply rooting for candidates or parties, but that we are seeking the common good. We need to realize a full prioritization of the common good in our policies and platforms, and not just the old war horses of identity politics. We need a new kind of political engagement in this country in this upcoming election.

In 2012 we already hear about the evangelical vote and the importance of specific values. Too much ink has been spilled on telling the wrong story, I believe. The media does not quite know how to tell the whole story. The Iowa caucus, every four years, they say, is a bellwether of where "values voters" are. We should pause and reflect that Governor Mike Huckabee, who won the GOP nod out of Iowa in 2008, and Senator Rick Santorum, who won in 2012, are not only so-called "evangelical candidates," but conservative Republicans who support federally funded programs to assist our global neighbors in greatest need. Both Huckabee and Santorum tirelessly advocated publicly for programs such as PEPFAR and the Global Fund, indicating that to be pro-life can and should also mean to comprehensively seek the welfare and common good of those now living. When choosing life, you cannot separate the two.

We live in difficult, trying times. Economic woes plague the United States. Wars and rumors of wars are a daily threat to living in peace. The broader culture and even the church are reexamining previously immovable pillars in the culture wars. An air of civility is hard to come by in a sound-bite, eye-for-an-eye culture. We can also flip through cable news and see devastating reports of underage children being sold into sex slavery. We can open up our e-mails and receive another request for disaster assistance in Haiti. We can scroll through Facebook and see a friend's post on devastations of climate change in the world's most vulnerable communities. Intense suffering and injustice flourish all around. That is a reality—not everyone is flourishing quite yet.

So, with all the work to do, it is essential that we be at prayer and seek the inspiration of the Word, together. Ruth Padilla DeBorst says it best. As a biblical preacher and rabble-rouser for social justice, she is a hero to me and many others. Just go on YouTube and look for her sermon on Ephesians 2 at the Third Lausanne Congress on World Evangelization in Cape Town, South Africa, in 2010. It's a barnburner. Contrasting the false peace of Rome with the true peace of Jesus Christ, she describes how God "breaks-in" to the oppressions and injustices of our day and declares that everyone is "indispensable, valuable, and beautiful."[12]

In an interview with *Christianity Today*, Ruth reflects on the ongoing struggles of the church in the world today, and suggests it's a matter of truly living biblically:

> I've been struck by how fragmented our reading of the Bible is. It's a kind of [a] Sunday school version of the Bible: all these isolated little Bible stories, taught out of their context. What we need to reclaim is the big story, the big picture. "In the beginning God..."—that's where we need to begin. In the end, we find the new Jerusalem and all people bowing before the Lord of all nations. The story between that beginning and that end is not divorced from human history.

Rather, it is a picture of God's involvement in history. It's the story of a people wandering closer and further away from his call and claim on their lives to serve as a light to the nations, an example of how people can relate to God and to one another in right and healthy ways. It's also the story of God calling his people back through the prophets, to the point of sending Jesus himself to say, *I am serious about this world; I love this world; I'm willing to suffer and die for this world.*[13]

It's time to live biblically in a twenty-first-century context. It's time to remember the promise of the Scriptures, especially Revelation, of when there will be no more hunger or pain in real time, real history. The resurrected One returns and brings the fullness of the promised kingdom, and the nations will bring their gifts, together, to worship and live in community. And all will be right. There will be no rich. There will be no poor.

There will be only *us*.

SECTION III

...and Redemptive Approaches in Public Life

16

Ending the Death Penalty

Timothy W. Floyd

The death penalty is among the most divisive issues in the United States today. Many support capital punishment on the grounds that to fully respect the dignity of the victim and to prevent future murders, justice requires the execution of the murderer. Others support it because they believe that the American death penalty is properly limited to "the worst of the worst" murderers—that is, the ones who commit the most heinous crimes. The debate sometimes includes biblical quotations hurled back and forth: proponents point to "An eye for an eye!" while others respond, "Judge not, lest ye be judged!"

As is often the case with such issues, debates about the death penalty are usually conducted at high levels of abstraction and emotion, and often without a full understanding of how the death penalty actually works in the American legal system. Not surprisingly, these kinds of discussions do not get us very far in healing our disagreements. Nor do they force us to take a hard look at a system that puts people to death on behalf of all American citizens,[1] or to really grapple with whether the American death penalty is consistent with our individual and collective religious beliefs. I believe that arguments for the death penalty break down when we examine the American death penalty as it actually exists, and that in fact the death penalty is both a broken system and inconsistent with the Gospel of Jesus Christ.

An analysis of the way in which the death penalty is administered reveals that it does not separate the wheat from the chaff. It does not ensure that only the worst of the worst—those most deserving of death—are executed. The vast majority of murderers do not receive the death penalty, and the factors that lead some murderers to be sentenced to death have very little to do with the severity of the crime or the depravity of the defendant. Other factors make the difference. Nor is there reliable evidence that the death penalty has a general deterrent effect in preventing murders.

The death penalty in the United States is actually quite rare. Although roughly 15,000 persons commit criminal homicide in the United States each year, fewer than 1 percent of murderers receive the death penalty. Only forty-three persons were put to death in the United States in 2011, and the number of persons sentenced to death and the number of persons actually executed has gone down dramatically in the past decade.

Moreover, it is not really accurate to talk about the "American" death penalty system, because most executions happen in a small handful of states. Sixteen states do not allow a defendant to be sentenced to death, while many states with the death penalty on the books rarely exercise that option. In the past thirty years, only ten states account for over 90 percent of all executions, and one state, Texas, has carried out nearly 40 percent of all executions in the United States. Mostly, the death penalty is a phenomenon of the American South; nearly 90 percent of executions in the past thirty years have taken place in the states of the old Confederacy.[2]

In its practice of the death penalty, the United States is increasingly isolated on the international scene. All the countries of Europe have abolished the death penalty, as have nearly all the other countries of the Western Hemisphere. The United States is consistently among the five countries in the world with the most executions, along with China, Iran, North Korea, and Saudi Arabia.[3] On the global stage, this places us in very poor company with regard to respect for human rights, and as the only predominantly Christian nation among that group. In fact, American insistence on maintaining the death penalty has made cooperation with our allies much more difficult on issues of crime and security.

What accounts for the relatively few defendants who do receive the death penalty, while the overwhelming majority do not? The difference has little to do with the facts surrounding the murder, or with the person who committed the crime. Rather, the evidence shows that two factors make the most difference: the competence of the defendant's lawyer and the race of the victim. In addition, we know that the system is replete with mistake and error.

Incompetent Attorneys

Nearly every defendant charged with a capital murder is too poor to hire an attorney. Therefore, their attorneys are appointed by the state and paid for their services at a rate much lower than what a private attorney would charge. Moreover, indigent defendants do not have access to adequate funding to put on a defense, such as the ability to hire expert witnesses or to conduct scientific testing, including DNA testing. In many cases, the appointed attorneys have too high a caseload to meet the demands of a complex capital murder trial. Even worse, many lack sufficient trial experience. Studies show that these lawyers have at times been completely unprepared for the sentencing phase of the trial, offering no mitigation evidence that might lead to the imposition of a life sentence rather than the death penalty. Appointed attorneys have slept through parts of the trial or arrived at the court under the influence of alcohol or other drugs. Persons have been executed after their lawyers filed no motions and raised no objections at the trial; other defense lawyers could not name a single criminal case from the United States Supreme Court. The process of sorting out who is most deserving of death does not work when the most fundamental component of the adversary system, competent counsel, is missing.[4]

Bias and Unfairness

Empirical studies underscore a persistent pattern of racial disparities in death penalty cases. The primary disparity is not in the race of the defendant, as one might suspect, but rather in the race of the victim. Persons who kill white people are four to five times more likely to receive a death sentence than are people whose victims are African Americans or other persons of color. The highest chance that the prosecution will seek the death penalty comes when the defendant is black and the victim is white. This is the case even though black persons are disproportionately the victims of murder. This kind of racial disparity has been found to exist in every state that regularly employs the death penalty.[5]

Additionally, geography—where the crime is committed—has much more to do with who will receive the death penalty than does the nature of the crime or of the defendant. A few states regularly sentence people to death, while most other states never do. Even within a state such as Texas, certain counties seek the death penalty much more than do others. Harris County (Houston) accounts for one-third of Texas's death row, while Dallas has only one quarter of Houston's total despite a higher murder rate. Likewise in Pennsylvania, convicted murderers in Philadelphia are far more likely to receive a death sentence than those in Pittsburgh or any other community in the state.

Other arbitrary reasons—those having nothing to do with the severity of the crime—also contribute to who gets the death penalty. Because death penalty cases are so expensive, factors such as when the case comes up during the fiscal year and whether the county has already had its limit of capital cases make a difference in whether the defendant will live or die. The nearness in time of the next election for the prosecutor can also be a significant factor in whether the prosecutor seeks the death penalty.

Mistakes

Perhaps the most disturbing aspect of the death penalty in the U.S. is that so many mistakes are made. A shocking number of persons have been freed from death row nationwide because they were proven innocent years after conviction. Since 1973, 139 people in twenty-six states have been released from death row because they were innocent.[6] Many of these cases were resolved not because of the normal appeals process, but rather as a result of new scientific techniques, investigations by journalists, and the dedicated work of expert attorneys—something not generally available to the typical death row inmate.

These cases show that our current system allows far too great a risk of executing the innocent. In addition to those who have been released from death row because their innocence has been proven, examples exist of persons being executed who are almost certainly innocent of the crime. To take only two examples: (1) Georgia recently executed Troy Davis in the face of compelling evidence of his actual innocence. After he had been sentenced to death, seven of the nine eyewitnesses against him recanted their testimony. Notwithstanding the substantial doubts about his guilt, the state of Georgia and federal courts allowed the execution to go forward. (2) Texas executed Cameron Todd Willingham for the arson/murder of his children in 2004. It has now been established that the expert testimony offered against him at trial was seriously flawed; in fact, arson experts now agree that the fire was accidental and that there was no murder at all.[7]

A common justification offered for the death penalty is that executing murderers deters other persons from committing murder for fear of future execution. However, no evidence supports the opinion that the death penalty is an effective general deterrent. Over 200 studies have been conducted to determine whether the death penalty acts as a deterrent, and the evidence overwhelmingly indicates that it does not. In fact, the murder rate is higher in those states that have the death penalty than in states that do not.[8]

Christians and the Death Penalty

Arbitrariness, bias, unfairness, risk of mistake—these are ample reasons for all Americans to reject our current practice of the death penalty. For Christians, however, the death penalty should be especially problematic. Christian supporters of the death penalty should struggle with whether it is contrary to the will of God as revealed in the teachings of Jesus. Jesus commands us: "Judge not, lest ye be judged." "Blessed are the merciful." "Love your enemies." "Pray for those who persecute you." "If anyone strikes you on the right cheek, do not strike back, but turn the other cheek."[9]

Paul's admonitions to the Romans (in chapter 12) strike much the same note: "Bless those who persecute you… [D]o not repay anyone evil for evil… [N]ever avenge yourselves. 'Vengeance is mine, I will repay, says the Lord.'" Vengeance is for the Lord alone"(from vv. 14–19, NRSV). The New Testament's ethical witness is diverse, and different strands of that witness have many different emphases. Still, strikingly, the New Testament speaks with one voice in rejecting violence and vengeance as a means of achieving justice.[10]

To be sure, the Gospel message of loving enemies and avoiding vengeance runs very much against the grain of American culture and common human nature. Every death penalty case begins with a brutal murder, and a desire for vengeance is an understandable and common human reaction to evil acts such as these. For those of us who are committed to the Gospel of Jesus Christ, vengeance is not and cannot be the response. Responding to violent acts with violence of our own is antithetical to the Gospel. We put our trust in a Lord who rejected the powers of this world and their ways of violence and vengeance. Our Lord "humbled himself and became obedient to the point of death—even death on a cross."[11]

Moreover, trusting the state to make the "right" decision as to who deserves to live and who deserves to die is problematic for Christians. It is idolatrous to trust in government as the ultimate giver and taker of life. Although many Christians cite Paul in Romans 13:1–7 as endorsing the power of the state to take life, Romans 13 should be read together with Romans 12 immediately preceding it, which counsels Christians not to repay evil with evil nor to exercise vengeance. The government has a proper role in restraining evildoers (as Paul acknowledged), but deciding who deserves to die is properly reserved only to God.

In the face of this overwhelming New Testament witness, it is a curious fact that evangelical Christians express support for the death penalty at higher rates than do most other Americans.[12] What explains this support for the death penalty?

The reasons are many. Sometimes persons who identify themselves as Christians express support for the death penalty without specific reliance upon or even thought about its relationship to Christian faith.[13] In our highly polarized political climate, support for the death penalty may simply result from allegiance to a political party or to political ideology. In that case, support for the death penalty is simply the position of "our side" in the ongoing cultural wars; to put it crudely, if secular liberals are opposed to the death penalty, some evangelicals will automatically support it.

On the other hand, political views do not explain all support by Christians for the death penalty. Many Christian supporters of the death penalty have given careful thought to the death penalty in light of their faith. It seems clear that support for the death penalty among some Christians is influenced by certain understandings about human nature and about the nature of God. However, the understandings of human nature and divine judgment that underlie support for capital punishment are not, I submit, fully adequate conceptions of the Gospel. Support for the death penalty may be grounded on an inadequate appreciation of the biblical understanding of human nature. The death penalty is often justified on the ground that certain people are wholly evil and are incapable of redemption. The very premise of the idea of reserving the death penalty for the "worst of the worst" is that the very "worst" are so bad that they have forfeited their right to live. In fact, this belief affects the way individual cases are litigated. To convince juries to sentence defendants to death, prosecutors often portray the defendant as less than or other than human—as an "animal" or as a "monster." Conversely, good defense lawyers work hard to convey to the jury that, although the defendant did a horrible act, he is still a human being. To the extent that jurors perceive that the defendant is a deeply flawed human being who nevertheless is not different in kind from the rest of us, they are much less likely to sentence the defendant to death.

Although this is a common underlying premise in death penalty litigation, Christians should reject this notion. Believing that certain persons are so evil that they do not deserve to live is not faithful to the biblical witness about humanity. A biblical view of human nature insists that no one in this fallen world is beyond the possibility of redemption. God's mercy and grace are available to all. Indeed, we are commanded to love our enemies precisely because God loves them.

Acting out of this biblical understanding is perhaps most difficult in this context. It might be one thing to extend God's grace to others or to expect the possibility of redemption for certain kinds of sins. We, however, are called to do so even when one has committed the sin of taking another's life, even in a particularly heinous way.

According to Scripture, individual human beings are created in the image of God and have sacred worth in the eyes of God. Sound Christian faith teaches that God's creation is good, including human beings.[14] God made humankind in God's image.[15] The psalmist asserts, "God has made humans a little lower than the angels, and crowned them with glory and honor."[16]

As Christians, we are also called to remember that all persons are sinners. "All have sinned and fall short of the glory of God."[17] Human beings live in a fallen world and are themselves all sinners. Starkly dividing humanity into the "good" and the "evil," which is a basis for the death penalty, is not compatible with that biblical understanding. As Solzhenitsyn put it, the line between good and evil runs through every human heart.[18] As Jesus tells us (notably in the command to love our enemies), God makes the sun to shine on the good and the evil, and the rain to fall on the righteous and the unrighteous.[19] Christians are required to do the hard work of seeing this humanity in all persons and of leaving the ultimate judgment of life and death to God rather than to governmental authority.

This is not to say that punishment is wrong, but rather that death is different. Society has an obligation to protect persons from those who have committed and may commit crimes of violence. Confining and restraining those who pose such a risk is essential, and imprisoning some people for life is the appropriate response for the worst crimes and for the most dangerous criminals. Christianity calls us to stop at life imprisonment; it is not right for the state to go further and take a person's life.

Moreover, a biblical respect for human fallibility would counsel humility and the avoidance of self-righteousness. The possibilities of mistake, as exemplified by the many cases of innocent persons sentenced to death, are a stark reminder of the fallibility of human judgments. If an innocent person is sentenced to prison, the possibility remains to correct the injustice and free that person; an execution cuts off that possibility.

In addition to the understanding of human nature, a second theological understanding may contribute to evangelicals' support for the death penalty. This factor rests in a particular view of the crucifixion and of the role of Jesus' death in our salvation. It is ironic (and not always remembered) that Jesus himself was the subject of capital punishment by the governing power of his day. Of course, no one forgets that the crucifixion is at the center of the Christian faith; the cross is the central symbol of Christianity. All Christians agree that Jesus' death on the cross is essential to our salvation. How Christians understand the nature and significance of Jesus' death on the cross plays a powerful role in their understanding of the nature of God and of divine judgment.

One view of the crucifixion is that the killing of Jesus was brought about by God's will. Many believe that God required the suffering and death of

Jesus as retribution for our sins. The sins of all humanity call for divine punishment, but the sacrifice of Jesus on the cross satisfied the divine need to punish. In this view, God would not, perhaps could not, save us without the violent torture and killing of Jesus.

Accordingly, if God required a death as penalty for sin, it would not be surprising to find that many Christians believe that the proper response to especially heinous acts is to insist on death as the punishment. In other words, the belief that a vengeful God requires suffering and a violent death as payment for sin influences many to believe that when people commit especially heinous or brutal crimes, justice requires that an execution is the only appropriate response.[20]

I submit, however, that a view of atonement that starkly separates the divine person into a judgmental and punitive Father and a merciful and gracious Son is an inadequate understanding of the unity of God. Although the Trinity is a mystery and the doctrine is not easy to understand, I do believe in a triune God. I also know God is One in three persons. The God who creates and judges us is the same God who forgives, redeems, and sustains us. If the doctrine of the Incarnation means anything, the God who made us is the same God who suffers with us, the God who experienced torture and death on the cross. A punitive understanding of the atonement unduly separates God and pits the persons of the Trinity against one another. That view is not consistent with the unity of God. The crucial theological doctrine here is the Incarnation: God became flesh and is present with us in our suffering, even unto death.

Although "penal atonement theology" is predominant among American Christians, especially among evangelicals, it not the only way to view the crucifixion and atonement. Other narratives and viewpoints appear in the Christian tradition. I submit that the crucifixion is God's emphatic rejection of violence and retribution. The evil Powers of this world tortured and killed Jesus, but Jesus did not resist with violence. Instead, he forgave his tormentors. In his death, Jesus gained victory over those Powers, because he rose from the dead and now reigns as Lord.

Jesus' suffering and death were not caused by God. The evil Powers of this world bear full responsibility for killing Jesus. Nonetheless, the crucifixion *is* central to our salvation. Jesus' death on the cross manifests God's love for humanity, and most importantly the resurrection vindicates God's justice in triumph over the evil Powers of the world. As a result, the way of vengeance—of repaying those who do evil with acts of cruelty and violence—is not open to followers of Jesus.

Conclusion

At the transfiguration, God tells the disciples: "This is my child, my beloved, with whom I am well pleased—listen to him!"[21] For Christians, the answer to the death penalty debate, as with other contentious social issues, is to focus more centrally on the life, ministry, and teachings of Jesus. If we will listen attentively to Jesus and follow his teachings and his example, we will reject vengeance and the death penalty. May we work together to hasten the day when our government no longer exercises the ultimate punishment.

17

Making Peace

Paul Alexander

Introduction

Imagine life in early first-century Palestine. Roman occupying forces abuse and demean the local people. Taxes are exorbitant. Revolutionaries occasionally gather followers to fight guerrilla warfare for freedom. Roman occupying forces crucify revolutionaries and their families by the hundreds, sometimes thousands. Roman law allows for occupying soldiers to force local Palestinians to carry their military packs for a mile. Occupation forces can commandeer farmers working in their olive groves, shepherds tending their flocks, merchants selling their wares, or carpenters crafting a piece of furniture.

Jesus' Third Way

I am going to argue for active peacemaking and against violence and passivity by listening to Jesus' teachings and the stories about Jesus and his followers. In the good news—welcome information for the public—according to Matthew, Jesus teaches his followers:

> You have heard that it was said, "Eye for eye, and tooth for tooth." But I tell you, do not resist an evil person. If someone strikes you on the right cheek, turn to him the other also. And if someone wants to sue you and take your tunic, let him have your cloak as well. If someone forces you to go one mile, go with him two miles. Give to the one who asks you, and do not turn away from the one who wants to borrow from you.
>
> You have heard that it was said, "Love your neighbor and hate your enemy." But I tell you: Love your enemies and pray for those who persecute you, that you may be children of your father

in heaven. God causes the sun to rise on the evil and the good, and sends rain on the just and the unjust. If you love those who love you, what reward will you get? Are not even the tax collectors doing that? If you greet only your brothers, what are you doing more than others? Do not even pagans do that? Be perfect, therefore, as your heavenly father is perfect (Mt. 5:38–48, auth. translation)

To explore what Jesus could have meant, we need to remember back to a time when sevenfold retribution was a common understanding of justice in the Ancient Near East. Imagine you and I are working in a field clearing trees so that we can plant crops so that our families do not starve to death. Since it is the Stone Age, we have sharpened rocks lashed to the ends of our sticks, and we are cutting down trees. The lashing on my axe comes loose, and the axe head flies off the handle and hits you in the face. Your cheek is bashed in, your eye is hanging out, and blood runs everywhere. I apologize profusely, help you home, and then head to my place to fix my axe.

A few days later, with my newly repaired axe in hand, I am on my way to the fields early in the morning, whistling. You, with your eye and face bandaged, along with a few of your brothers or sisters, ambush me from behind a boulder and beat, stone, and kick me to death. Justice demanded sevenfold retribution, sevenfold payback, and that is what your family did to me—paid me back at least seven times the damage I inflicted on you. You lost your eye; I lost my life.

I am survived by a brother who is about six feet three inches tall, and several big cousins as well. After my death they wait a few weeks and then sneak into your tent in the middle of the night and slit the throats of you, your spouse, and your children. Sevenfold retribution, sevenfold justice, the accepted and just way of many communities. I lost my life; you lost your family. But your clan will not stand for this atrocity. They eventually decide to attack my clan. Then my tribe has to get involved to defend the honor of my clan. This spirals down into inter-tribal warfare. This is the spiral of escalating violence supported by traditions that teach it is necessary to pay back more violence than one receives. "You have to show them that they cannot do that to you and get away with it." "Violence is the only language they speak; it's all they know."

This story is not meant to portray a historical event. It narrates a tradition of manifold retaliations for offenses that has been present in humanity for millennia. It is even present in Genesis when Lamech boasts to his wives, "Adah and Zillah, listen to me; wives of Lamech, hear my words. I have killed a man for wounding me, a young man for injuring me. If Cain is avenged seven times, then Lamech [is avenged] seventy-seven times!"[1] Sevenfold retribution was present in the cultures of the Ancient Near East, and some, exemplified by Lamech, thought that even retaliation multiplied by seven was not sufficient justice. We still encounter people today who think it is necessary to give back more violence than is received, so one-fold retribution teaching in the Hebrew Scripture was radical then and is still radical today for some.

For the sake of the story, imagine that you, your family, and your friends have been accustomed to a culture of sevenfold retribution. You know that the proper response to an offense, the logical response, the just response, is to dish out more pain and suffering than you received. You even have a story about God threatening this on behalf of Cain so you know it is right. Someone now enters into your story and dares to suggest, dares to claim, that God desires something quite different. According to Exodus and Leviticus, Moses received God's law and shared it with the people. The presentation of much of this teaching could have sounded something like the following.

"I know that you have heard that when someone takes your eye, you are supposed to kill them. You have heard that when someone kills someone else, the victim's family is supposed to kill the other family. But how about when someone knocks out your eye, if you have to do something, just gouge out their *one eye*. Don't kill them. If someone kills someone else, if you have to retaliate, just kill *that one person*. Don't kill their entire family."

As recounted in the Bible, it sounds like this: "But if there is serious injury, you are to take [only] life for life, eye for eye, tooth for tooth, hand for hand, foot for foot, burn for burn, wound for wound, bruise for bruise." (Ex. 21:23–24)

…And also like this: "If anyone takes the life of another person, only the one who kills can be killed…. If anyone injures a neighbor, only whatever was done can be done back to them: fracture for fracture, eye for eye, tooth for tooth. As that person has injured another, that is the only way they can be injured…. You are to have the same law for immigrants and the native-born" (Lev. 24:17–22, auth. translation).

The tradition of limiting one-fold retributive "justice"—pay back only the same as the offense committed—is significantly different from retributive "justice" that seeks a force multiplier greater than one. One-fold retribution was not unique to the Hebrews or the Hebrew Scriptures, for the *lex talionis*—"law of retaliation"—is found in many cultures. The Jewish rabbinic tradition emphasizes that it was and is intended to *limit* retribution; it was not a command to enact retribution. Although one-fold retribution is often heard as calling for more retaliation in place of doing nothing, it was, in fact, a call for less retaliation rather than more. Most contemporary Christian and Jewish scholars read these laws as limiting retribution, and that is the trajectory that Jesus continued to live in and teach.

Jesus lived in an occupied territory where people were tortured, murdered, raped, and crucified. He lived with and addressed people who were familiar with the desires for retributive "justice" that traditions like Cain's sevenfold retribution and Lamech's seventy-sevenfold retribution seem to provide. They were also familiar with the Mosaic one-fold limitation of retribution in "only eye for eye and only tooth for tooth." Jesus lived in a culture in which people suffered and in which some wanted to do violence to end the suffering, while others wanted to ignore it to survive to live another day. In the midst of this, Jesus taught, and the early church repeated, "You have heard that it was said, 'Eye for eye, and tooth for tooth.' But I tell you, Do not resist an evil person. If someone strikes you on the right cheek, turn to him the other also" (Mt. 5:38–39, auth. translation).

I think Walter Wink offers a largely convincing interpretation of what Jesus meant by "if someone strikes you on the right cheek, turn to him the other also."[2] Wink argues that in the domination system of the first century, a strike on the right cheek would have been a backhanded, insulting, violent slap with the right hand. Raise your right hand across your body and swing a *backhanded* slap through the air. Notice that you would hit the right cheek of someone if you swung backhanded with your right hand. Since most people are right handed, that is the way oppressors would violently insult, degrade, and "put in their place" people they perceive to be beneath them in society—such as slaves, servants, foreigners, poor people, children, or women. Echoes of this violent, insulting action are heard in the derogatory slang "pimp slap," which refers to the way a pimp hits a prostitute to control her with violence. Hitting on the right cheek is a violent action of the oppressor against the oppressed, of those who exploit against those who are exploited, of the self-proclaimed superiors against the "inferiors." The right cheek is the cheek of insult, rejection, and inferiority.

When two self-perceived equals fought (since most people are right handed and the left hand is the unclean/dirty hand), they would strike with a fist and their right-handed fists would land on the *left* cheeks of the opponents. Make a fist with your right hand and swing. Notice that it would hit the left cheek of the opponent. The left cheek is the cheek of equality, dignity, and respect. Throwing a "fair" punch at an equal in society would hit that person on the left cheek. Slapping or backhanding an equal in society was punishable by stiff fines.

The mishnaic tractate *Baba Kamma* specifies the various fines for striking an equal: for slugging with a fist, 4 *zuz* (a *zuz* was a day's wage); for slapping, 200 *zuz*; but "if [he struck him] with the back of his hand he must pay him 400 *zuz*." Damages for indignity were not paid to slaves who were struck.[3]

When Jesus says, "If someone strikes you on the right cheek," he is saying this to people who have certainly experienced it. When the author of Matthew writes it for the community of followers of Jesus, many people hearing it would have certainly experienced it. To understand the power of Jesus' teaching, we need to explore the two most common normal human responses to being violently insulted. The first normal human response is to hit back, to give back violence for violence received. When a person is attacked, we find it understandable for that person actually to try to fight back, to hit if possible, to attack with violence. Maybe even to rip out the other person's jugular vein if possible. Violent insults seem to call for retaliation, and many people are ready and willing to oblige. Fighting back is logical. Fighting back makes sense.

The second normal human response is to run away, to passively take it, leave, go home, and legitimately complain about the injustice of being violently accosted—probably not for the first time—by the oppressor who is violently dominating one's life. Sometimes the road is so hard, the violence so prevalent, the pain so intense, that flight is the preferred path. By responding to being hit on the right cheek with passivity, one can perhaps survive for another day. The violent slap sends one to the ground. Rather than getting up with fistfuls of rocks and fighting back, one just slinks away. Or perhaps with the right cheek burning in pain, one just walks away with as much dignity as possible, leaving the oppressor in his illusion of superiority. Flight is logical. Flight makes sense.

To a group of people who understood both fighting back and passively walking away (perhaps to plan how to fight back later), Jesus offered a third possibility. Jesus said to turn the *other* cheek. Turning the *other* cheek requires one to stand your ground and not to leave. It is not passive. Envision it. Turn your head sharply to the left as if you have been hit hard on the right cheek. Plant your chin in your left shoulder. While in that position, think about fighting back and think about walking away. Realize that the cheek of inferiority is still exposed to the oppressor. When in the position of having had your inferiority cheek hit, Jesus taught neither fighting back nor walking away; neither violence nor passivity. Jesus said to stand there, or get back up, and face the oppressor with your cheek of dignity, respect, and equality— your "I am also made in the image of God" cheek. Now turn your cheek as Jesus said, from the left shoulder where it was hit to where your chin is over your right shoulder. If your neck stretches or strains a little bit be careful, but get your right cheek facing behind you so much that the oppressor in front of you cannot reach it. You are preventing this person from hitting your insult cheek again. It cannot be reached. You are facing your oppressor down with your "made in the image of God" cheek.

This is an action. It is an action that does not fit the normal expectations of human behavior: hit back or run away. It is an action that refuses to be passive and thus leave the oppressor in his illusion, to leave him in the lie that he is superior. Turning the cheek is also refusing to become the oppressor, refusing to use the same tactics of violence that were perpetrated. Turning the cheek can say, "You do not know who I am. I am more than you think I am. I am more valuable than you think I am. I am not going to walk away and let you keep thinking and acting as if I'm inferior because it is damaging for you and for me and for many others. I am also not going to hit you back because I am not you, and you are worth more than that. If I hit you, then the truth will not be known, and we will continue to live in a lie. If I walk away, the truth will not be known, and we will continue to live in a lie. The way for the truth to be known is for me to stand here and turn my cheek to you—which affirms my value and your value at the same time—and invite you into a new, more truthful reality."

Turning the cheek confronts the oppressor, the one who violently accosts those beneath him, and offers new options for him to live into. The attacked one, standing there with the cheek of dignity facing forward and the cheek of indignity firmly turned away, offers the violent one new possibilities. Just like the one who was hit had three "options"—hit back, walk away, or turn the cheek—the one who hits now has three "options" as well. Now, these "options" are influenced significantly well in advance by who one already is, who one is already becoming. What one would do in such a situation is a matter of what possibilities one knows and how one has been trained in one's community, so the habits and virtues that shape one's life affect a response. But new, unexpected possibilities can emerge spontaneously as well.

First, although unlikely, it is possible that the oppressor could hit the left cheek with a fist. It is unlikely because to hit the cheek of dignity with a fist would be to accept the slave, the servant, the woman, the "inferior" person as equal. A major worldview shift would be taking place in the life of the attacker if he responded to a turned left cheek by making a fist with his right hand and punching the left cheek. But if it did happen, it would be significant. It would signify to the surrounding crowd of other "inferiors" as well as to other "superiors" that were present that this person of perceived low status was being treated like an equal to the master.

The backhanded violent slap on the right cheek had been a public insult attempting to put the low status person back in a low status place. When that low status person lives into Jesus' third way and responds by turning the cheek of dignity and equality, the oppressor knows exactly what it means. The one who struck knows that it means, "I am your equal." The one who struck knows that if he hits the person with a fist on the left cheek, everybody watching will know that the low status person "got in the head" of the oppressor. The internal emancipation of the oppressed—realizing their own value before God in their minds, in their hearts, in the depths of their souls—leads to the power to work to liberate the oppressor as well. Their hopes for liberation lie together. The action of turning the left cheek toward the oppressor opens up the possibility of mutual liberation. If the oppressor, in the presence of witnesses who are generally present in a situation such as this, clenches the fist and delivers a bone-crunching blow to the equality cheek of the oppressed, then this one little subordinate has nonviolently affirmed his own dignity and has had it affirmed violently by the oppressor. Turning the cheek is firm action, standing in the presence of the violent, confronting them with their violent defense of their lies. It may indeed evoke more violence from them. Direct nonviolent love can elicit violence.

Second, the oppressor may walk away, refusing to acknowledge the dignity and equality of the oppressed, even with violence. This is the passive response, available even to the oppressor who struck on the right cheek in the first place. With a violently insulted person standing his ground and asserting his dignity to the face of the oppressor, some oppressors may try to ignore the deep truth of such an assertion and try to avoid its power by vacating the premises. The backhanded violent insult had been sufficient in the past; it had worked to sustain the illusion of superiority and the exploitive domination system which benefited the oppressor. Now, that plausibility structure was being challenged in a creative, innovative, and confounding way. The surprising nature of the left cheek turn leaves the attacker bewildered. When the "victim" deviates from the expected public script of violence or passivity, fight or flight, the "victim" is not playing the role of victim that the oppressor expects.[4] An attacker who walks away, having the "victim" nonviolently assert his dignity, could be thinking and feeling many things. Whether the attacker feels disgust at the impudence, aloofness at the arrogance, frustration at the audacity, confusion at the perhaps never-before-considered humanity, or intrigue at the courage, a crack has opened up. God's truth is present in the world in a way it was not before the turning of that one particular left cheek. That oppressor is now walking in a new world. That person has experienced an invitation to consider him- or herself differently, to see the oppressed differently, and even though the oppressor is walking away from the person who offered freedom, this inbreaking of the kingdom of God has become a part of the oppressor's life story.

The third possibility requires some kind of faith. I do not expect many people to even think it is a possibility. If there is a God, and if the Holy Spirit is working in this world, and if murderers like Saul can become saints like Paul, then the third way of Jesus can make way for the third way for oppressors. The oppressor could repent. Nothing guarantees this will happen. Yes, it is all but absurd to think it is possible. When the oppressor is confronted in this firm, direct, loving, and nonviolent way, the oppressor at least has the opportunity to realize his (or her) oppressiveness, his exploitation, his sin. For, beyond asserting the denied dignity of the oppressed and beyond respecting the humanity of the oppressor, turning the left cheek creates real space and time for transformation. Turning the left cheek is an accusation, and sometimes the accused can see and realize that the accuser is correct. Of course, even the realization that the accuser is correct does not mean that the accused oppressor will confess destructive ways and begin the difficult work of becoming a less oppressive person. But this accusation that is also an invitation has opened up a redemptive story line and creates the potential for the enemy to become a friend.

It seems a little overly dramatic to imagine the attacker falling to his knees in confession and repentance, asking forgiveness from the oppressed person who had the courage to respond in such a way to being struck. The most unexpected redemptive possibilities must be named and included in the possible ways a story such as this could go, especially since turning the cheek is often dismissively connected with allowing an enemy to kill you. If the attacker did in fact confess the sin and ask forgiveness, we can imagine that a follower of Jesus discipled so deeply, living the story of Jesus so faithfully, as to turn the cheek, would of course forgive the oppressor. In fact, the turning of the cheek rather than responding with violence already signifies that forgiveness is available and manifestly offered. Turning the left cheek could bring about confession, repentance, forgiveness, and a new story in which conciliation, equality, and dignity are possible. If the attacker does not enter into the offer of forgiveness at once and instead hits again or walks away, the oppressor is still living in a world where he has been accused without violence and where forgiveness and deliverance are available. The oppressor's violence presents three broad story possibilities for the follower of Jesus who is hit: resisting with violence, not resisting at all, or resisting with active love by standing and turning the cheek. Jesus teaches explicitly against the first way, does not address the second way, and explicitly teaches the third way.

"Do Not Violently Resist Evil"

Unfortunately, this phrase has often been mistranslated "do not resist evil" or "do not resist an evil person" rather than "do not violently resist with evil"[5] or "do not resist an evil person with evil." Based on the most common first-century usage of *antistenai* (violent resistance), *me antistenai to ponero* in Matthew 5:39 should be translated "do not violently resist evil" or "do not violently resist an evil person."[6] Josephus used *antistenai* as violent resistance fifteen of seventeen times.[7]

Jesus' teaching against violent resistance has been misunderstood as supporting passivity and nonparticipation in resistance of any kind. It is as if a statement such as, "Do not participate in armed revolution against evil," has been translated as, "Do not disagree with or oppose evil." It is as if, "Do not be a violent revolutionary," was translated as, "Accept oppression and injustice." These are not the same teachings. "Do not be a violent revolutionary," does not necessitate the accepting of oppression and injustice. This mistranslation has had a profoundly adverse effect on understanding Jesus' teaching to lovingly resist evil and to overcome evil with good. On carefully argued exegetical grounds, David Wenham concludes that Matthew's, "Do not resist evil," and the Pauline/Petrine, "Do not return evil for evil," should be seen as differing versions of the same saying of Jesus, and that the latter is the more original.[8]

Giving God's Underwear

In addition to teaching a third way to respond to violence, Jesus taught a third way to resist and respond nonviolently to economic exploitation as well. "When someone sues you for your outer garment, give them your undergarment as well." This is yet another seemingly absurd teaching of Jesus. Give more material goods to your enemy, even as they take practically the last remaining shred of clothing and dignity you have left. The context for this teaching was the indebtedness that many people in the Roman occupations experienced. Low wages, laws that favored the wealthy, and high tribute led to increased debt, which led to loss of land to pay debt, which led to more debt for the landless peasants who labored on the increasingly large estates of the wealthy, which led to the wealthy and landed lenders suing the poor for the shirts off their backs as collateral for the loans.

Picture a Sanhedrin-type courtroom with judges, witnesses, prosecutors, observers, and the accused poor person. The poor person would be the poorest of the poor if all this person has for collateral is his outer garment, his robe. Perhaps this *campesino* (farmer) has lost his land because of imperial policy that consolidates land in the hands of the few, thus creating an overabundance of people who will work for poverty wages and who accumulate debt just to survive. The prophet Amos condemned this behavior and addressed this type of situation: "They who trample the head of the poor into the dust of the earth…lay themselves down beside every altar upon clothing taken as collateral" (2:7–8, auth. translation).

The rich began seeking nonliquid investments to secure their wealth. Land was best, but it was ancestrally owned and passed down over generations. No peasant would voluntarily relinquish it. Exorbitant interest, however, could be used to drive landowners ever deeper into debt. Debt, coupled with high taxation required by Herod Antipas to pay Rome tribute, created the economic leverage to pry Galilean peasants loose from their land. By the time of Jesus, we see this process already far advanced: large estates owned by absentee landlords; managed by stewards; and worked by tenant farmers, day laborers, and slaves. It is no accident that the first act of the Jewish revolutionaries in 66 C.E. was to burn the temple treasury, where the record of debts was kept.[9]

A poor person with no land, no assets, and no money is being sued for his shirt to make sure that he repays his debt. All he has are his clothes and his body. When the judge says that the poor person is to give his outer garment to the creditor, the poor person is told by Jesus to strip off all his clothes and stand there completely naked in the courtroom. In front of everybody, in public, expose their injustice and corruption and greed and exploitation by exposing your own body. The only way to make this stronger would have been for Jesus to have said, "and after you give them your underwear and are completely naked, start cutting off your hair and give that to them as well. Then your fingers, one at a time, cut them off and as you bleed onto the floor of the courtroom hand them your fingers. Then your toes, then your ears, then your eyes, and then cut out your heart and give that to them as well. Give them your body one piece at a time until you have nothing left to give."

Jesus' teaching left the poor person's body intact and whole, only naked and exposed. That nakedness did not shame the poor person as much as it shamed the people who caused it to happen: the one suing as well as the system that allowed such an atrocity to happen. Humiliating oneself humiliated the oppressors, or at least it focused attention on them in a new way so that respect for their business acumen was undermined rather than undergirded.

This is a third way of dealing with economic exploitation and abuse that is neither violent nor passive. One way would be to slit the throat of the creditor for destroying so many lives, or organize a revolution to change the system so that the debts could be forgiven. Imagine a revolution in the USA that included the credit card accounts in corporate computers being erased and citizens of the USA having one trillion dollars of credit card debt erased. Imagine a revolution where the billions of dollars of debts owed by countries in the global South to billionaires in the global North were just erased. Millions, no *billions*, of people would rejoice and there would be a very few very pissed-off millionaires, billionaires, and investors. The final scene in the movie *Fight Club* shows the destruction of skyscrapers that house credit card corporations. There are violent ways to reduce debt and set the oppressed free. That is why those who own the loans have access to such powerful militaries—to make sure violent debt reduction options are less likely to happen.

A passive way to deal with having the shirt sued off your back is just to go along with it silently. Give them your clothes and go home. At least you still have your underwear. Nobody else has to suffer, just you and your family. The wages they paid for working all day, every day, could not cover the costs of rent and food, so you had to borrow just to be able to feed your family. Now they are taking your clothes, your robe that keeps you warm at night, to make sure you pay back the loan and interest on food your family has already eaten. That is just the way it is. The world is unjust. "The rich get richer, and the poor get children."[10] There is no sense in trying to do anything about it. What can a poor person do anyway? You can't fight city hall.

Jesus did not say, "When someone sues you for your outer garment, you're probably going to lose the lawsuit so just give it to him and then go home and be glad you still have your undergarment." Jesus did not say, "When someone sues you for your outer garment, give it to him but then ambush him on his way home and bash his head in. Then take your garment back." Jesus did not say, "When someone sues you for your outer garment, join the revolution and overthrow the imperialist pigs and burn the debt records."

Jesus taught neither violence nor passivity in response to financial exploitation. Jesus instead taught a prophetic, nonviolent, and active way to respond to economic oppression and injustice. He empowered the disenfranchised. Jesus said that when someone seeks to exploit you economically, take off all your clothes in public. You think I'm naked? You know what's really naked? Your self-interest.

Going God's Second Mile

What would it be like to live in a homeland occupied by a foreign military that claims to be bringing you peace? You have to work from dawn until dusk just to try to feed your family and pay the extorting tax collectors who keep as much as they can and pass the rest up the chain of command to the foreign power. What would it be like to have one of those soldiers drag you away from *your* work and make you do *his* work? As noted earlier, Roman imperial soldiers could press local people into service and force them to carry military packs for a mile or so.[11] *Angareia*, as it was known, was practiced widely and abused so often that many authors addressed it and complained about it to Roman officials: "Many soldiers without written requisition are traveling about in the country, demanding ships, beasts of burden, and men, beyond anything authorized, sometimes seizing things by force… to the point of showing abuse and threats to private citizens. The result is that the military is associated with arrogance and injustice."[12] Josephus, a first-century Jewish historian, wrote, "An infantry man is almost as heavily laden as a pack-mule."[13] Horsley notes that the reference to the second mile emerges from "the sphere of imperial political-economic relations."[14] When a soldier pulls a carpenter away from his craft, the carpenter has to quit working, carry the pack as far as the soldier says, and then walk all the way back to his shop. It could waste half a day or more. At the end of the mile (or more) a commandeered peasant could respond to the soldier in either of two standard ways. Of course, Jesus offered a third way.

First, the person could drop or throw down the pack, run a ways back, pick up some rocks and shout, "Get out of our country, you stinking Roman dog! Anathema on you! May the God of Abraham, Isaac, and Jacob destroy you and your blasphemous empire! This is Yahweh's holy land!" Being out of the range of the soldier's sword, the legitimately angry peasant could chuck stones at the soldier, continue to curse him in the name of Yahweh, and outrun him through the countryside if the soldier tried to pursue.

A person forced to labor for the enemy may not do this the first time, but resentment builds during occupations and it is certainly realistic to consider that cursing, stone throwing, and obscene gestures might ensue at the end of the first mile. Another violent possibility at the end of the first mile could be attempted killing, or even actual killing. Jewish revolutionaries, commonly called Zealots in the New Testament but known by various names, made their livings in occupations such as farming and fishing while they simultaneously planned guerrilla warfare and assassinations.[15] The Sicarii, or "assassins," carried curved daggers on the inside of their thighs and trained for the opportunity to kill Roman soldiers and Jewish "collaborators" such as the high priest, if ever they had the chance to slit a throat or slip a blade cleanly and silently through the seams of their enemy's armor.[16] Josephus wrote, "The festivals were their special seasons, when they would mingle with the crowd, carrying short daggers concealed under their clothing, with which they stabbed their enemies…"[17] The peasant carrying the pack could actually be a warrior who planned his attack carefully enough to be able to swiftly carry out the kill, or at least be willing to fight to the death for the freedom of his people. It is important to realize that some of Jesus' own disciples were freedom fighters/revolutionaries. Many more gathered in his audiences. Folks who were not revolutionaries themselves certainly had friends or relatives who were. When Jesus taught on this topic, people with these experiences listened intently. They knew what could happen during or at the end of that mile.

A second realistic possibility at the end of that first mile is passively laying down the pack and walking back home. No cursing out loud, no throwing rocks, no pulling out a dagger or fighting to the death—just resignation to the depressing fact of occupation and oppression. A wasted afternoon is only a wasted afternoon; it could be worse. The peasant could simply walk the mile (or more) back and rightfully complain to his family and friends about what happened. The soldier did what he could legally do. The peasant did what he was told to do, and the status quo remained unchallenged and unchanged. Sometimes acceptance of oppression and injustice seems like the wisest way to survive.

Before we explore what Jesus did teach, we should think about the possibilities that Jesus did not teach. Jesus did not say, "When someone forces you to go one mile, refuse from the beginning because it is unjust." Jesus did not say, "When someone forces you to go one mile, at the end of the mile curse him in the name of God and throw stones." Jesus did not say, "When someone forces you to go one mile, be prepared so that you can kill him during the journey." Jesus did not say, "When someone forces you to go one mile, go the one mile to fulfill your legal duty and then return home."

Jesus did teach a third realistic possibility that is neither violent nor passive. Jesus said to carry the enemy's pack an additional mile. After the soldier diverts the peasant, the fisherman, the carpenter from their work or craft for an afternoon, they should, Jesus instructed, give more time, more energy, and more space to this enemy. Each step farther down that road away from home is one step that has to be made on the way back. What does Jesus expect his followers to do during this second mile, during this new story that is now being created as the peasant spends time with the soldier? The first mile belonged to the Empire of Rome, to the oppressor, to the soldier. It was demanded forcefully. This second mile belongs to the Empire of God, to the oppressed, to the peasant. It is given freely. It is God's mile.

What did Jesus expect his followers to do during the second mile with the oppressor? His other teachings intimate the answer to this question. Jesus told his disciples to be aware of their relationships with other people. When they realized an offense stood between them and someone else, they should drop their gifts to God and go work for reconciliation. Forcing someone to carry a military pack is certainly offensive. Jesus also told his followers to

give food and drink to their enemies. In light of these teachings, I imagine
that the second mile Jesus intended was not a quiet second mile consisting
only of donated labor. Donated labor creates the context in which something
more powerful can happen. Moving the pack and the soldier down the road
one more mile is not Jesus' main point. Although carrying the pack another
mile does get the soldier farther away from one's family, it also alleviates the
burden of a fellow Palestinian who will not have to lug it a mile himself.
The potential of what can happen *during* the second mile holds the power.

A follower of Jesus who has listened to the Sermon on the Mount and
who seeks to put Jesus' teachings into practice could engage in conversation
with the soldier. Perhaps a conversation could go like this, "How long have
you been stationed in Palestine?"

"A little over three years."

"Do you have any family?"

"Yeah, I have a wife and three kids."

"Have you been able to get home to see them at all?"

"No, and I don't get to head back for another two years."

"Where are you from?"

"Tuscany."

"Oh, do you get much good home cooking?"

"Not at all! They don't like us around here too much. They put stuff in
our food that gives us diarrhea."

"Well, how about you come over to our place. We'll make you some
good hummus and falafel. We'll feed you right. We'll eat out of the same
bowls and share the same bread so you'll know it's good."

At this point in a conversation like this the soldier could respond in
various ways. The soldier could hit the peasant upside the head with the
broad side of his sword and accuse him of being a guerrilla fighter trying to
lure the soldier into an ambush. Or the soldier could just refuse the invitation.
Or the soldier could engage in further conversation and ask the Palestinian
Jew more about himself and his family.

What is the *proyecto historico*, the preferred future, of carrying the pack a
second mile? In *Mujerista Theology*, Isasi-Diaz explains that Latinas seek to live
into their preferred future, their *proyecto historico*.[18] This is similar to asking,
"what is the *telos*," the end, the goal, toward which carrying the pack a second
mile leads? What is the preferred future toward which this additional work,
conversation, and engagement with the enemy are journeying? I think that
it includes the hope that the occupation soldier from Italy would begin to
follow Jesus and become a disciple, too. It includes both "less" and "more"
than that as well. Walking with that particular soldier for that particular

extra mile includes that soldier in the love of God in a particular way that would otherwise be less manifest.

During the second mile that belongs to God, the Spirit-empowered peasant who is "flipping the script" of domination can talk with the soldier, humanize him- or herself, and invite the enemy to his home for a meal. The peasant may also speak even more truth in love and tell the soldier that commandeering locals into service is a source of extreme frustration and leads to more support for the revolutions. Commandeering local men from their work generates more resentment and more guerrilla fighters. Is the relief provided by one peasant for one mile worth the cost of fueling more animosity? Some soldiers may think that it is, but others may start relating to the locals in less oppressive ways. The follower of Jesus does not say, "Carry your own damn pack, you stinking Roman dog." The follower of Jesus might create a situation in which this message might be listened to, without the insulting racial slur at the end.

The *proyecto historico* for many Jews in the first century probably included less forced pack carrying, but we know they also hoped for an end to the occupation and domination by the Romans. If followers of Jesus humanize (sacralize?) soldiers by walking second miles and humanize (sacralize?) themselves in the process, it is possible that some soldiers would stop coercing locals into carrying their packs. Matthew 28:19–20 reports that Jesus said, "As you go into all the world, make disciples in every ethnicity [of all nations/ *ethne*], baptizing them in the name of the Father, and the Son, and the Holy Spirit, and teach them to obey everything I have taught you." If discipleship included teaching what Jesus taught, then when Roman soldiers, or anyone else, started to become followers of Jesus and entered into the journey of discipleship, they would be taught to become people who love their enemies, turn their cheeks, carry occupier's packs, and give their underwear when sued.[19] Jesus' teachings in the "Sermon on the Mount" provide substance to the "make disciples" and the "teach them everything I have taught you."[20]

When Jesus said, "Blessed are the peacemakers, for they are the children of God" (Mt. 5:9, auth. translation), I think these ways of being and living are what he was talking about. When followers of Jesus worked and sacrificed to make peace by turning their cheek of dignity to a violent enemy, by carrying a military pack farther down the road than required, by stripping naked in front of a courtroom full of people, they were acting like God's children. This making of peace differs dramatically from acquiescing to the status quo or fighting the oppression with violence. It makes something new. It makes a new world.

18

Abolishing Nuclear Weapons

Tyler Wigg-Stevenson

The logic used to go like this: we have the Bomb to keep others from using the Bomb against us. We don't want to use it, but it's a necessary evil for the world we live in. During the Cold War, the argument could be made in good faith. Though nuclear deterrence has always been "morally problematic," to use Chuck Colson's phrase, it is certainly morally superior to nuclear war.

The problem is that deterrence can't keep us safe anymore.

First, it doesn't stand up to the threat of nuclear terrorism. If terrorists acquired a nuclear weapon, or the material to manufacture one, they could deliver it anonymously, via boat or truck. Nuclear deterrence only works when you've got a state to threaten retaliation against.

Second, nuclear deterrence was a challenging balance to maintain during the essentially bilateral struggle of the Cold War. Even then it came close to breaking down in the Cuban Missile Crisis, our survival of which was attributed to luck, not brains, by then-Secretary of Defense Robert McNamara. The brute force strategy of deterrence—club us, and we'll club you back—doesn't function in the complicated political game of a multipolar world, with competing centers of interest ranging from Washington to Brussels to Beijing to Brasilia to Moscow to Delhi. There are simply too many adversaries rubbing borders with each other, such as Pakistan-India-China. In no other field of human endeavor do we expect a record free of accidents, but nuclear security requires it.

Third, time is not on our side. Senator Sam Nunn, former Chairman of the Senate Armed Services Committee and one of the world's preeminent experts on nuclear security, says that we are walking a line between cooperation and catastrophe. This is because the spread of nuclear weapons has mostly been kept in check by the Nuclear Non-Proliferation Treaty (NPT), a voluntary agreement in which the nuclear powers committed to negotiating the elimination of their own weapons, the non-nuclear powers agreed not to acquire nuclear arsenals, and every signatory gained the right to nuclear power. Held together by this vision of cooperative security through a world without any nuclear weapons, the NPT has survived for four decades and counting.

Now, it is beginning to fray at the seams. What had seemed like an agreement for the good of all is now starting to look like a permanent discriminatory norm, favoring the mid-twentieth century powers with the unique right of wielding existentially threatening weapons against everyone else. Potential breakout crises such as in Iran are thus not isolated incidents, but early signs of failure in a structure that has been foundational to U.S. and global security for generations. Two decades after the end of the Cold War, the nuclear club remains small—the U.S., UK, France, China, and Russia, as well as Israel, India, Pakistan, and North Korea, which are the four nations that have not signed the NPT. But if nuclear-capable nations such as Turkey, Saudi Arabia, Japan, or South Korea decide that their security would be better obtained through their own nuclear arsenals than it is through the NPT, the nuclear club could grow by leaps and bounds. The spread of nuclear material, technology, and related conflicts will grow then, too, hastening the day when deterrence breaks down and a nuclear weapon is used in war, terrorism, or accident. We face a similar danger if a rapid expansion of nuclear power is employed to address climate change, since the same technology can be used to develop weapons.

The situation thus boils down to this: the continued existence of nuclear weapons will result in their eventual use. Their continued possession cannot defend us from their effects. The only possible course of action that can prevent the disaster of their use is their verifiable and global elimination. This course of action has been endorsed by President Obama and former Russian President Medvedev, as well as many other heads of state. It has the nonpartisan support of Cold War eminences who built the nuclear system, including two-thirds of all former U.S. secretaries of state, secretaries of defense, and national security advisors—including George Shultz, Henry Kissinger, and William Perry, who, along with Senator Nunn, have publicly championed this work.

In this situation of crystalline moral clarity—abolish the Bomb or see it used—evangelicals are adding a new chapter to their complicated history with nuclear weapons.

A Complicated History

Religion and nuclear weapons have been paired since the latter were developed in the deserts of the American Southwest. The language of theology and apocalypse, both Christian and other, was the only sufficient vernacular available to describe the awesome power released through the splitting of the atom. Thus even Robert Oppenheimer, the father of the Bomb, famously quoted from the *Bhagavad Gita* after witnessing the first nuclear test (itself called "Trinity" after the Christian Godhead): "I am become Death, destroyer of worlds."

The recognition that nuclear weapons posed a potentially existential threat—a potential that was realized with the development of the hydrogen bomb and its pairing with intercontinental ballistic missile technology— profoundly discomfited many evangelicals. Traditional peace churches took public stands against the Bomb, and the theologian Karl Barth anonymously authored a letter declaring that the manufacture or use of nuclear weapons could not be conducted Christianly—that such a matter held *status confessionis* for followers of Jesus Christ. Later, nearer the Cold War's end, conservative evangelical statesmen such as John Stott and Billy Graham, as well as more progressive voices such as Ron Sider, Jim Wallis, and Tony Campolo, renounced the indiscriminate effect of nuclear war.

Other evangelicals, however, saw this same apocalyptic power as an indicator of God's sovereign hand guiding us to the end times. Passages such as 2 Peter 3:10–12 took on new significance in the atomic age: "But the day of the Lord will come like a thief. The heavens will disappear with a roar; the elements will be destroyed by fire, and the earth and everything done in it will be laid bare... [L]ook forward to the day of God and speed its coming... [T]he elements will melt in the heat." In other words, nuclear disarmament opposed the divine will by delaying the day of God when they would be used. Books such as Hal Lindsey's bestselling *The Late Great Planet Earth* popularized such mindsets, leading to evangelical indifference to nuclear weapons, or even active support.

In recent years, however, evangelicals have begun to take a leadership role in a particular anti-nuclear movement of the post-Cold War, post-9/11 era. The Two Futures Project has staked out a biblically grounded theological case against nuclear weapons in this particular context. The New Evangelical Partnership has made nuclear abolition a focal point of its work, with Rich Cizik also serving as a prominent spokesman for the Global Zero movement. In 2010, the National Association of Evangelicals (NAE) joined the U.S. Conference of Catholic Bishops in supporting the ratification of the New START agreement reducing U.S. and Russian nuclear arsenals.

In October 2011, the NAE Board of Directors adopted without opposition a new policy position calling for reductions in nuclear arsenals, ratification of the Comprehensive Nuclear Test Ban Treaty, and reconsideration of the moral basis for deterrence. The World Evangelical Alliance has formed a Global Task Force on Nuclear Weapons, which will bring evangelical public opinion to bear on international measures like the quinquennial NPT review. Such efforts have also generated a new interest in the theological and ethical ways that humans engage our most dangerous creation.

Thinking Theologically about the Bomb

As conventional wisdom has it, since nuclear weapons can never be uninvented, we will need nuclear deterrence to prevent their use. The conventional wisdom is half right, because it realizes that humans must now live with the consequences of knowing how to build and deploy nuclear weapons. It was not a necessity of human history that our species learn how to release, with devastating effect, the energy that binds atomic material together. Having done so, however, we cannot now collectively unlearn it. The "Bomb in the mind," as Jonathan Schell calls it,[1] will always be with us. This once contingent knowledge has become a necessity of all future history. This is the condition for all our theological and ethical reflection.

The conventional wisdom on deterrence is fatally flawed, however. It conflates the necessity of the knowledge of the Bomb with the necessity of the primary tactic—deterrence—used to manage its destructive potential during its first historical era, the Cold War. It treats deterrence as inherent to the Bomb as an oak tree is inherent to an acorn.

But there is not a logically necessary connection between the Bomb and deterrence. There are many ways for a country to avoid being attacked with nuclear weapons. Threatening the use of nuclear weapons is one of them. In some circumstances, deterrence may well seem indispensable. But—and this is important—nuclear security and deterrence are not the same thing. The latter is one conceivable means to the former.

By decoupling knowledge of the Bomb and the strategy of deterrence, we clear the playing field of our moral imagination. We do not have to ask, "How can we morally manage this unavoidable condition of deterrence?" Instead, we can ask the much broader question: "What is the range of acceptable moral ends toward which nuclear weapons technology can be dedicated?"

This question reveals the morality of nuclear security to be, fundamentally, the morality of technological management: what moral norms should circumscribe this particular technological knowledge? Ironically, this is a rather quotidian task: every complex technology or body of knowledge is subject to management, official or otherwise. Technology gives us new capacities, and we conform these new capacities to what we believe are morally acceptable ends.

This is not the usual mode of conceiving nuclear morality, especially within Christian communities. A far more common approach is to ascribe moral worth to one or more of the management strategies—e.g., disarmament, nonproliferation, arms control, counter-proliferation, deterrence, etc. What we often overlook in such arguments is that morality does not inhere to any particular strategy, but is actually conditional on the strategy's efficacy in attaining another, morally normative goal. Because this goal is often assumed and rarely articulated, nuclear moral judgments often have the character of commenting on the quality of someone's driving, without ever evaluating whether they are on a road that leads to their desired destination.

So, this is the fundamental question to those of us deliberating in the light of faith: What is the morally normative goal to which nuclear weapons technology should be oriented?

Once we have clearly articulated that goal, we then have a basis and universal organizing principle for all subsequent engagement. Does this or that nuclear policy, practice, device, etc., build toward or detract from the morally normative end?

In taking these two questions as fundamental, we do two things as Christians.

First, we isolate our core contribution to the nuclear weapons "issue" as essentially moral and theological in nature. This allows us to speak from our strength—which is not properly ours, but the wisdom of the cross—rather than as amateur nuclear planners.

Second, we establish with unequivocal clarity a standard that everyone can understand, including the people in the pews—*this* is what we are for, and why. We thus create a position for the *church*, not technocratic experts.

A Christian Moral Norm

So: what is an evangelical moral norm for nuclear weapons?

The "Just War" tradition cannot be ignored as perhaps the singularly determinative arbiter of nuclear ethics for many Christians worldwide—though a robustly theological Just War tradition will acknowledge that it offers only a tiny fraction of Christian resources on war and peace, for it speaks only about the situations of last resort. If we do not get lost in too-frequent use of Just War criteria as tick boxes for the purpose of legitimizing war, we can see that Just War is the (often futile) demand that even the practice of human violence be subject to the justice of God's coming kingdom.

Within traditional Just War loci, three points speak especially to nuclear weapons. The *principle of discrimination* precludes any use of weapons of mass destruction against civilians. The *principle of proportionality* requires that the use of force be relative to the conflict. Both situations are difficult to imagine, given the power of modern nuclear weapons. For people already disposed to hate nuclear weapons, these arguments are enough. But serious nuclear technocrats who are paid to imagine worst-case scenarios can deploy hypothetical exceptional scenarios—an unforeseeable global war, with a military target far removed from noncombatants—that may, in fact, satisfy proportionality and discrimination. As these are the people who are in charge of the nuclear establishment, we do ourselves no favor by not taking them seriously.

But the nuclear technocrats cannot avoid stumbling, ethically speaking, with scenarios that underestimate the significance of maintaining the taboo against nuclear use. The Just War demands consideration of macro-proportionality: that the good from a given action exceed the predictable harm. And there is simply no case to be made for the benefits of a given tactical situation, no matter how dire, outweighing the costs of rupturing a sixty-six-year-and-counting taboo against nuclear weapons as legitimate instruments of war. All strategic planners' justifications to the contrary give undue consideration to their own nation's hypothetically exceptional circumstances, while diminishing the fact that there is a difference between an absolute norm and an exceptional norm. The use of nuclear weapons by a state actor in any circumstance would open a door that could not readily be shut, and through which hell itself could race.

It is this Just War standard, that good must outweigh harm, which fixes an immobile and absolute moral norm against the use of nuclear weapons—a norm of non-use that can then be used as an operating principle for developing and evaluating policy. This means that the morally normative goal of all nuclear technology management should be to ensure that no nuclear weapon is ever used. Having accepted this, it is a step—but not a long one, given the quality of policy analysis by security experts and our theological conviction about the predictable depravity of humankind—to the conviction that the only macro-strategy capable of aspiring to this goal of non-use is abolition.

Toward a More Humane Future

During the Cold War, nuclear weapons were so all-consuming that their strategy and ethics constituted entire fields unto themselves. Our present climate pushes us beyond the specific parameters of nuclear weapons ethics, however, into broader concerns about Christian engagement in a world facing global, transnational crises. The popular apocalyptic imagination has certainly shifted from nuclear-only to a pantheon of world-ending phenomena—climate change, nano- and bioengineering, pandemics, resource scarcity, etc. In this context it is both right and good to treat nuclear weapons not only as an isolated ethical question but also to situate Christian engagement with nuclear weapons in the broader concern of peacemaking in a globalizing era.

In the same text that seeded the Christian Just War tradition, St. Augustine described Christian engagement in human government as the pursuit of peace, which he defined as *tranquillitas ordinis*, or the tranquility of order. Our task is to conform our earthly social order, as best we are able within the confines of a fallen creation, to the perfect order of heaven. This work seems eminently timeless and applicable today. Though the crises attending globalization present unique challenges of complexity and scale, our marching orders remain the same—attend to the job at hand, with the tools available, and with eyes fixed on a heavenly blueprint.

The question to us is thus tactical. Churches, after all, do not possess nuclear weapons. We cannot directly eliminate them. So how should we understand what is the faithful and wise way to manifest our conviction regarding the norm governing nuclear weapons, and related policy steps?

In immediate terms, the course appears relatively clear: strengthen the global commitment to a world without nuclear weapons and take decisive steps in that direction. The U.S. and Russia, who together possess more than 90 percent of the global nuclear stockpile, must take the lead in bilateral reductions, but the other nuclear nations should be brought in as well in a workable timetable. The development of nuclear weapons free zones, including the Middle East, would increase Israel's security and curb any ambitions by Iran. The ratification of the Comprehensive Test Ban Treaty by the U.S. would push the treaty closer to entry into force, establishing a high bar against new nations joining the nuclear club. UN Secretary General Ban Ki-moon has proposed a Nuclear Weapons Convention, much like those governing biological and chemical weapons, which would ban the use of nuclear weapons and thus provide powerful assistance toward their dismantlement. Bomb-quality fissile material (highly enriched uranium and plutonium) forms the wasp's-waist of the supply chain for developing the Bomb—you can't build a nuclear weapon without it, and it can't be found in nature or made without a massive industrial effort—so efforts such as the Nuclear Security Summit and its campaign to account for and secure all nuclear material worldwide are absolutely vital. Each of these steps will increase the security of all nations, which is critical; if nuclear abolition makes powerful nations more vulnerable, self-interest will simply prevent it from ever happening.

If we are successful in such steps, the movement toward a world without nuclear weapons will itself raise significant ethical questions. At lower numbers, for example, the strategic calculus around nuclear weapons shifts, and strips away the illusion that deterrence is based in threatening an adversary's military assets, rather than cities and population. Simply put, to get to zero we will have to go through a numerical phase of armaments that reveals the barbarism underneath deterrence's respectable Savile Row suit, and which is categorically beyond Christian ethical sanction. Dealing with this will be critical—will it require a nuclear weapons convention, which would ban nuclear weapons, and thus at least relegate the threat to annihilate civilians to the level of implicit possibility, rather than stated nuclear doctrine? Furthermore, ethical evaluation of the end-state—a device of global governance that could predictably counter any nuclear breakout—will also be important. These, and other questions, must be seriously engaged.

As suggested above, we need to figure out how to pursue the work of *tranquillitas ordinis* in the midst of globalization. This merits some careful thought. Often, Christian activists can respond to problems with instincts that are drawn more from activist circles than from the church (and I have been the chief of sinners in this regard, on occasion). That is, confronted with a challenge, we resolve to get this or that petition signed, or this or that resolution passed, or lobby this or that official, or aspire toward action grounded in the notoriously ephemeral discourse of activism: "raise awareness," "take a stand," "speak out," "raise our voices," "advocate." None of these tactics (such as they are) are adequately distinctive or authentic to who we are as Christians or, even less, the church. Nor are they sufficient to the challenge of nuclear disarmament.

Toward this end, it will continue to be good and necessary for Christian organizations to make moral pronouncements about the conduct of governments. This teaching role is important. We all know that we have a hard enough time getting our congregations—or ourselves!—to behave according to the moral imperatives of personal holiness. If a law carved in stone by God's own finger could not compel perfect obedience, how much less so will any resolution by our imperfect church bodies?

As we pursue our work, therefore, we might do well to remember the difference between moral imperatives of "thou shalt/not" and the morality of love and compassion. It is one thing to obey an ethical command to help "the poor," and quite another to respond in love to someone in need.

Though both are moral impulses, our Lord's teaching—e.g., the parable of the Good Samaritan—seems to favor the latter. This shift is challenging to make with nuclear weapons, which are potentialized threats that are invisible and unreal to most people's daily lives. Their iconic image is a mushroom cloud photographed from miles away, distance obscuring the human conflagration at its heart. Add to this the emotionally fraught terrain of revisiting Hiroshima and Nagasaki, especially in an American context, and we see why it is extremely difficult to put a face to the issue that would enable a moral response grounded in the particularity of relationship and compassion, rather than the abstraction of imperative (however well-reasoned!).

Yet there is no group better suited to this important task than evangelicals, whose concern for individual salvation and discipleship dedicates us to the welfare of persons, more than causes. The task of rendering and remembering nuclear weapons on a human scale, and in light of their human cost, may well be the most extraordinary contribution that evangelicals can make toward their eventual elimination.

19

Overcoming Global Warming

Jim Ball

Introduction

Overcoming global warming is a marathon we will be running the rest of our lives, but it is a race we should have started long before now. Serious impacts have already occurred. Even with our best efforts billions of people will be adversely impacted, especially the poor. The rate of change needed to overcome global warming is tremendous: we need a tenfold increase in carbon productivity in forty years. By comparison, we achieved a tenfold increase in labor productivity during the Industrial Revolution, but the overcoming-global-warming-clean-energy-revolution must take place in one-third of the time.[1]

We still have time to overcome global warming. To do so we must:

1. avoid catastrophic impacts by seriously reducing the causes, and;
2. adapt to the consequences that will befall us.

As I discuss more thoroughly in my book,[2] it is not a matter of whether we have the means and the know-how to overcome global warming. We do. It is a matter of the will. No individuals by themselves can overcome global warming. Every individual has a part to play. As individuals, we must work together: in our families, our churches and schools, our businesses, our communities, our states, and as one nation under God. Then all the nations of the world must work together. With global warming we are all in this together, and everyone's efforts count. We cannot do this alone; all are needed.

So ultimately our collective efforts and our collective will as a nation, itself made up of millions and millions of individual efforts, will overcome global warming.

For the world to have a shot at overcoming global warming, emissions of greenhouse gases must peak between 2015–2017 and decline after that.[3] Given that the world's economies are powered primarily by the burning of fossil fuels—the major cause of global warming pollution—we are already seriously behind in being able to achieve this. We have barely begun to grapple with how to adapt to the climate change that will occur.

Put together, all of this means that the 2012 election is the most important U.S. election there will ever be when it comes to overcoming global warming. The world cannot meet this great challenge without strong leadership from the United States, and that in turn will require strong leadership from the next president.

So, again, what is needed is the will, both individually and as a nation. Then we must have the collective will of all nations.

Where will we find the will?

For Christians, this brings us to the most important fact about global warming: the Risen LORD is leading the way in overcoming it. As such, overcoming global warming is now an important part of Christian discipleship for all Christians.

Overcoming global warming is tailor-made for those who actually follow the Risen LORD. It presents a tremendous near-term challenge, but much of the "payoff" is decades into the future, and for people in distant lands we will never meet. It calls us to act in love and righteousness and wisdom, and to do so with perseverance. Therein lies a huge part of the problem.

Overcoming global warming is ultimately a spiritual challenge, for it has to do with faithfully following the Risen LORD. Thankfully we have been given the spiritual resources to run this race in the form of Christ's grace and God's presence with us.[4] In overcoming global warming, we have our loving heavenly Father watching over us, the Holy Spirit within us, and the Risen LORD beside us leading the way.

Three Stories

To provide encouragement and guidance for the journey, let me tell you three stories.

The first comes from the Narnia book *Prince Caspian*. At one point we meet Lucy—the youngest of the brothers and sisters from England who find themselves in the magical world of Narnia. There, even though they are children, they are regarded as kings and queens. Lucy sees the great Aslan, a lion who is the real ruler of Narnia. But the other children—Peter, Susan, and Edmund—don't see him.[5]

"Look! Look! Look!" cried Lucy.

"Where? What?" asked everyone.

"The Lion," said Lucy. "Aslan himself. Didn't you see?" Her face had changed completely and her eyes shone.

"Do you really mean...?" began Peter.

"Where did you think you saw him?" asked Susan.

"Don't talk like a grown-up," said Lucy, stamping her foot. "I didn't *think* I saw him. I saw him."

"Where, Lu?" asked Peter.

"Right up there between those mountain ashes...the opposite side of the way you want to go. He wanted us to go where he was—up there."

"How do you know that was what he wanted?" asked Edmund.

"He—I—I just know," said Lucy, "by his face."

The other children remain doubtful as to whether Aslan was really there. The children then take a vote, which goes against Lucy. They continue along the way that seems the most straightforward and reasonable. Later that night while everyone else is asleep, Lucy is awakened from a deep and restful slumber by a voice calling her, "a voice she liked best in the world." She sees the trees are dancing, and she joins them, dancing her way toward the voice that was calling her.

She never stopped to think whether he was a friendly lion or not. She rushed to him. She felt her heart would burst if she lost a moment. The next thing she knew was that she was kissing him and putting her arms as far around his neck as she could and burying her face in the beautiful rich silkiness of his mane.

"Aslan, Aslan. Dear Aslan," sobbed Lucy. "At last."

The great beast rolled over on his side so that Lucy fell, half sitting and half lying between his front paws. He bent forward and just touched her nose with his tongue. His warm breath came all round her. She gazed up into the large wise face.

"Welcome, child," he said...

For a time she was so happy that she did not want to speak. But Aslan spoke.

"Lucy," he said, "we must not lie here for long. You have work in hand, and much time has been lost today."

"Yes, wasn"t it a shame?" said Lucy. "I saw you all right. They wouldn"t believe me. They're all so..."

From somewhere deep inside Aslan's body there came the faintest suggestion of a growl.

"I'm sorry," said Lucy, who understood some of his moods. "I didn't mean to start slanging the others. But it wasn't my fault anyway, was it?"

The Lion looked straight into her eyes.

"Oh, Aslan," said Lucy. "You don't mean it was? How could I—I couldn't have left the others and come up to you alone, how could I? Don't look at me like that...oh well, I suppose I *could*. Yes, and it wouldn't have been alone, I know, not if I was with you. But what would have been the good?"

Aslan said nothing.

"You mean," said Lucy rather faintly, "that it would have turned out all right—somehow? But how? Please, Aslan! Am I not to know?"

"To know what *would* have happened, child?" said Aslan. "No. Nobody is ever told that."

"Oh dear," said Lucy.

"But anyone can find out what *will* happen," said Aslan.

Lucy returns to her sleeping brothers and sister and finally is able to rouse them from their slumber and get them to follow her, and eventually they, too, see Aslan.

So when it comes to overcoming global warming, what is it that "Lucy" can see but that others can't just yet? It's the key spiritual fact about this tremendous challenge and spiritual opportunity. The real truth about global warming is that it is the Risen LORD who is leading the way in overcoming it. For Christians, this is what global warming is really all about: following the Risen LORD as he leads the way.

The second story is about an orphaned baby girl named Muya Val, and about the woman she was named after, Dr. Val Shean, a veterinarian and missionary.[6]

For nearly twenty years Val has shared Christ's love in both word and deed among the seven sub-tribes of the Karamojong. These folks live in an arid region of Uganda called Karamoja, the driest area of Uganda and home to over a million people. Val has had years of firsthand experience as to what global warming has been doing to the poor.

The Karamojong are semi-nomadic agro-pastoralists, meaning that the men take their cows away from the village to graze while the women work to provide food via rain-fed agriculture.

The arid and semi-arid regions of the poor countries of the world, regions like Karamoja, are on the front lines of climate change. That's because one of the main consequences of climate change is how it is disrupting when rain comes and how much comes or doesn't come. As a result there will be more floods and droughts, and these floods and droughts will be more intense. For the poor who depend upon rain-fed agriculture to survive, especially in naturally dry places like Karamoja, such consequences can mean the difference between life and death.

According to Val, that's exactly what is happening in Karamoja—and why Muya became an orphan.

Muya's mother was one of Val's friends from their village, a woman named Aleache. For three years Aleache's ability to grow crops to help feed her family had been thwarted by the changing climate. For two of these years the rains came at the wrong time for planting, and when they did come it wasn't enough to stem the drought. Then in the third year they had what Val described as "a horrible flood," all the more remarkable since they've never had flooding. So for three straight years Aleache's family didn't have enough food. Her husband became so enraged at this that he threw her out of the home for being a bad wife and mother because she couldn't make her contribution to feeding the family. But of course it wasn't Aleache's fault. It was because of global warming. And yet she was blamed.

Once her husband threw her out, Aleache went to another village and lived with another man and became pregnant. On her way back to her home village Aleache had her baby, named Muya, but died after giving birth. Muya was then brought to the local church, who asked Val to be her guardian.

Because they didn't know who the father was, Muya was given Val's name as her last name, becoming Muya Val. All of this happened the week before Val came to speak in D.C. to a conference on climate change and the poor that my organization helped arrange. So before Val came, she had to leave Muya Val at an orphanage.

Unfortunately, in the years to come, many more climate change orphans such as Muya Val will populate our villages and drought areas. Indeed, in our lifetime billions of the world's poor will be impacted by global warming, and millions will die.

The final story is a well-known one from Jesus, that of the Good Samaritan. Right before this parable in the Gospel of Luke, an expert in the Law tests Jesus, "'Teacher,' he asked, 'what must I do to inherit eternal life?'" (10:25b). Jesus then asks the expert what answer he finds in the Law, and he replies with the Great Commandment. Jesus affirms his reply and then says, "'Do this and you will live'" (10:28b). With this Jesus essentially connects a true life today with life in the kingdom when it comes in its fullness.

Do you want to know what real life is? Do you want to truly live? Do you want to taste a glimpse of God's future for his people and the rest of his creation right now? Then love God with everything you've got and your neighbor as yourself. Do this and you will live, really live.

The expert, mister smarty-pants, wants to show off what he knows (and maybe put Jesus in his place). "He asked Jesus, 'And who is my neighbor?'" (10:29b). In other words, who am I required to "love" to earn the prize of eternal life, and who are not my neighbors and thus can be treated in less than a loving manner?

This weasely question sets up the parable of the Good Samaritan.

During Jesus' time Jews regarded Samaritans with utter contempt. They understood Samaritans to be the ancestors of those peasant Jews left behind when the ruling elites were taken into exile, who then intermarried with the foreigners brought in by the Assyrians to repopulate the land. Over the ensuing centuries they sometimes aligned themselves with the enemies of the Jews. They were thus considered traitorous half-breeds, and from inferior Jewish stock to boot. Perhaps more importantly, the Samaritans had their own version of the Torah and their own temple on Mount Gerizim, which the Samaritans claimed was the proper place for the temple, rather than Jerusalem. Thus, religious and ethnic differences that would appear small to outsiders fueled the strong distaste each group had for the other. John 4:9 puts it mildly when it says, "Jews do not associate with Samaritans." In response to the desire of the expert to know legally where love ends, Jesus provides a story. In this story, one of those heretical, traitorous, half-breed Samaritans shows us what it means to love your neighbor.

> A man was going down from Jerusalem to Jericho, when he fell into the hands of robbers. They stripped him of his clothes, beat him and went away, leaving him half dead. A priest happened to be going down the same road, and when he saw the man, he passed by on the other side. So too, a Levite, when he came to the place and saw him, passed by on the other side. But a Samaritan, as he traveled, came where the man was; and when he saw him, he took pity on him. He went to him and bandaged his wounds, pouring on oil and wine. Then he put the man on his own donkey, brought him to an inn and took care of him (Lk 10:30–34).

The biblical lawyer was looking for the love loophole: "We're just talking about our neighbors, right, and by that I mean the appropriate kinds of neighbors. So I don't have to love those other people, right?"

By having the Samaritan demonstrate love by his actions, Jesus in effect says that everyone is our neighbor—even or especially others we hold in contempt. Furthermore, those of us who think of ourselves as religious, as doing the right things to appease God and look righteous to others, better think again.

Here is where this parable and global warming intersect for us. The priest and the Levite were not the ones who robbed the man, just as in our time we didn't create the conditions of poverty, a situation that makes the poor much more vulnerable to the impact of global warming. But the priest and the Levite did pass by on the other side. Righteousness and love are the presence of good and loving acts, not simply the absence of bad ones. By not helping the man in the ditch, the priest and the Levite made his plight worse and failed to love God and be who God created them to be.

Today, collectively, we are in fact making the plight of the poor worse through global warming. Knowing their plight and not doing what we can to help to overcome global warming is like passing by on the other side. We may be highly observant of the outward signs of what it means to be religious in our community. So, too, I'm sure, were the priest and the Levite. That's exactly why Jesus chose them to be characters in his parable. If we don't help the poor who, through no fault of their own, find themselves victims in the ditch of global warming's impact, then all the religiosity in the world won't bring us closer to the LORD.

Why? Matthew 25 lets us in on a little secret about the parable of the Good Samaritan. (You will recall that in Matthew 25 Jesus says that what we do to "the least of these" we do to him.) While the Good Samaritan is Christlike in his behavior, *Jesus himself is the man in the ditch*. To get close to the LORD is to tend to him when he's in the ditch. The point of the parable is to be a neighbor, to be a Good Samaritan, to go and do likewise.

In terms of the problem of global warming, right now, as a Christian, it is as if you are approaching a victim of global warming in the ditch. You are just within sight of the person. You don't yet quite know what is going on. Is it risky to go over to this person? You can't quite yet tell anything about who it is—just that a lump in the ditch looks human. Whoever it is could be drunk—maybe not a victim at all! As you venture closer, you come to find a child, not a man—a young baby girl. It is actually Muya Val. She is in distress. Is she sick? Weak from hunger? Both? Maybe she has an infectious disease. Where are her parents? Who is responsible for this baby girl? How did she get in this situation? Suddenly you notice that someone else is in the ditch with her. It is the Risen LORD.

Here we must ask ourselves some questions about the spiritual resources God has given us in our journey with the Risen LORD.

Who are we becoming with the spiritual blood of Christ's saving grace flowing in our veins? Who are we becoming with the uplifting strength and guidance of Christ's Spirit, the Holy Spirit, residing in our hearts? Who are we becoming with the Risen LORD walking beside us, with his glorious face reflecting the compassionate fire of the Father's love? Who are we in light of this? Are we becoming religious people who will pass by on the other side and ignore the victims of global warming? Or are we becoming those who let our passion for the LORD transform us into those who have the courage and strength to love others as ourselves, whoever and wherever they may be, in whatever situation they find themselves? What will our response to the impact of global warming on others, especially the poor, say about our walk with the Risen LORD?

Right now you may be like Lucy. You've grasped the great spiritual fact about global warming; you've seen the Risen LORD as he is leading the way in overcoming global warming.

Just like Lucy's brothers and sisters didn't believe that she had seen Aslan and voted against going the way she knew Aslan wanted them to travel, it could be that some of those close to you don't yet believe that the Risen LORD is leading the way.

In the movie *Prince Caspian*, Lucy says, "I knew it was you, the whole time, I knew it. But the others didn't believe me."

Aslan replies, "And why would that stop you from coming to me?"

20

Reducing Abortion

Charlie Camosy

Introduction

The polarization of those involved in debate over abortion has been nothing short of devastating. Perhaps more than any other factor, it is responsible for the culture wars in the United States and for dominating whole segments of our society's political attention during elections, judicial appointments, and even debates over other issues, such as foreign aid. Through this lens many look at a host of other important issues: stem cell research, assisted suicide, removing life-sustaining treatment, animal rights/welfare, and health care reform. The 2012 elections will once again be dominated by this kind of polarization.

Perhaps just as importantly, the abortion debates keep many from cooperating toward common goods. Instead of trying to find overlap of ideas and public policy goals, many self-identify at a core level with intense opposition to their ideological and political opponents over abortion. We see this even in relatively strong Christian communities such as the University of Notre Dame—where the debate over Obama's strong pro-choice voting record and his worthiness to receive an honorary degree tore that community apart. Different types of evangelical Christian communities also find it difficult to cooperate due to these kinds of divides.

The polarization is so deeply rooted in our national psyche that many fear the debate is intractable. Many public policy intellectuals now refuse to touch the topic, and many who have tried to move it forward in the past are now suffering from abortion fatigue. Abortion is even used by certain kinds of academic ethicists as a prime example of the failure of the Enlightenment project—their argument being that despite our appeals to a baseline of secular "reason," the different contexts and narratives associated with the various positions have produced principles that simply cannot be reconciled with each other. According to this argument, there is therefore no hope for anything beyond stalemate in the abortion debate.

Especially when thinking about Christian communities, I reject this pessimistic understanding of the situation. In teaching bioethics to many different kinds of students, doing academic research on abortion and related issues, planning conferences designed to find common ground, and doing various public presentations on these topics, I have found that the disagreement over abortion can be attributed in large part to participants defining themselves in opposition to certain positions, groups, and movements before (or even in spite of) a full exploration the debate. I strongly believe that when Christians start consistently applying their values of nonviolence and concern for the vulnerable to abortion-related questions, instead of idolatrously grasping onto a "liberal" or "conservative" ideology as their source of ultimate concern,[1] we can see a way forward in the abortion debate.

Moving Forward Together

Christians of many different kinds can work together to reduce abortion. In many circles this is thought to be a "liberal" approach to the problem, but given that illegal activity will still take place, even a public policy that bans abortion will only *reduce* the number of abortions.[2] In thinking about the way we should go about reducing abortion, Christians, I argue, should employ a consistent ethic of life. As I highlight in the conclusion to a new book that attempts to foster dialogue between Christians and utilitarians,[3] the feminist and progressive writer Mary Meehan wrote the following words back in 1980:

> Some of us who went through the anti-war struggles of the 1960s and early 1970s are now active in the right-to-life movement. We do not enjoy opposing our old friends on the abortion issue, but we feel that we have no choice. We are moved by what pro-life feminists call the "consistency thing"—the belief that respect for human life demands opposition to abortion, capital punishment, euthanasia, and war.[4]

Just three years later the Roman Catholic archbishop Joseph Cardinal Bernardin would deliver his now famous Gannon Lecture at Fordham University in New York City, titled "A Consistent Ethic of Life: An American-Catholic Dialogue." This ground-breaking talk began his defense of an ethic that requires consistent reasoning across the issues of genetics, abortion, capital punishment, modern warfare, and the care of the terminally ill.[5] Bernardin would go on to refine his view and add poverty and welfare reform, health care, and civil rights to what he called the "seamless garment" of concern for life.[6] The Consistent Ethic frames Jesus' biblical command to love within reason's requirement of logical consistency in the application of principle.

This is no mere academic or obscure ivory-tower approach. The far and powerful reach of politically active groups such as Democrats for Life, and grassroots groups such as Feminists for Life, is evidence of the fault lines shifting in a way that reveals that many are beginning to apply pro-life principles more consistently. Those who adhere to a consistent ethic of life, in my view, should do the following:

- Acknowledge the moral value of all life: humans, nonhuman animals, and the broader ecological world.
- Have a presumption against using violence, especially that aimed at death.
- Have a presumption *for* aiding those in need, especially those who will die without aid.[7]
- Foster a special concern for the most vulnerable regardless of age, condition of dependency, net contribution to the economy, race, gender, class, health, wealth, power, or moral condition.

The remainder of this essay will attempt to show how both "liberal" and "conservative"[8] Christians can use a consistent ethic of life to think about how to reduce abortion in the United States.

Reducing Abortion: Insights from the "Liberal" Narrative

The lens of the consistent ethic can help us see why abortion is such a complex issue: it involves two vulnerable people in the moral equation, whose interests sometimes appear to be in conflict. Liberals, and rightly so, often have a particular focus on the vulnerability of the pregnant mother, for she lives in a world of structures created by a gender that cannot become pregnant. She must contend with economic and other social expectations that see pregnancy as a burden to be overcome, rather than an opportunity to cooperate in the gestation of a human person in the most intimate way possible—perhaps the greatest earthly gift that God can give a human being. Indeed, it is a gift that, if rightly understood, should cause us to push other goods (profit maximization, social mobility, etc.) to the side.

Instead, women are forced to participate in a culture that has the "burden" understanding of pregnancy. When they find themselves financially dependent on others (a spouse or other partner, family member, etc.), pregnancy becomes a different kind of burden—and perhaps one that is even more keenly felt. Indeed, if a woman is dependent on someone else for her economic well-being, then her burden may actually even coerce her choice. It cannot be left unsaid that pregnancy can often cause a woman very serious health problems, and may even threaten her very life.

For these reasons, many "liberals" focus particularly on the vulnerability of the pregnant mother. However, they also may point out that this kind of focus, in addition to defending vulnerable women, may also end up reducing the number of abortions—even if we maintain a pro-choice public policy. Consider that many other countries have made dramatic attempts to subordinate the goals of the market to the goal of supporting pregnant women. Embarrassingly, a recent study found that the United States was one of only a handful of countries (a total of 168 were studied) that did not have some kind of paid maternity leave.[9]

The study shows that Sweden, for instance, offers a whopping sixteen months of leave—at 80 percent pay—to be split between both parents. The United Kingdom offers fifty-two weeks of maternity leave, thirty-nine of which is paid—and also offers "Sure Start" grants for expenses related to being a new mother, as well as free milk, fresh fruit and vegetables, infant formula, and vitamins to certain pregnant women and children.[10] Perhaps unsurprisingly, studies in the mid-1990s found that the abortion rates were substantially higher in the United States than in these countries. Indeed, while the teenage abortion rate in the United States was 29 per 1000 women, it was 22 in the UK and 18 in Sweden.[11]

Structures of poverty are very important forces driving abortion choice in the United States. Poor women (defined as those in families making less than 100 percent of the federal poverty level) accounted for 42 percent of all abortions in 2008, and their abortion rate increased 18 percent between 2000 and 2008, from 44.4 to 52.2 abortions per 1000 women aged 15–44. In comparison, the total abortion rate for 2008 was 19.6 per 1000, reflecting an 8 percent decline from a rate of 21.3 in 2000.[12] Race, especially because it is so tied to economic and other kinds of injustice, also plays an important role. Consider that in 2008 the abortion rate among African American women was dramatically higher than the rate for both Hispanic and non-Hispanic white women: 40.2, compared with 28.7 and 11.5, respectively.[13]

"Liberals" generally understand the need to focus on the underlying structures of poverty and push for structural change in American public policy in this regard. They argue that this is not only a matter of justice for women—especially for those who are structurally disadvantaged in our culture—but many will also highlight the examples of Sweden and the UK as evidence that changing such structures in favor of women will lower the abortion rate as well. An important success was recently achieved on this front with the passage of several provisions of health care reform. Much of the "Pregnant Women Support Act" ended up becoming the law of the land.[14] It included the following:

- Funding for colleges to provide pregnancy and parenting resources located on campus or within the local community and improve such resources, including:
  - ~ The inclusion of maternity coverage and the availability of riders for additional family members in student health care
  - ~ Family housing
  - ~ Child care
  - ~ Flexible or alternative academic scheduling to allow students to stay in school
  - ~ Education to improve parenting skills
  - ~ Maternity and baby clothing, baby food, baby furniture, and similar items
  - ~ Postpartum counseling and support groups
- Funding for programs that help pregnant or parenting teens stay in or complete high school and prepare for college or vocational education by providing resources and assistance
  - ~ Assistance to states in providing intervention services, accompaniment, and supportive social services for pregnant victims of domestic violence, sexual violence, or stalking
  - ~ Additional resources for public awareness and outreach so that pregnant and parenting teens and women are aware of services available to them
  - ~ Elimination of pregnancy as a pre-existing condition
  - ~ Enhancement of Adoption Tax Credits

Insofar as "conservatives" focus only on the legality of abortion in their public policy proposals, they not only miss the fact that abortion involves at least two vulnerable persons, but they miss out on the chance to change public policies in ways that have been shown to actually reduce abortion and save the lives of our prenatal children.

Though this critique responds to a caricature of the "conservative" position on abortion, I take it as an important critique nonetheless. Abortion is a far more complex issue than simply determining whether or not it should be legal. However, it is also more complex than the above "liberal" narrative is prepared to consider. And it is to some of these complexities we now turn.

2 2 2

Complications for the "Liberal" Narrative

The fact that an astounding 1.2 million women have an abortion every year in the United States certainly cannot be reduced to issues of structural poverty. Indeed, even with many of the kinds of social structures that "liberals" want to have in place in America, Sweden and the UK now have comparable abortion rates to that of the U.S. While there might have been a large gap in the mid-1990s, by 2003 this was no longer the case. In the 20–24 age range the United States still had an abortion rate higher than other comparable countries, but rates among American women aged 30 or older were *lower* than those in many developed countries with energetic social welfare. And the teenage abortion rate in the United States (22 per 1,000 women) was comparable to that of England (23) and *lower* than that of Sweden (25).[15]

For many women, rather than an exceptional choice to be used only in dire circumstances, abortion has simply become another kind of birth control. Remarkably, over half of American women who have abortions in a given year have already had at least one abortion.[16] In addition, 61 percent of women who have abortions in the United States already have at least one child.[17] In a particularly disturbing example of this phenomenon, *The New York Times* had a recent story about a couple who, after getting pregnant through *in vitro* fertilization, "reduced" twins to a singleton pregnancy through abortion. The reason?

> "Things would have been different if we were 15 years younger or if we hadn't had children already or if we were more financially secure," she said later. "If I had conceived these twins naturally, I wouldn't have reduced this pregnancy, because you feel like if there's a natural order, then you don't want to disturb it."[18]

Like many IVF users, this couple were in their 40s, and with pregnancy in one's 40s comes an increased risk of Down's Syndrome and other issues. This, unfortunately, is another major reason why many women have abortions: the prenatal child is prenatally diagnosed as not meeting the desires of his or her parents. The abortion rate of babies with Down's is high in the U.S., but it is worse in the UK, where 9 of 10 women who have prenatal children with Down's Syndrome end up aborting the pregnancy.[19] Denmark has pledged to become "Down's Syndrome free."[20] Taking it up one more discriminatory notch, Sweden has even proclaimed that "gender-based" abortion should be protected by law.[21]

No, while a certain level of social (and familial) support seems to reduce the abortion rate a significant amount, the problem of abortion—because it involves the violent killing of millions and millions of our vulnerable and utterly dependent children—will remain a grave and overwhelming evil *even if* the necessary social supports for women are in place. If we wish to reduce abortion in a way that is consistent with Jesus' call to resist violence and to support and defend the most vulnerable, we need to do better.

Reducing Abortion: Adding "Conservative" Insights

The claim that the fetus is a person with full standing as a member of the human family is one that is shared by many "liberals" and "conservatives" of various kinds.[22] However, though there are some exceptions that "prove the rule," "conservatives" generally take this claim far more seriously than do "liberals." Indeed, they are more willing to use legal force to see that the full dignity of prenatal children is articulated and defended in our public policy. Too often, "liberals" will punt on the question of equal protection of the laws for our prenatal children—and instead default to the well-rehearsed (but often not seriously investigated) position that such protection is impossible or impractical. Equal protection of the laws for the marginalized (hardly a "conservative" position in contexts of race and gender) has always had its "realist" detractors. If we care about justice for this vulnerable population, we need to do far more than default to "liberal" realism. Not only are our current prenatal children owed legal protection, but a pro-life law's pedagogical function would help create a world in which all of us are taught about their value, leading to the protection of future generations of such children.

The American Supreme Court is deeply divided on the issue of abortion, with four justices supporting broad legalization and four favoring broad legal restriction. Justice Anthony Kennedy is the wildcard—having supported *Roe v. Wade* "in principle" in his *Planned Parenthood v. Casey* opinion, while also supporting important restriction in cases such as *Gonzalez v. Carhart*. But the legal reasoning that supported *Roe* has crumbled: post-*Casey*, the legal issue now before the Court is not a right to privacy, but what kind of abortion restrictions constitute an "undue burden" on women. When the Supreme Court hears the next challenge to *Roe/Casey*, it is not clear how Justice Kennedy will rule on this question—nor is it clear what the makeup of the court will be at the time this happens. Should Kennedy change his understanding of how broad abortion restrictions burden (or do not burden) women, or should a strong pro-life Supreme Court justice be nominated and confirmed, equal protection of the laws for our prenatal children—at least in some states—suddenly becomes a very realistic possibility.

But what many folks are worried about is not the *principle* of equal protection of the laws for our prenatal children, but (1) whether making abortion broadly illegal will actually reduce abortion and protect prenatal children, and/or (2) whether making abortion illegal adequately protects another vulnerable population: pregnant women. Unfortunately, the pre-*Roe* statistics for illegal abortions, and how they affected women, are far from clear and have been manipulated by those on multiple sides of the debate. The physician and public health scholar Mary S. Calderone, writing over a decade before *Roe*, claimed that abortion, whether legal or illegal, "is no longer a dangerous procedure." Indeed, while the maternal death rate related to abortion was going down "strikingly" from 1921 through 1957, we know that the population and birth rate were dramatically rising. How can both be true? Calderone explains:

> Two corollary factors must be mentioned here: first, chemotherapy and antibiotics have come in, benefiting all surgical procedures as well as abortion. Second...90 per cent of all illegal abortions are presently being done by physicians. Call them what you will, abortionists or anything else, they are still physicians, trained as such; and many of them are in good standing in their communities.[23]

It seems, then, that dramatically fewer women die from abortions today, not primarily because abortion is legal, but because medical technology has improved so dramatically. There would certainly be a number of illegal abortions performed even if the practice was recriminalized, but given that trained physicians would still be doing the vast majority of such abortions (to say nothing of our improvements in emergency and other kinds of medical care), it is unlikely that the maternal death rate from abortions would rise significantly if most abortions were made illegal.

And just how many illegal abortions would be procured if abortion were made broadly illegal in the United States? The answer is unclear and depends on which studies and estimates one chooses to examine and highlight. In the last decade or so in the United States, about 1.3 million abortions occurred per year. About 22 percent of all pregnancies during that time have ended in abortion.[24] More than 30 percent of American women have at least one abortion by the age of 45.[25] However, according to a study of 22,657 women from the late 1930s by demographer Raymond Peal, only 1.4 percent of all pregnancies among white women ended in illegal abortion (0.5 percent for black women). Despite taking place during a time when abortion estimates were being revised sharply higher, the Kinsey studies at the University of Indiana conducted in the 1950s found that only 22 percent of the women they surveyed had had at least one abortion by the time they were 45.[26]

Perhaps the most telling trend can be found when examining statistics just after abortion was legalized in all fifty states in 1973. In that first year after *Roe* there were approximately 750,000 women who had abortions in the United States, or one abortion for every four live births. However, just seven years later the numbers had risen dramatically to 1,600,000 women, or one abortion for every 2.25 live births.[27]

It is frustrating and difficult to try to extrapolate from the historical data to what is (or could be) happening in our contemporary American culture. But what about a Western country like Ireland, similar to the United States in many ways, with restrictive abortion laws? Could we use it as a means of comparison? Spurred by the aftermath of *Roe* in the United States, Ireland pushed back against a similar pro-choice movement growing on the Emerald Isle.

Following a 1983 referendum, the Eighth Amendment, known as the "Pro-Life Amendment," came into existence to deter the legalization of abortion in the future. The amendment contained three assertions: the unborn's right to life must be protected; the unborn's right to life was equal to that of the mother; and, this right to life would be defended to the greatest degree practicable.

Just two years later, a pro-life campaign began to push back against various pregnancy counseling groups giving information about obtaining abortions outside of Ireland. The Irish courts supported the pro-life argument and made distribution of such information illegal.[28] Less than a year ago, the European Court of Human Rights in Strasbourg also upheld the Irish public policy. They found that there is no broad legal right to abortion and that European member states had the freedom to enact their own abortion public policies.[29]

On the one hand, the Irish policy looks like it has been effective. According to Planned Parenthood's research arm, the best estimate of the abortion rate in Ireland in 1996, for example, was 5.9 per 1000 women. Just across the water in England/Wales the abortion rate that year was almost triple that of Ireland: 15.6 per 1000 women.[30] But in addition to the cultural differences between the two areas, which are certainly affected by the pedagogical function of the law,[31] there is the complicating factor that a number of Irish women travel to England (and other places in Europe) to have abortions. The total numbers are disputed, but according to the BBC, in 2009 there were 4600 women seeking abortions in Britain (along with 391 in the Netherlands) who gave an Irish address.[32] It is also worth noting that recent trends with regard to this practice are going down: there were 2000 more Irish women seeking abortions in Britain in 2001 than in 2009, and the number from the Netherlands cited above has fallen from 451 in 2007. The numbers of Irish who go elsewhere to obtain abortions, therefore, are not high enough to substantially change the general conclusion that Irish women have abortions at a far lower rate than do their British counterparts.

In light of what has just been presented, can we make any responsible and fair conclusions about what happens in a modern, developed, Western democracy when abortion is criminalized? Given limitations of the data, I would hesitate to make too many claims, but I do think we can take away two important points.

First, though it is not clear how much either the law or one's cultural ethos affects one's behavior (indeed, they seem to mutually reinforce each other), it is certainly possible for a Western country to criminalize abortion and have far fewer abortions than similar countries that have not criminalized it. The claim that *the same* number of abortions will *necessarily* take place in a given country whether abortion is criminalized or not, even if we posit a significant number of illegal abortions or abortions done in other countries, cannot be sustained given what has been shown above. Criminalizing birth-control abortion would save a significant number of our prenatal children—especially given its pedagogical power over the long run.

Second, well before abortion laws were liberalized in places such as the United States and Western Europe in the late 1960s and 1970s, the numbers of women dying from illegal abortions had become very low due to improved technology and the fact that trained physicians were the ones doing the overwhelming majority of illegal abortions. If the United States decided to afford our prenatal children equal protection of the law, it is not likely that large numbers of women would be killed via illegal abortions. Such a public policy—both through criminal penalty[33] and its long-term pedagogical effect—could protect large numbers of our vulnerable prenatal children from being killed. A small (but still significant) number of women would die from illegal abortions, but these numbers would not be significantly different from the numbers of women who currently die from legal abortions.

Reducing Abortion: Toward a "Magenta" Approach

Attempts to view complex issues such as abortion through the lens of binaries like liberal/conservative and red-state/blue-state hide more than they reveal. In part because this method requires one to define one's position (and perhaps even one's very identity) against the other side of the binary, the complexity of the issues is often lost in favor of easy answers—or, even worse, in favor of political agendas. It is high time that Christians refuse to use abortion (and, by extension, prenatal children and pregnant women) as pawns in a political battle. Rather than make an idol out of "liberal" or "conservative" ideologies, we should instead consistently follow our ancient Judeo-Christian principles wherever they lead us. If we find them matching up too closely with Democrat or Republican party platforms, we should turn a skeptical eye inward and honestly ask ourselves how likely it is that political agendas formed in the twentieth-century United States match up with a Christian faith that began in the ancient Middle East.

Rather than accepting the red-state/blue-state binary, Christians should take a "magenta" approach to abortion. This means accepting and incorporating the "liberal" insights about there being two vulnerable people to consider, as well as the structural reasons that women often choose to have abortions. However, it also means having an unflinching zeal to see that all vulnerable populations live under equal protection of the laws— and especially when, as in the case of our prenatal children, they cannot advocate on their own behalf. Whether we are talking about abortion or some other issue, Christians should be among the first to resist making the false choice between stamping out social structures that perpetuate injustice, and identifying those "least ones" who are in special need of justice and equal protection of the law.

21

Resisting Consumerism

Jennifer D. Crumpton

For the longest time, I thought something was seriously wrong with me. Over the twelve years I spent in the corporate marketing world as an advertising executive for global entities such as Citigroup, MasterCard, and the ad agencies that animate their brands, it became an increasingly perplexing problem. Even as I developed high-profile campaigns and promotions for my clients, I felt distracted and uneasy with the work. Sitting in meetings, it seemed everyone was speaking an odd language I couldn't wholly follow, a vernacular inspired by a buy-in I could not seem to achieve. I gave myself pep talks. I beat myself up for not appreciating my "glamorous" job. I tried my best to heed the corporate creed, pledging loyalty to a doctrine that, while logical on a spreadsheet, made zero sense internally. Why was I so bored at board meetings? Why couldn't I force myself to care more about the office politics or the latest buzz products in the financial sector? Why was it starting to get so hard to get out of bed in the mornings? Maybe I just didn't have what it takes.

Three and a half years ago I left the corporate world and followed a call to seminary. In the process, I realized that my trepidation in my former career had nothing to do with me—and everything to do with me. Nothing was wrong with my career efforts, my business practices, or my level of intelligence—all things I had started to question. The answer was that the core of my being—the person I am at heart—deeply rejected every slippery acquisition presentation that promised unreasonably higher profit margins, every business plan that banked on the instinctual insecurities and mutated desires of consumer culture. Because of my faith, my perception of reality—or truth—is embodied by a man whose nature was to give everything and take nothing, who did not have a place to lay his head yet held the weight of the world on his shoulders, and who was willing to risk and lose life to give others a chance at it. Clearly, the reality of Christ has a "Return On Investment" that would not be attractive to the big banks. They are two very different ideas of what's "priceless."

So, as a Christ-follower, what does it mean to live a truly "priceless" life as a redemptive approach to public life, one that does not hinge on buying or being bought? It involves a recognition of our imposed consumer identity, a reassessment of what we believe makes us and others whole, and a refusal to worship the consumer idol. This, of course, is easier said than done, especially when our pervasive addiction to consumerism does not stand out in society as a problem, but rather as a sign of success. It is also difficult when many of our jobs, our very livelihoods, are dedicated to pumping the consumer pedal. But the important thing is that we begin to shift our internal perceptions and think differently about how we do our jobs and the potential within them. If we each pay closer attention every day and increasingly dare to question the things we see going on within our own spheres of influence, then we will have made big strides.

Seeing Stuff for What It Is

The ultimate goal of my corporate work all those years had been to shape human behavior into a spending pattern, to categorize life into occasions to buy, to open up a bottomless hole of desire and then promise to fill it with something that leaves people ultimately unsatisfied, so their longings could be exploited again and again. We most openly witness the consequences of this daily carrot-dangling every year when "Black Friday" rolls around and people trample, pepper spray, and even kill one another over slightly discounted products. The average, day-to-day effect of consumerism may seem less harmful, but considering that we may see up to 5,000 ads a day, depending on our habits, it becomes a powerful force without our realizing it. When our vulnerabilities, our need for love, and our tender psychological wounds are consistently addressed by buying temporary relief, beauty, or distractions, dangerous compensational behaviors are formed and normalized. Even considering the relational, emotional tug of the MasterCard "priceless" commercials, the experiential payoff of each sweet scenario depends upon a preceding purchase path. Dependent upon credit worth and buoyed by buying power, the moment of truth is based on lies.

Yet at this point in human history, we hardly know any other way to find relief and we rarely recognize true, lasting beauty. Hence, there are office buildings full of untold numbers of people whose job it is to keep us crawling down the rabbit hole on a wild chase for some semblance of wholeness, to hold up the distorted mirror to our faces, to incessantly fill our ears with a language crafted to our credit worth. Not to say that purchasing or having things is innately evil, or that the enjoyment we get from buying something we like is all bad. But our tendency to seek pleasure takes those good feelings and the sense of security we may get from the ability to buy things to new levels of dependence—when buying things becomes the only way we can find a fleeting moment of fulfillment, when we give more weight to our money and possessions than other aspects of life, when our reality becomes more stuff-centric than purpose-centric. It is increasingly easy to become confused about the purpose of being, especially when the Kardashians are American role models and the typical politician or presidential candidate has multiple homes. It is rare to find people in the spotlight or in positions of power who model true dedication to purpose. Rarely do we find corporations that consider the human soul and the plight of other creatures in their business plans. Our very sense of awareness about what we watch, what we consume, who we listen to and emulate can make a big difference. How can we seek to follow Christ when we are gorging ourselves with the identities and priorities of antithetical examples? One way is to revisit what we really believe it means to love God.

At Union Theological Seminary, where I studied for the ministry, the academics did not tend toward sentimentality, but I learned more in those three years about the action of loving God with all my heart and loving my neighbor as myself—the social justice aspects of my Christian faith—than in the lifetime of Christianity I had claimed. My understanding of Christianity shifted from a Jesus I was supposed to "believe in" or else go to hell, to a Jesus who called me to actually emulate him, called me to awareness of injustice and action on behalf of others. This is not that self-help Jesus who is like a magic genie of happiness for the individual who stays on the straight and narrow and prays diligently for good things to happen. Nor is this the one who keeps his judging eye on everyone and whose primary interest is in whether we utter a curse word or go to Sunday school. The Christian idea that we are to strive to "become more like Jesus" has little to do with leading a perfect, sinless life or praying dictated words for personal salvation, and everything to do with, well, acting like Jesus. Jesus inaugurated his ministry with words from Isaiah 61, saying: "The Spirit of the Lord is on me, because [the Lord] has anointed me to proclaim good news to the poor. [The Lord] has sent me to proclaim freedom for the prisoners and recovery of sight for the blind, to set the oppressed free, to proclaim the year of the Lord's favor" (Lk. 4:18–19).

The foremost concern of Jesus was addressing human oppression and need.

I also confirmed in my own experience the presence of the Holy Spirit I learned about back in my early upbringing as a Southern Baptist in Alabama. It is a deep and wide Spirit that lives within each of us if we will allow room for it, and it will not let us live by any other standard than that of the greatest commandment without sounding an alarm in the core of our beings. However, it *can* easily get drowned out by other voices, images, demands, and norms. Still, consider Mary, who got a visit from an angel who told her this Holy Spirit would come upon her, and she would conceive and give birth to Jesus. And even before Mary delivered Jesus, Luke had her deliver a song, one "Magnificat." Have you ever stopped to hear what she really says in Luke 1:46–55?

"My soul glorifies the Lord
   and my spirit rejoices in God my Savior,
for he has been mindful
   of the humble state of his servant.
From now on all generations will call me blessed,
   for the Mighty One has done great things for me—
   holy is his name.
His mercy extends to those who fear him,
   from generation to generation.
He has performed mighty deeds with his arm;
   he has scattered those who are proud in their inmost thoughts.
He has brought down rulers from their thrones
   but has lifted up the humble.
He has filled the hungry with good things
   but has sent the rich away empty.
He has helped his servant Israel,
   remembering to be merciful
to Abraham and his descendants forever,
just as he promised our ancestors."

Mary is not waxing poetic about the joys of pregnancy or her personal salvation. She is making a very clear political statement. God is concerned with the poor and the hungry and has filled her womb with the one who would rise up and speak out against social injustice and economic oppression, and die for showing the rest of us humans how to do it. Is that why most of us do not emulate Jesus? Fear of scarcity, fear of poverty, fear of death?

By comparison to our lifespans today, Jesus only had a short time on earth, and his ministry is estimated to only have been about three years. But every moment of Jesus' life was spent challenging the status quo to help us imagine a better way.

Moments of Hole-ness and Wholeness

MasterCard has kept the "priceless" campaign going for well over a decade now, because it works really well for selling financial products and making big profits. But if the moments we are all taught to cherish as a society are dependent upon a purchase pattern, what does that make our experiences? What does that make our memories? What does that make us? If a person does not have the means to purchase the products and services we believe are needed to create the ideal moments we see in advertisements, what kind of life can he imagine for himself in relation to all that he sees around him? If he cannot buy what it takes to live this particular life, does he fail to really live? If a person chooses to be at home more and present for her family, but therefore cannot work enough hours to give her children the newest clothes or toys or lessons, what kind of person is she? Are her priorities out of order? Because she does not match the consumer schema, has she failed to give her children an ideal life or good memories? If her family does not make a blip on our consumer indices, do they exist? Society may see people who earn less and consume less as less successful than others, but are they also less human? Some of the most powerful, profitable industries do not even register the existence of people who do not fall into their target markets based on certain socio-economic barometers and buying history. Media messages do not speak to them, but mock them with images of a "perfect" life they will never have. A whole world moves past them and does not see them.

Sound familiar? These are the people about whom Jesus was most concerned in the New Testament, those who fell into the margins, those who did not make a blip, those who were left in the dust and not seen. In the first century, it was the widows, the orphans, those crushed by Roman taxation, those who were blind or lame. Today, many additional sets of circumstances can define the disenfranchised. Jesus was about restoring them into community. He operated by reminding us what it means to be human and pointing us back to our intrinsic value. As Christ followers, we must reinvent restoration for the twenty-first century. Each of us has a unique contribution to make, unique actions to take in our families, offices, and communities.

Yet our normalized consumer culture has an edge in that it is omnipresent, easily accessible for many of us, and frankly just a matter of course. It becomes hard to look past the construction of what we have and what we buy, to see what really makes up who we are. In some communities, we may notice a trend of judging a person's morality and level of "blessing" by the evidence of possessions and the ability to maintain certain social standards. Why do we tend to see our level of ability to be consumers as a blessing from God? It has been an odd yet longstanding, unspoken superstition that those who live uprightly can be identified by their possessions, by the appearance of success and "having it all together." We even tend to judge ourselves this way, thinking that if we backtrack in any area of our lives, that if we are not consistently upwardly mobile, that we must not be fulfilling God's will for our lives, must not be doing something right, must not be blessed to the extent of others who have more. We forget that we are valued because we are God's children, and that our purpose in life may not lead us to a place where we can afford the same house, the same cars, the same luxuries as our peers.

Why is it so hard to keep in mind that our purpose is more important than our purchasing power? Some of it may trace back to early biblical tales of God promising to prosper those who did God's bidding, whether with livestock, healthy crops, many servants or slaves, or large numbers of children and descendants, all of which translated equally into wealth and the ability to buy and multiply, and wield the power that ability affords. Some of it also derives from the concept of the American Dream and the pursuit of happiness embedded in our nation's history as symbols of a new world of unprecedented freedom and long-awaited opportunity to make one's own way, whether in our religious practices, our educational endeavors, or our business and financial goals. But what happens a couple hundred years later when personal liberty and autonomy are taken for granted by a large part of the population, especially those in power? What happens when the definition of happiness changes, growing ever more consumption-oriented, and all-consuming?

Worshiping the Dream?

Although the United States subscribes to a separation of church and state, our national patriotism and its associated elements of doctrine—such as the "American Dream" and the "Pioneer Spirit"—nonetheless have a relationship to all other structures of society, much like that of the heart to all other organs of the body. The core, or heart, of our nation has throughout history pumped the lifeblood of the "American Way" into our secular lifestyles, our trade practices and economics, our business sector, our political scene, our governing structures, and our state educational systems. The American Way is a common national ethos in play since the seventeenth century that is based in American exceptionalism, and derives from the expectation that unbridled national economic production and expansion, added to the individual formula of willing self-exploitation of one's talent and level of ability, plus ruthless engagement in fierce competition, plus dedication to incessant, tireless hard work, will invariably equal a high standard of living for anyone who can "do what it takes" to "make it happen."

We are taught that this equation equals "life to the fullest." That notion is solidified by our families, our friends, our social experiences, our media intake, and our education. If not before, then the training certainly begins within the structure of kindergarten, an early childhood education concept we borrowed from the Germans, the same institution that was hijacked at one time by Hitler in order to shape the minds of children tightly around his evil, corrupt nationalistic ideals, citing the virtue of tender minds "consciously shaped according to principles which are recognized as correct." As the leader of the Nazi Teacher's League, Hans Schemm, put it: "Those who have the youth on their side control the future."[1]

Advertisers know this concept well, and are investing heavily to create brand loyalty at alarmingly early ages. Today, children consume a lot of media via television, the Internet, videos, and games, and since an increasing number of kids actually possess significant access to parents' cash and credit, advertising executives are targeting messages to people as young as three years old. The Campaign for a Commercial-Free Childhood is kept tremendously busy fighting the barrage of ads targeted specifically at kids. For example, Florida, Kentucky, Missouri, New York, Rhode Island, and Washington are all currently considering bills that would allow ads on school buses for everything from junk food to violent and sexualized media. The Campaign is also proposing changes to the Children's Online Privacy Protection Act that provide important safeguards protecting children from the technologies and techniques that advertisers use to identify, track, and target kids online and on mobile devices. The seduction starts at birth, and today there are many easy avenues for the consumer voice to travel into young minds.

Today, standard consumer ideology echoed from the classroom to the desktop to the pulpit to the political podium teaches us early on to dream the "American Dream," which by its modern definition makes our top priority and life goal that of procuring property, wealth, and uncountable personal possessions. The fondly remembered "pioneer spirit" is hailed as the undaunted courage of ancestors who conquered the great unknown and wrangled it into something we now have a right to consume in its entirety. The seductive undertones of aggression and entitlement hiding in stories of forcible land theft and unconscionable genocide infiltrate our psyches without the benefit of being raised into the light and exposed for what they are, and, hence, it is for these elements of the human spirit we annually give "Thanksgiving."

Today, another version of the pioneer spirit moves corporations to propose dangerous projects such as the Keystone XL Oil Pipeline, which would expose miles of Midwestern terrain to crude oil leaks, and which originally would have run right through the sensitive Ogallala aquifer—the single most important source of water in the American High Plains region, providing nearly all the water for residential, industrial, and agricultural use in the region. This is a perfect example of how profits come before people in shockingly counter-intuitive ways, especially under the pressure of competitive markets and corrupt politics. On the surface, pioneering capitalist ideas can seem innocently inspiring and more noble than evil, but underneath in the dim depths, a giant iceberg of greed and self-aggrandizement moves like a monolith, ready to blow a fatal hole in the delicate ship of human decency, and, sometimes, human well-being.

These events should bring Mary's Magnificat back to our minds. God sent Jesus into the world in human trappings to challenge those in positions of power who would operate by methods of control, of starving the people and the land, of exploiting the vulnerable who could not do anything about their plans for profit. Becoming aware of such issues, educating ourselves, standing up and speaking out against the misuse of power and profits, and acting to stop them are all things Jesus showed us how to do, and then said, "Follow me." He met all of the disciples at their places of labor, work, and livelihood and said, "Put it down and follow me." Not, "Pray this prayer," or, "Attend this Bible study," or, "Only associate with people just like you,"... but, "Follow me."

The church in America has not been exempt from buying into consumerism and destructive counterfeit realities, as we all know. There are many familiar criticisms of Christianity in the U.S. today, particularly the legacy of holding to ideologies that are fatal to the human spirit, such as racism, sexism, exceptionalism, the bizarrely anti-Jesus-like support of ongoing war, and a blindness to global human rights violations blatantly antithetical to the message of the Gospel. American ideologies of the individual pursuit of happiness (which is popularly equated to power, money, excess comfort and privilege, and the potential for fame and notoriety), and the resulting competition and fear, the myth of scarcity, and the obsession with self-preservation continue to set the common lifestyle standard. The consumer mindset says that we have not just the right to the pursuit of happiness as stated in our Declaration of Independence, but it also plays upon our drive to "do what it takes" to "make it happen," to compete, fight hard, and, above all else, *win*—academically, athletically, socially, physically, financially, and in our careers. Where in the definition of "win" does caring about the needs of others come in? Why wouldn't the people who make up the Christian church likewise respond like programmed robots to these implicit, unquestioned, shallow assumptions, and fall in line with the American status quo?

Is it any wonder that modern churches allow the American Way to thwart them from the true goal of actually following the way of Christ (going where he goes) and functioning as his body in the world (doing what he does)? After all, most people under the influence of nationalistic American ideology would say that Jesus didn't win. How can turning the other cheek, taking the risk of speaking out on behalf of others, and ultimately dying be seen as success? Consumerism and capitalism are based in a free market where we see who can win, weeding out the less efficient and profitable options—even if the less efficient and profitable companies are considering the safety of creation, and considering the needs of people who do not seem to "count" by any other standards. The paradox is obvious. Was it Jesus who lived backward back then? Is it we who live backward now? Are we following Jesus or are we worshiping the "Dream"?

In light of the great commandment to love God with all our hearts and to love our neighbors as ourselves, it's easy to see that many (most?) of our societal norms are backward—the consumption of far more than is needed by many, while others barely survive or do not survive; the widespread preferential treatment of people who exhibit certain physical qualities or social status; an economic system based on the callous exploitation of animals, natural resources, and the beauty and utility of creation. Yet we are impervious, desensitized, senseless. We don't get it. Besides, giving of ourselves to nature, to others, without expectation of a generous ROI would threaten our precious "standard of living." Yet this was not the expectation or the standard by which God came to Earth.

This, it seems to me, is also the message of Occupy Wall Street, which is a movement harshly condemned by many Christians as an "orgy" or a "bunch of lazy hippies." Yet if we set our preconceived notions aside and look deeper than a few isolated incidents of individual impropriety, we see that there is a valuable spirit that will not let the occupiers rest in a world of gross inequality, unquestioned greed, and oppression of the vulnerable as it stands. It is an undeniably holy spirit. Media, politicians, and pundits are continually confused about what OWS is up to; however, OWS is simply refusing to be forced to think and act backward in order to succeed.

While criticized for a perceived lack of leadership, decorum, demands, or action plans, OWS picked up on something far more profound, something that has the potential to change the world. If it came in the form of a business plan or a savvy political scheme led by a select few who had the power or clout to make it take off in popularity, it would not be a forward-thinking idea with a better sense of priorities than our current systems. This movement had to live into the paradox the same way Christ came in a baby's body, laid in an embarrassingly smelly manger, and surrounded himself in his adulthood with an unwieldy, often irresponsible group of ne'er-do-wells who meant well. And OWS looks as suspect as Jesus did to the haughty folks who wondered what good could come out of Nazareth. But isn't it oxymoronic to demand compassion? Isn't it counter-intuitive to carefully construct a publicity campaign for spontaneous acts of passionate protest, for extemporaneous takeovers to inspire extreme makeovers in the most crucial sectors of society?

Occupy Faith NYC, a multi-faith group of clergy who support the new democratic spirit of Occupy Wall Street and associated groups around the country, sensed the subversive potential present in the rag-tag appearances of the movement. Faith communities of all types have unified behind OWS because the movement comes the closet of any effort of late—religious or nonreligious—to illuminating the sheer life-and-death nature of our choice to obey (or not) the principles of economic justice, social responsibility and merciful dealings that all scriptures and interreligious ideologies promote. In the Bible, God asks the people repeatedly to care about one another as they care about themselves, to want the best for everyone regardless of circumstance, even it if means compromising or taking less than one might believe one has earned or otherwise deserves. Is it impossible for human beings to actually care about one another? Or it is that many of us who are powerful—or even just comfortable—don't know how to care for others because we don't know what it means to truly care about ourselves anymore?

In his new book *The Price of Civilization*, world-renowned economic advisor and scholar Jeffrey Sachs describes the current economic crisis as a moral crisis, a product of "the decline of civic virtue among America's political and economic elite."[2] He begins his entire narrative by saying:

> A society of markets, laws, and elections is not enough if the rich and powerful fail to behave with respect, honesty, and compassion toward the rest of society and toward the world. America has developed the world's most competitive market society but has squandered

its civic virtue along the way. Without restoring an ethos of social responsibility, we cannot experience a meaningful and sustained economic recovery.[3]

Before we fix our glare on politicians, Wall Street, capitalism, corporations, and absurdly compensated CEOs alone, Sachs reminds us that "[the] breakdown of politics also implicates the broad public. American society is too deeply distracted by our media-drenched consumerism to maintain the habits of effective citizenship."[4] People generally know more about "American Idol" than American socio-economic policies and political procedures. People generally buy into more of the reality show's ideas, brands, personas, and products, too. So, which one shapes our goals and priorities? As Christ-followers in particular, Christ is supposed to shape our goals, priorities, and behaviors. Shouldn't we be on the cutting edge of leadership in civic virtue, social responsibility, respect, honesty, and, most of all, compassion? Shouldn't this be evident in our political choices, our vocations, and practices of consumption?

Jeremy Rifkin, president of the Foundation of Economic Trends and advisor to the European Union, wrote *The Empathic Civilization*. He argued that the overall arc of history bends toward an increasingly compassionate and unified global culture, if for no other reason than our common, ill-fated environmental conundrum. Rifkin points out that no matter who or where we are, we all ultimately want and need the same things: to keep our planet from self-destructing and to ensure positive economic, social, and environmental prospects for our children and those we love.

To realize our shared goal, it is imperative to recognize certain realities. Individual or nationalistic advantages are at stake. These competing advantages make agreeing on the right course of action a contentious proposition. Our fate as a species depends on our ability to loosen our tightly wound self-interests and cooperate. Only then can we pull off the sizable revolution that will be "saving the world" and restoring humanity to a sustainable future.

As a pastor, a theologian, and an activist, I have to believe Rifkin is right: human beings are on a trajectory of experience, growth, and change. More intensely with each passing decade, this trajectory evokes our empathic sensibilities, encouraging the practice of compassion toward the "other." The advent of technology fosters global interconnectedness, and the rate of realizing the benefits of collective care increases with each passing day. To propel us along this trajectory, we must face challenges, correct setbacks, and point out our missteps to one another. We must speak out about systemic malfunctions. "Christian charity" cannot sustain us; the systems that either provide or deny avenues for education, training, support, and opportunities must be reworked to promote human dignity and allow real change that lasts. This is why we urgently need protests, movements, occupations. This is how humankind provokes the movement of God in the world:

> The LORD rises to argue [the] case;
>   [a]nd stands to judge the peoples...
> It is you who have devoured the vineyard;
>   the spoil of the poor is in your houses.
> What do you mean by crushing my people,
>   by grinding the face of the poor? says the Lord God of Hosts.
>   (Isaiah 3:13–15, NRSV)

The tempting truth is that, in our profit-driven world, thinking backward makes bank, and consumerism is the national religion. As people of faith, alive with the Spirit, we are called to live out of our conscience into a new consciousness. This is the coming of a new reality that some may call the kingdom of God, some may call social responsibility, and some may call an empathic evolution of humanity. God's presence is called forth by our rejection of the status quo. We follow Jesus in our desire for a new way of being. It is easier said than done, but didn't Jesus tell us that following him would be like that?

22

Standing Fast Against Torture

David P. Gushee

Introduction

In August 1550 the Dominican friar Bartolomé de Las Casas was summoned by King Charles V of Spain to debate Catholic theologian Juan Ginés de Sepúlveda on this question: "Is it lawful for the king of Spain to wage war on the Indians, before preaching the faith to them, in order to subject them to his rule, so that afterwards they may be more easily instructed in the faith?"[1] The judges included fourteen of the most eminent theologians, lawyers, and government officials of the entire Spanish kingdom.

The contestants, who disagreed sharply over the matter they were discussing, never appeared before the council at the same time. Sepúlveda summarized his case for the affirmative in three hours. Las Casas came the next day and made the case for the negative by reading a prepared manuscript over five days, until the judges couldn't take it anymore. (And that was not all. There was a second round of this disputation, which lasted more than a month in the spring of 1551.)

Why do I tell you this story? Because I have been writing about Las Casas for a new book.[2] He is a hero for me. Figures such as him have been formative in shaping my Christian ethics. The main reason is because this story strikes me as having some obvious parallels to the debate about the moral legitimacy of torture that we continue to have in the United States today.

Those parallels include:

- Both cases involve the question of the use of force by the state to accomplish its valued ends;
- Both cases have sometimes evoked reasoning that mixes legal, factual, moral, and even religious claims, including the use of Just War Theory;

- Both cases were debated by churchmen with an interest and commitment to what would today be called public policy, in debates that were of interest to both church and state.

I would suggest one final parallel:

- Respectfully but clearly, I must say that both cases are morally repugnant. I believe that one day our Christian descendants will look back on our early twenty-first-century evangelical Christian debates about torture with the same sense of repugnance that they have when they consider the Las Casas-Sepulveda debates of 1550. They will wonder how torture could even have been an open question.

But the debates of 1550–1551 happened. The debate about torture has happened. This chapter is a kind of retrospective. I am looking back on an argument that riveted the nation about six years ago. With the Bush Administration long gone, it might seem we have no need to continue this old conversation. But the issue remains alive, opinion remains divided, and evangelical Christians as a whole have not yet stood fast against torture.

I will offer my paper in two rounds. I will do so by first summarizing the case for "enhanced interrogation techniques" as practiced for several years by the Bush-Cheney Administration. My core source here will be the massive 2010 book by former Bush official Marc Thiessen, *Courting Disaster*.[3] I have chosen this book because it is fairly recent, it is thorough, it is warmly endorsed by both Dick Cheney and Donald Rumsfeld, it is written by someone with inside information and direct contact with the principal figures involved, and it clearly represents the views of that part of the former administration most ardently supportive of the "tough" interrogation policies.

After summarizing Thiessen's claims, I will offer rebuttals.

In a brief concluding section, I will reflect on what can be learned about the church, the discipline of Christian ethics, and Christian engagement with U.S. public policy through this analysis. It is there that I will speak to issues of methodology, passions, and loyalties.

You will notice two methodological moves from the beginning.

First, I will stipulate that the issue I am considering is not an abstraction called torture, but instead the moral justifiability of known and documented Bush-Cheney interrogation practices that were called by that administration "enhanced interrogation techniques" (EIT). I loathe the term and believe it be to a euphemism for torture.

However, I will accept for purposes of discussion the existence of the term and will stipulate that it included, as officially approved individual techniques or in combination, the following: *the "suffocation by water" practice known as "waterboarding," continuous solitary confinement and indefinite incommunicado detention, hooding and other forms of sensory deprivation, extended sleep deprivation and use of ear splitting loud music, "wallings" (or "beatings by use of a collar," involving detainees being propelled forcefully against walls), face and belly slapping, grabbing, beating and kicking, confinement in a box, prolonged standing in stress positions, prolonged forced nudity, exposure to cold temperatures and cold water, prolonged use of handcuffs and shackles, threats of various kinds, forced shaving, and dietary deprivation/manipulation.*[4]

It is these specific governmentally authorized practices that I want you to have in mind. Ethics is done better in the concrete than the abstract. Therefore I will call these concrete practices periodically to our attention.

In a confidential February 2007 report from the International Committee of the Red Cross to the CIA Inspector General that leaked to the press, these techniques were named and their use on fourteen specific "high-value" detainees then being held at the U.S. facility at Guantanamo Bay documented. (Various combinations of these techniques were used on far more than these fourteen men.) The following summary evaluation of how to classify these acts was offered by the Red Cross, the body among whose official duties in international affairs is to monitor compliance with the Geneva Conventions and the treatment of prisoners of war:

> The allegations of ill-treatment of the detainees indicate that, in many cases, the ill-treatment to which they were subjected while held in the CIA program, either singly or in combination, constituted torture. In addition, many other elements of the ill-treatment, either singly or in combination, constituted cruel, inhuman, or degrading treatment.[5]

The authority of the Red Cross on such matters is sufficient that this report in itself gives reason for high Bush-Cheney Administration officials to fear prosecution for human rights violations, including torture. Again, rather than debate terminology, I will merely stipulate that my topic is the arsenal of so-called "enhanced interrogation techniques" employed by the Bush Administration, confirmed by Marc Thiessen, documented in Administration memos that have now been publicly released, and described in this 2007 Red Cross report.

Second, until the end of the chapter I will not entertain or make a religious argument of any type. I am doing this as a thought experiment. I want to see if specifically Christian reasoning makes any real difference in the moral debate about torture. It certainly hasn't seemed to make any real difference in helping most evangelical Christians stand fast against torture.

Summary of Thiessen's
Pro-"Enhanced Interrogation Techniques" Case

Marc Thiessen's 484-page book offers every conceivable argument for the counterterrorism policies developed and employed by the Bush Administration. Sifting through the many hundreds of claims made in the book yields what in my view are the following major assertions:

Enhanced interrogation techniques were necessary and effective.[6]

They were deployed to break hardened terrorists who had been trained to resist less coercive interrogation techniques, such as those traditionally employed by the U.S. military and the FBI. In a large number of significant cases these new techniques succeeded in gaining valuable intelligence. This intelligence enabled U.S. officials to better understand the internal structure, operations, and strategy of al Qaeda. It also was pivotal in leading to the disruption of several specific terror plots targeting U.S. interests overseas as well as in the United States. Less coercive methods had not gained this kind of information in the past and were not effective in gaining this information after 9/11. The new techniques contributed greatly to the fact that no successful terror attacks have occurred on our soil since 9/11. They have therefore made us safer. We continue to benefit from their residual effects even though they have been mistakenly rolled back in recent years by law and Obama executive branch policy.

Enhanced interrogation techniques were legal.

By definition, this claim means that those acts approved as enhanced interrogation techniques were not torture, because torture is a felony under U.S. law.

Thiessen's legal claims involve several different kinds of arguments. He says first that they were legal because they did not violate U.S. statutory law, such as the 1996 War Crimes Act, which makes torture a felony offense. The reason we know that they did not violate the War Crimes Act is primarily because this was the ruling offered by the authoritative Office of Legal Counsel (OLC) in the Justice Department in memos upon which the CIA and the Administration relied in developing and implementing interrogation policies from early 2002. If the OLC declared the specific acts authorized by the Bush-Cheney Administration to not constitute torture, this is authoritative.[7]

To the argument that the treatment of detainees violated the standards of the Geneva Conventions, notably Common Article 3, which bans "outrages upon personal dignity" and "humiliating and degrading treatment" of prisoners of war, Thiessen offers two main retorts.[8] The first is that the Bush Administration was correct in concluding that the Geneva Conventions do not apply to members of non-uniformed terrorist organizations. They apply only to uniformed military personnel. The second, made in passing, is that these Geneva standards are "vague and undefined."[9] Thiessen notes but does not rely on the more aggressive claims made in the (in)famous 2002 John Yoo/Jay Bybee "Standards" memo, in which the OLC authors argued for expansive Commander in Chief powers, including the claim that the Constitution would permit the president to trump torture laws if necessary for national security.[10]

Thiessen does acknowledge the existence of events that occurred in interrogation or imprisonment contexts during the Bush-Cheney years that were unlawful in that they violated the limits clarified by the OLC and established by the CIA and the Pentagon for actual interrogations—or were simply abuses, such as what occurred at Abu Ghraib prison in Iraq.[11] The fact that investigations and sometimes prosecutions were undertaken of those who violated the legal standards, in his view, can be adduced as evidence for the lawfulness of the *approved* techniques and a general commitment to the rule of law on the part of the Bush Administration.

Enhanced interrogation techniques were tough but humane.

Thiessen concedes that these techniques, named by the Red Cross as "in many cases…constitut[ing] torture," were "tough." He concedes that they were "unpleasant."[12] But he also echoes an interrogator's claims that they were "very respectful,"[13] that they did not gratuitously inflict pain, and that they were undertaken by highly trained interrogation personnel monitored by medical professionals.[14] He goes further to claim that at least one high value detainee, Abu Zubaydah, actually thanked his interrogators for the enhanced interrogation techniques used on him. On the basis of conversations with interrogators, Thiessen claims that the reason for Zubaydah's gratitude is that al Qaeda operatives were taught that they were morally obligated to resist to the limits of their endurance, but that after they had reached those limits they were permitted to speak the truth to their captors. Therefore the use of enhanced interrogation techniques actually lifted the burden of resistance off the shoulders of al Qaeda members, which was a relief to them.[15]

Enhanced interrogation techniques were and are supported by the American people.

Thiessen reports the results of Pew Research Center polling over the last four years.[16] Pew has framed its questions in terms of actual support for "torture" rather than EIT. In the April 2009 poll, 71 percent of Americans say that "torture to gain important information from suspected terrorists is justified." (That included 15 percent who answered "often," 34 percent who answered "sometimes," and 22 percent who answered "rarely.") Only 25 percent answered "never." He cites a variety of other polls that reached similar results. The "never" torture group has not reached higher than 36 percent in any recent poll. Thiessen concludes that most Americans agree with the policies developed by the Bush Administration and employed by the CIA until they were (mistakenly) terminated.

Enhanced interrogation techniques were consistent with our nation's highest moral values and ideals.

Thiessen quotes some Bush Administration officials, such as former Director of National Intelligence Mike McConnell, who do accept that there was something of a tradeoff between the value of enhanced security and the value of upholding our highest moral ideals.[17] Former Vice President Dick Cheney is also quoted to suggest that EIT was actually the proper *moral* choice. Cheney claims that it would in fact have been immoral to forego the opportunity to collect intelligence using these tough techniques. Failure to do so, he says, would have violated the oath of office that both he and the President had taken. Cheney does not use tradeoff language to describe these policies.[18]

Enhanced interrogation techniques bear no real resemblance to torture as practiced by totalitarian regimes or the Spanish Inquisition.

Critical comparisons of Bush-Cheney EIT to the torture techniques employed by odious regimes such as Nazi Germany, Imperial Japan, Pol Pot's Cambodia, or the Spanish Inquisition are important enough to Thiessen that he feels compelled to raise them and respond.[19] Therefore his book includes lengthy descriptions of these techniques, including especially their version of water tortures,[20] which he wants to distinguish clearly from what he understands to be the quite different techniques employed by the United States in the administration he served.

Rebuttals

Let me offer the following brief assessment of each of these claims. Again, I am bracketing all specifically Christian analysis or commentary at this time.

Enhanced interrogation techniques were necessary and effective.

Whether "enhanced interrogation techniques" were necessary is a matter of dispute among intelligence professionals. Throughout his book, Thiessen quotes a large number of high-ranking Bush Administration officials who make the claims that these techniques were necessary because less coercive techniques did not work. Of course, they were and are deeply committed to such a belief, and in some cases they may face legal action if those claims were to be negated in a court of law.

Among the interrogators who have become fairly well-known for rejecting these claims are Ali Soufan and Matthew Alexander.

Ali Soufan, a retired FBI agent with extensive field experience as an interrogator, has claimed that his interrogation of high value detainee Abu Zubaydah had resulted in actionable intelligence, such as discovering the identity and mission of now-convicted terrorist José Padilla; and that thereafter, when he was taken off the case and CIA waterboarding was performed on Abu Zubaydah, the flow of intelligence stopped.[21] Thiessen claims that Soufan is incorrect in these assertions.[22] But Soufan's claims were supported by the CIA Inspector General's 2004 Report, the 2008 Department of Justice's Inspector General Report, and the Department of Justice's 2009 Office of Professional Responsibility Report.[23]

Matthew Alexander (pseudonym), who played a key role in tracking down Iraqi terrorist leader Abu Musab al-Zarqawi, says this intelligence was achieved "using interrogation methods that had nothing to do with torture."[24] Other former interrogators and intelligence officers from the military, FBI, and CIA have made similar claims about some of their own work. Alexander is a loud and visible opponent of EIT and torture.

Whether enhanced interrogation techniques were effective in disrupting terrorist plots is also hotly disputed. Certainly, in some cases leads supposedly offered through EIT were based on false information. One such case was that of Ibn al-Shaykh al-Libi who had confessed under EIT that Iraq had trained al Qaeda in the use of weapons of mass destruction. This was then used as justification for the subsequent invasion of Iraq. Al-Libi's confession is now known to be false.[25]

In 2007 the U.S. Intelligence Science Board, sponsored by the Defense Intelligence Agency and the Pentagon's Counterintelligence Field Activity, reported that almost no scientific evidence supports the U.S. intelligence community's use of controversial interrogation techniques in the fight against terrorism, and that some painful and coercive approaches could actually hinder the ability to get good information.[26] The general tenor of the results of this authoritative study is indicated by the following comment: "There is little or no research to indicate whether [coercive] techniques succeed… [But the preponderance of reports seems to weigh against their effectiveness… Psychological theory…and related research suggest that coercion or pressure can actually *increase* a source's resistance and determination not to comply (emphasis in the original)."[27]

The claim that enhanced interrogation techniques have made us safer depends in part on the disputed factual claim just discussed. It also depends on a very difficult calculation of the long-term implications of the use of such harsh and tough techniques, especially on the U.S. moral standing in the world. Sometimes this is described in terms of U.S. "soft power," including the power of our good name and any good will (or bad will) generated by our actions. The perception of straying from the moral high ground affects the opinions of others about the United States and therefore affects our interests.

Enhanced interrogation techniques were legal.

Thiessen and I concur that torture is a felony in violation of the War Crimes Act. We do not concur in the judgment that because the Office of Legal Counsel in a series of memos ruled that specific interrogation techniques were lawful, that they were indeed lawful. More precisely, I concur with former Bush Administration State Department legal adviser Philip Zelikow in his secret memo from 2005 that the OLC's interpretation of the Constitution and the War Crimes Act was not a reasonable interpretation. Zelikow has since described the actions authorized as torture.[28] I conclude that the way the Bush Administration was able to label its menu of enhanced interrogation techniques as not constituting torture was by narrowing the definition of torture in an illegitimate way. That itself may be unlawful, and it certainly does not render the authorized actions lawful.[29]

As for the Geneva Conventions, I simply side with the Supreme Court in its 2006 ruling in the *Hamdan* case that contrary to what the Bush Administration advocated, the customary laws of war apply also to the "War on Terror," which includes the Geneva Conventions, as these have been incorporated into the ordinary laws of war and the statutory Uniform Code of Military Justice.[30] The basic principle is that the President is not simply permitted to set aside U.S. legal obligations due to the supposed exigencies of the War on Terror.

As to Thiessen's acknowledgment of events that occurred in interrogation or imprisonment contexts during the Bush-Cheney years that were unlawful in violating even the (unreasonably) narrow limits as interpreted by the OLC and then established by the CIA and the Pentagon for actual interrogations, I say that history demonstrates that when regimes open the door to cruelty and torture they have rarely proven able to prevent its spread beyond the contexts and techniques originally intended. The fact, acknowledged by Thiessen, that at least one hundred prisoners died in American custody,[31] as well as the fact of well-documented abuses at Abu Ghraib and Guantanamo, such as religious and sexual humiliation,[32] supports my claim.

Enhanced interrogation techniques were tough but humane.

I am grateful that Thiessen concedes that *the "suffocation by water" practice known as "waterboarding," continuous solitary confinement and indefinite incommunicado detention, hooding and other forms of sensory deprivation, extended sleep deprivation and use of ear splitting loud music, "wallings" (or "beatings by use of a collar," involving detainees being propelled forcefully against walls), face and belly slapping, grabbing, beating and kicking, confinement in a box, prolonged standing in stress positions, prolonged forced nudity, exposure to cold temperatures and cold water, prolonged use of handcuffs and shackles, threats of various kinds, forced shaving, and dietary deprivation/manipulation*, were "tough" and "unpleasant." I find it hard to take seriously the claim that they were "very respectful." I doubt that there is a survivor of harsh, tough, enhanced interrogation techniques anywhere in the world who would claim that they felt respected in the process. Seriously, I doubt that any one of us—to speak of the Golden Rule for a moment—would believe that it would be very respectful to have such experiences inflicted on oneself, or one's son or daughter.

The claim that the techniques were developed and undertaken by highly trained interrogation personnel has been disputed numerous times. It is now well known that the CIA interrogation strategies were based on work done by psychologists James Mitchell and Bruce Jessen in the Air Force's Survival Evasion Resistance Escape (SERE) program.[33] Thiessen acknowledges the role of the SERE program in developing EIT.[34] The CIA contracted with the two psychologists to develop alternative, harsh interrogation techniques. Neither of these men had any experience in conducting interrogations; they simply reverse-engineered the SERE techniques. It was on this dubious basis that CIA interrogators were trained to use dubious techniques they had never employed before.[35]

The claim that the sessions were monitored by medical professionals, including physicians and psychologists, appears to have been true, but the professional associations of both groups have reaffirmed their absolute rejection of any legitimate involvement of medical professionals in these practices.[36]

The claim that Abu Zubaydah and other al Qaeda operatives were actually grateful to have the moral burden of continued resistance off their shoulders seems extremely hard to believe. If it is true, I would simply ask this question: if they were permitted to provide information when they "reached the limit of their ability to withhold it in the face of psychological and physical hardship," what does that say about the nature of the suffering we inflicted upon them?

Enhanced interrogation techniques are supported by the American people.

I accept the fact that after ten years of Fox's *24*, with its hourly torture scenes, and after just about as many years of being told by respected government officials that "enhanced interrogation techniques" are crucial to national security, a majority of Americans are unwilling to rule it out. The polls are reasonably consistent. I do not agree that this says anything valuable about the legality or morality of torture. It does say a lot about the power of media and leaders to degrade a nation's morality.

Enhanced interrogation techniques were consistent with our nation's moral values and ideals.

Let's postulate for argument's sake that X percent greater security on a given day in 2005 was purchased at the cost of edging closer to or over the moral line that separates tough interrogation from torture. Thiessen quotes some Bush Administration and Pentagon officials who explicitly state their willingness to buy this incrementally greater security at that price, as well as some who were not. If one takes the tradeoff view, then EIT would be described as the right thing to do *despite being inconsistent* with our nation's highest moral values and ideals.

Dick Cheney makes the stronger claim that EIT was actually the moral choice, because it would be immoral to forego the opportunity to collect intelligence using these tough techniques. The error in this reasoning is the reduction of morality to enhanced security, as if there were no other considerations involved in morality. Vice President Cheney has lost the tradeoff here.

I also note in passing that the weakness of the language of "moral ideals" is one reason why I never use the phrase. "Ideals" are a Greek rather than biblical concept, and their very airy perfection and unreachability makes it all too easy for us to sacrifice them in the world of the "real" as we understand it at the time.[37]

Enhanced interrogation techniques bear no real resemblance to torture as practiced by totalitarian regimes or the Spanish Inquisition.

For my money this is the most rhetorically interesting move Thiessen makes, and in some ways the most problematic. I believe he is successful in showing that, yes, the interrogation techniques authorized by the Bush Administration were not as severe as those employed by Nazi Germany, Imperial Japan, Pol Pot's Cambodia, or the Spanish Inquisition. This loses some of its force when we ask whether we really want to be involved in practices that bring to mind those tyrannical regimes and force such comparisons. This is a race to the bottom, and even the winner of such a contest loses.

Second, I can only ask the reader to compare the thorough descriptions offered by Thiessen of the various water tortures employed by these various police state regimes and of the waterboarding techniques we authorized and used. It's in chapter 4, called "You Did the Right Thing." After quoting long stretches of the 2005 Steven Bradbury OLC memo, which describes approved water suffocation techniques in excruciating detail, Thiessen says, "Any American who reads these words should take enormous comfort and pride in the care taken by the Justice Department and the CIA to ensure that the detainee is not harmed during the procedure."[38] On the contrary, precisely as an American, what I see is a bureaucratic and legalistic euphemizing and cleansing of a technique historically employed by some of the world's most abusive regimes. Thiessen wants me to feel comforted and proud. Instead I feel dirty and ashamed. I take no comfort at all.

Christian Reflections

I was initially intending to write an entirely separate section of this chapter on specifically Christian grounds for arguing for and against torture, or the Bush-Cheney "enhanced interrogation techniques."

Many readers of this manifesto will already be familiar with the kinds of Christian ethical arguments I and my colleagues have made against torture. You will have followed my work as president of Evangelicals for Human Rights, the predecessor organization to NEP. These include my 2006 *Christianity Today* article,[39] or our 2007 *Evangelical Declaration Against Torture.* The Declaration worked its way from a foundation in the God-given sacredness of each human life, through a defense of human rights, to a rejection of then-current administration policies as a violation of both. Readers may also be familiar with the kinds of counterarguments made by those who have criticized that declaration or my other writings about torture. In a 2009 presentation at the Society of Christian Ethics,[40] I grouped opposition to my arguments related to torture under ten primary headings:

1. Those who oppose Bush counter-terror and detainee policies are politically motivated "leftists."[41]
2. Those who oppose these policies are pacifists-in-disguise who do not support the legitimate use of force to defend our country.[42]
3. Torture is a much worse problem around the world, and especially on the part of the very terrorists we are capturing. That is where those worried about it should focus their attention. Failure to pay proper attention to such problems reveals that opponents are at least anti-Bush, if not anti-American.[43]
4. The evangelical anti-torture movement is divisive within the Christian community and should be dropped on grounds of Christian unity; besides, there are far more important concerns facing us.[44]
5. The struggle against Islamist terrorism is a new kind of war requiring new means.[45]
6. Terrorists are not protected by international law and its conventions.[46]
7. Those in the anti-torture movement have failed to define torture adequately.[47]
8. Just War Theory permits considerable coercion in defense of national security, the protection of which is government's primary responsibility.[48]
9. Any argument made about torture that is not offered within Just War Theory's canons of argumentation is by definition invalid. Our work approaching torture via a sanctity-of-life argument is overly emotive and even irrational.[49]
10. Some argue that torture (narrowly defined) should be banned and not employed; others argue that it should be banned in principle but possibly applied in emergency circumstances with later accountability.[50]

Arguments 1, 3, 5, 6, 7, and 10 are either suggested or addressed directly by Thiessen. I spared you some of that, but most of these claims are present, and I have sought to address his most substantive arguments. Argument 2 is untrue factually. Argument 4 is a red herring; differences of conviction within Christianity on moral issues exist, different people rank moral issues at different levels of significance, and to take a position on a disputed moral issue is not a violation of canons of Christian unity.

Arguments 8 and 9 related to Just War Theory are really the only serious arguments that have been made from an explicitly Christian perspective against the view taken in *EDAT* or in some of my other work about torture.

Let me take just a minute to comment at a metaethical level on the role of Just War Theory in Christian moral argument.

I respect Just War Theory. I see its value. But much of my work over the last several years has led me to deep suspicion of its continued employment as the default paradigm for all Christian moral reasoning about war and peace. As long ago as 2004 I argued that there was a fracture in Just War Theory between those who seem to find in it warrant for every American war and every tactic employed in every American war, and those who do not.[51] More recently in my work on the sacredness of life, understood broadly, I have seen historical examples of Just War Theory being deployed to justify every possible ridiculous battle during the Middle Ages, often in the name of Christ. This is not to mention the Crusades themselves, which were justified on just war grounds, or the wars of conquest in the New World, which had a whole lot of Crusade mentality going while also being justified on just war grounds. It may be appropriate for more than a little "hermeneutics of suspicion" to be employed in relation to the employment of Just War Theory, even on the part of those who, like myself, do not rule out the moral legitimacy of some uses of force by the state.

Just War Theory is one form of Christian tradition, borrowed and adapted from the classical world, handed down through Catholicism, borrowed and adapted further by evangelical Protestants, borrowed and adapted further again in U.S. military tradition and practice and in international law. It has value; rightly interpreted, I think its value would include its ability to generate a total rejection of torture. That is how it has been interpreted by such stalwart "just warriors" as James Turner Johnson of Princeton.[52]

Just War Theory is not divine revelation. It is not Scripture. It carries no intrinsic authority. Its capacity to help Christians discern right from wrong in the issue of war is limited. It is a form of moral reasoning about war. Human moral practices are shaped by more than our named and official forms of moral reasoning. Just War Theory in itself does not appear capable of preventing Christians from being swayed by their loyalties to nation or party or president, or by their passions of anger and grief and fear, such as those that swept our nation after 9/11. We are more than reasoning creatures, and the way we use our reason reflects our deepest loyalties, passions, trusts, and fears.[53] I believe those led us astray after 9/11.

The pro-EIT arguments of a Marc Thiessen, faithfully channeling Dick Cheney and Donald Rumsfeld, amount essentially to a utilitarian justification of a euphemism for torture in the name of national security. I think that most Christians who have supported EIT or torture itself have done the same thing but have dressed it up a bit with some Just War Theory. I think that distinctively Christian categories of thought have had little to nothing to contribute to the perspective of those Christians who have supported either EIT or torture.

These days Christian political theology and ethics evidences something of a recovery of a distinctive entity called *the church*. Stanley Hauerwas was a pioneer here. He has been followed more recently by all kinds of really fine theologians and ethicists who are trying to help the church recover its distinctive calling, identity, and witness. These are good developments.

For decades Christian moral thinkers have tagged along and tried to play the nation's political games in the way the nation's politicians and theorists played them. This has been true on the right and the left. We have offered a decorative veneer of legitimization to our favored party and politicians. We were helpful to Caesar as long as we delivered for Caesar some political cover or some access to a favored voting bloc. In return we got the illusion of access to power.

But the one, holy, catholic, and apostolic church has a different Lord, a different sacred text, a different mission, a different history, a different politics, a different accountability than does the American state, or any other one.

I am glad that on the issue of torture I have encountered numerous fine American citizens who are fully able to discover solely in the laws, traditions, interests, and values of America grounds for total opposition to torture by any name. I think these purely "secular" resources are and ought to be sufficient for public moral opposition to torture. I also see certain vulnerabilities in American moral resources and reasoning per se, notably the risk under conditions of fear that we will follow Dick Cheney in reducing all morality to the question of what will provide 100 percent security for the American people.

Here a church that knows who it is and *whose* it is ought to be able to feel the stirrings of its distinctive identity, calling, and mission. We are just a different kind of people than this. We just need to remember who we are. Maybe new evangelicals can help remind the church of its own identity.

In the face of the question of whether we who follow Christ can support the *"suffocation by water" practice known as "waterboarding," continuous solitary confinement and indefinite incommunicado detention, hooding and other forms of sensory deprivation, extended sleep deprivation and use of ear splitting loud music, "wallings" (or "beatings by use of a collar," involving detainees being propelled forcefully against walls), face and belly slapping, grabbing, beating and kicking, confinement in a box, prolonged standing in stress positions, prolonged forced nudity, exposure to cold temperatures and cold water, prolonged use of handcuffs and shackles, threats of various kinds, forced shaving, and dietary deprivation/manipulation*, I find myself driven back to a community that once thought like this:

> For since we…have learned from His teaching and His laws that evil ought not to be requited with evil, that it is better to suffer wrong than to inflict it, that we should rather shed our own blood than stain our hands and our conscience with that of another, an ungrateful world is now for a long period enjoying a benefit from Christ, inasmuch as by His means the rage of savage ferocity has been softened, and has begun to withhold hostile hands from the blood of a fellow-creature. —Arnobius (ca. 300), *Against the Heathen.*

Or maybe this:

> There is nothing remarkable in cherishing merely our own people with the due attentions of love, but that one might become perfect who should do something more than heathen men or publicans, one who, overcoming evil with good, and practicing a merciful kindness like that of God, should love his enemies as well… Thus the good was done to all men, not merely to the household of faith. —Cyprian (200–258), *Epistle to the Carthaginians.*[54]

It would be nice to hear a bit more of that part of our tradition as we, once again, Christian brothers and sisters, debate the fine points of the ethics of torture.

An earlier version of this chapter was published by the Huffington Post, *November 2010.*

Appendix

The New Evangelical Partnership for the Common Good: "Here We Stand"[1]

The following are important principles, issues, and causes we are pursuing in the name of Jesus Christ.

We stand *against human degradation and for the human rights of all people,* especially the rights of the most vulnerable and despised. We are working for human rights in areas such as torture, the conditions in our prisons, immigration, and religious freedom.

We stand *against war and for peacemaking.* We are committed to peacemaking efforts between the world's major religious traditions and especially in the Middle East, where tensions remain high. We are working toward nuclear disarmament and a world without nuclear weapons.

We stand *against the devaluing of human life and for a society in which no woman feels that abortion is her only choice.* We are involved in creative efforts to prevent unintended pregnancies, support pregnant women, improve our adoption laws and practices, and change cultural attitudes and practices—all with the primary goal of reducing the number of abortions in our country.

We stand *against environmental denialism and for God's endangered creation.* We are deeply involved in efforts to address major environmental challenges facing our world, including climate change, species loss, and green energy.

We stand *against needless human suffering due to lack of health care and for human health.* We are involved in efforts to expand health care access in the United States and around the world and to reduce the current threats to human health already present due to the growing toxicity of the environment that we are polluting.

We stand *against the collapse of marriage and for stronger family life.* We are involved in efforts to strengthen the fading institution of marriage and thereby protecting and enhancing the well-being of children. We do not believe that denigrating the dignity and denying the human rights of gays and lesbians is a legitimate part of a "pro-family" Christian agenda, and will work to reform Christian attitudes and treatment of lesbian and gay people.

We stand *against poverty and economic injustice and for dignified and decent economic conditions for all.* We seek to be involved in creative efforts to build a more fair and humane economic order here and around the world.

We stand *against tyranny and for democracy, justice, and the rule of law.* We are involved in efforts to protect and strengthen the culture of American democracy, the unique legacy of religious liberty in this land, and the always fragile rule of law. We look for ways to support indigenous efforts to advance democracy, religious liberty, public justice, and the rule of law in other lands.

Contributors

Paul Alexander serves as Professor of Christian Ethics and Public Policy at Palmer Theological Seminary of Eastern University in St. Davids, Pennsylvania.

The Rev. Jim Ball, Ph.D., is author of *Global Warming and the Risen Lord* and Executive Vice President for Public Policy and Climate Change at the Evangelical Environmental Network.

Cheryl Bridges Johns is Professor of Discipleship and Christian Formation at the Pentecostal Theological Seminary. She is also co-pastor of the New Covenant Church of God.

Charles Camosy is Assistant Professor of Christian Ethics at Fordham University in New York City.

Rev. Richard Cizik is President of the New Evangelical Partnership for the Common Good.

Scott Claybrook is a minister, author, and blogger (scottclaybrook.com).

Rev. Jennifer Danielle Crumpton is a pastoral associate at Park Avenue Christian Church in New York City, where she facilitates The XY Factor, a spiritual growth and social justice ministry for those in their 20s and 30s.

Timothy W. Floyd is Professor of Law and Director of the Law and Public Service Program at Mercer University School of Law.

David P. Gushee, co-founder of the New Evangelical Partnership for the Common Good, is Distinguished University Professor of Christian Ethics and Director of the Center for Theology and Public Life at Mercer University.

Lisa Sharon Harper is the Director of Mobilizing at Sojourners. She is also co-author of *Left, Right, and Christ: Evangelical Faith in Politics,* and author of *Evangelical Does Not Equal Republican...or Democrat.*

Dr. Rick Love is President of Peace Catalyst International and serves as Consultant for Christian-Muslim Relations in the Association of Vineyard Churches, USA.

Paul N. Markham is Assistant Professor and Co-Director of the Institute for Citizenship and Social Responsibility at Western Kentucky University.

Rev. Steven D. Martin is a co-founder of the New Evangelical Partnership for the Common Good, a filmmaker, a husband, and a father of four.

Brian McLaren is an author, blogger, speaker, and activist based in Florida (www.brianmclaren.net).

Adam Phillips is an ordained minister in the Evangelical Covenant Church and Senior Manager, Faith Mobilization, at ONE. He has previously served congregations in Chicago and Washington, D.C. He lives with his wife, Sarah, an urban educator, in Baltimore.

Laura Rector is a Ph.D. candidate at Fuller Theological Seminary in Pasadena, California.

Glen Harold Stassen is Lewis B. Smedes Professor of Christian Ethics at Fuller Theological Seminary.

Andi Thomas Sullivan is co-founder of His Nets, has an M.Div. from McAfee School of Theology, and is currently pursuing an M.A. in International Affairs at American University in Washington, D.C.

Rev. Tyler Wigg-Stevenson, a Baptist minister, is the founding director of the Two Futures Project, and chairs the Global Task Force on Nuclear Weapons for the World Evangelical Alliance.

Notes

Introduction

[1]Evangelicals comprise 25 to 30 percent of the American population, 75-80 million people, according to the Institute for the Study of American Evangelicals, "How Many Evangelicals Are There?" http://isae.wheaton.edu/defining-evangelicalism/how-many-evangelicals-are-there/.

[2]Rodney Clapp, "Bad News Evangelicals," Christian Century (March 10, 2009).

1: The Church in America Today

[1]One could also make a case that higher college attendance rates indirectly contributed to mainline and Catholic decline, and lower college attendance rates to evangelical strength. See Robert Wuthnow, After the Baby Boomers (Princeton: Princeton University Press, 2007).

[2]Diana Butler Bass, *Christianity After Religion* (New York: HarperOne, 2012).

[3]For accessible overviews of the Christian churches in the U.S., I recommend Diana Butler Bass, *Christianity After Religion;* David Olson, *The American Church in Crisis* (Grand Rapids: Zondervan, 2008); David Kinnaman and Gabe Lyons, *UnChristian* (Grand Rapids: Baker, 2007); and David Kinnaman, *You Lost Me* (Grand Rapids: Baker, 2011).

[4]As the subtitle suggests, this is the major concern of my 2012 release, *Why Did Jesus, Moses, the Buddha, and Mohammed Cross the Road: Christian Identity in a Multi-Faith World* (Nashville: Jericho Books, 2012).

[5]http://www.nytimes.com/2011/12/11/opinion/sunday/americans-and-god.html?_r=1&ref=ericweiner.

[6]Mainline colleges have struggled with the opposite problem—of losing their Christian distinctiveness altogether. Catholic higher education has schools that display both leanings.

[7]Among Mainline Protestants, parallel "leading edge" groups have formed—such as the Gospel and Our Culture Network, Church Innovations, and (in the UK) the Fresh Expressions movement. What Phyllis Tickle calls "The Hyphenateds" especially exemplify leading edge space. See Phil Snider, ed., *The Hyphenateds* (St. Louis: Chalice Press, 2011). Catholic emergence is also underway, exemplified in the work, for example, of James Alison.

2: Where the Church Went Wrong

[1]See http://www.skepticism.org/timeline/april-history/5184-dietrich-bonhoeffer-talks-of-the-nazi-threat-to-germanys-churches.html.

[2]I am deeply indebted to Dr. Robert Ericksen and his book, *Theologians Under Hitler* (New Haven, Conn.: Yale University Press, 1985), and Dr. Manfred Gailus's research on Karl Themel.

3: A Disenchanted Text: Where Evangelicals Went Wrong with the Bible

[1]See the following: Barna Research Group (www.barna.org); the Bible Literacy Project (http://bibleliteracy.org); The Gallup Poll (www.gallup.com); *The Baylor Religion Survey* (Waco, Tex.: Baylor Institute for Studies of Religion, 2005).

[2]Gary Burge, "The Greatest Story Never Read: Recovering Biblical Literary in the Church," *Christianity Today,* August 9, 1999, pp. 45–50.

[3]James Smart, *The Strange Silence of the Bible in the Church* (Philadelphia: Westminster Press, 1970).

[4]Ibid., pp. 15–16.

[5]Max Weber, "Science as a Vocation," from *Max Weber: Essays in Sociology* (Oxford: Oxford University Press, 1946), p. 155.

[6]Ibid.

[7]Mark Noll, *Between Faith and Criticism: Evangelicals, Scholarship, and the Bible in America* (Grand Rapids: Baker Book House, 2d ed., 1991), p. 32.

[8]Charles Hodge, *Systematic Theology,* vol. 1 (London: James Clarke, 1960), pp. 1–2.

[9]B.B. Warfield, *Counterfeit Miracles* (Edinburgh: The Banner of Truth Trust, 1918), p. 66.

[10]Harold Lindsell, *The Battle for the Bible* (Grand Rapids, Mich.: Zondervan, 1976).

[11]James Davison Hunter, *Culture Wars: The Struggle to Define America* (New York: Basic Books, 1992), p. 152.

[12]George Barna, *Think Like Jesus* (Nashville: Integrity Publishers, 2003), p. 6.

[13]Ibid.

[14]Ibid.

[15] Ibid.

[16] Tim Conder and Daniel Rhodes, *Free for All: Re-Discovering the Bible in Community* (Grand Rapids: Baker Books, 2009, p. 47.

[17] Phyllis Tickle, *The Great Emergence: How Christianity Is Changing and Why* (Grand Rapids: Baker Books, 2008), p. 116.

[18] Ibid.

[19] James Smart, *The Cultural Subversion of the Biblical Faith* (Philadelphia: The Westminster Press, 1977).

[20] Conder and Rhodes, *Free for All*, p. 62.

[21] Ibid.

[22] John S. McClure, *Other-wise Preaching: A Postmodern Ethic for Homiletics* (St. Louis: Chalice Press, 2001), p. 17.

[23] Wesley A. Kort, *"Take, Read": Scripture, Textuality and Cultural Practice* (University Park, Pa.: University of Pennsylvania Press, 1996), p. 128.

[24] Ibid., p. 122.

[25] Ibid., p. 123.

[26] McClure, *Other-wise Preaching*, p. 19.

[27] Ibid., p. 21.

[28] John Webster, *Holy Scripture: A Dogmatic Sketch* (Cambridge: Cambridge University Press, 2003), pp. 14–15.

[29] Ibid.

[30] Ibid., p. 28.

4: My Journey Toward the "New Evangelicalism"

[1] Rodney Clapp, "Bad News Evangelicals," *Christian Century* (March 10, 2009).

[2] John Howard Yoder, as quoted in Clapp, "Bad News Evangelicals."

[3] For this document, see http://www.anevangelicalmanifesto.com/manifesto.php.

[4] Most of the documents cited in this section can be found in David P. Gushee, *The Future of Faith in American Politics* (Waco, Tex.: Baylor University Press, 2008).

[5] Benjamin Libet, as quoted in Daniel M. Wegner, *The Illusion of Conscious Will* (Boston: MIT Press, 2002).

[6] Scott McKnight, as quoted in Marcia Pally, "The New Evangelicals," The New York Times (December 9, 2011), accessed at http://campaignstops.blogs.nytimes.com/2011/12/09/the-new-evangelicals/.

[7] These numbers are drawn from Marcia Pally's important book, *The New Evangelicals* (Grand Rapids: Eerdmans, 2011), p. 108, in which she writes: "By 2008, the devout who identified themselves as outside the Religious Right came to 25 percent of the adult population. Making up the group were the Religious Left at 9 percent; "red letter Christians," also at 9 percent; and religious centrists, those with liberal theology and moderate-centrist politics, at about 6 percent." Her source was the Pew Forum on Religion and Public Life, "Assessing a More Prominent 'Religious Left,'" June 5, 2008.

[8] Michelle Gordberg, *Kingdom Coming: The Rise of Christian Nationalism* (New York: Norton, 2007).

[9] See Jim Collins' acclaimed book *From Good to Great* (New York: HarperCollins, 2001), p. 74.

[10] Collins, Good-to-Great, p. 74.

5: A Theology That "Works"

[1] See Paul N. Markham, "Searching for a New Story: The Possibility of a New Evangelical Movement in the United States," *Journal of Religion and Society* 12 (2010), pp. 1–22.

[2] N. T. Wright, *Simply Christian* (San Francisco: HarperOne, 2010).

6: God's Vision for the Church—Kingdom Discipleship

[1] Michael Westmoreland-White, Glen H. Stassen, David P. Gushee, "Disciples of the Incarnation," *Sourners* (May 1994). In the first half of this chapter, I shall quote from that programatic article without further citation. I believe it was prescient for developments that we see being revealed all the more in our present time.

[2] David Kinnaman and Gabe Lyon, *Unchristian* (Grand Rapids: Baker, 2007).

[3] Mike Slaughter, Charles Gutenson, and Robert P. Jones, *Hijacked: Responding to the Partisan Church Divide* (Nashville: Abingdon, 2012).

⁴Ryan Bolger and Eddie Gibbs, *Emerging Churches: Creating Christian Community in Postmodern Cultures* (Grand Rapids: Baker, 2005).

⁵Available in print from Fuller Theological Seminary.

8: Those Trafficked and Commodified

¹United Nations Office on Drugs and Crime, online: http://www.unodc.org/unodc/en/human-trafficking/what-is-human-trafficking.html?ref=menuside.

²CNN, "Held as slaves, now free," online: http://www.cnn.com/2010/CRIME/12/02/slave.labor.ring.busted/index.html?npt=NP1.

³Summary adaptation of a story recounted in "Teen Girls' Stories of Sex Trafficking in the U.S." ABC Primetime News online: http://abcnews.go.com/Primetime/story?id=1596778&page=1 Copyright © 2010 ABC News Internet Ventures.

⁴See http://afuturenotapast.org/resources/the-facts/.

⁵UNICEF, "Child protection from violence, exploitation and abuse," online: http://www.unicef.org/infobycountry/usa_46464.html.

⁶United Nations Office on Drugs and Crime, "Global Report on Trafficking in Persons," online: http://www.unodc.org/documents/human-trafficking/Global_Report_on_TIP.pdf.

⁷The Federal Bureau of Investigations, online: http://www.fbi.gov/news/pressrel/press-releases/occv_110810.

⁸From http://www.sp2.upenn.edu/restes/CSEC_Files/Exec_Sum_020220.pdf.

⁹Shelley Portet, "Social network accounts outnumber people on Earth", online: http://www.silicon.com/technology/mobile/2011/04/01/social-network-accounts-outnumber-people-on-earth-39747241/.

¹⁰Romero, D., S. Asur, W. Galuba, and B. Huberman, "Influence and Passivity in Social Media." HP Labs Research, 2010, online: http://www.scribd.com/doc/35401457/Influence-and-Passivity-in-Social-Media-HP-Labs-Research.

¹¹Youth Radio, online: www.stopsellingsex.com/trafficked-teen-girls-describe-life-in-the-game/.

¹²Eran Fisher, *Media and the New Capitalism in the Digital Age: The Spirit of Networks* (New York: Palgrave MacMillan, 2010), p. 1.

¹³Pew Internet and American Life Project, "Social Media and Young Adults," online: http://www.pewinternet.org/Reports/2010/Social-Media-and-Young-Adults/Part-3.aspx?view=all.

¹⁴Advanced Interactive Media Group LLC, online: http://library.constantcontact.com/download/get/file/1103423277228-22/EscortAdsMonthlyReport0311.pdf (accessed 20 Apr 2011).

¹⁵Byron Acohido, "Sex Predators Stalk Social Media" in USA Today online: http://www.usatoday.com/printedition/news/20110301/1apedophiles01_st.art.htm.

¹⁶David Gushee and Glen Stassen, *Kingdom Ethics* (Downers Grove, Ill.: InterVarsity Press, 2010).

¹⁷Ibid., ch. 1.

¹⁸A Future. Not a Past, online: http://afnap.org/content/young-new-york-city-girls-are-targets-for-sex-trafficking/.

¹⁹Amity-paye,"Young New York City Girls are Targets for Sex Trafficking," online: http://www.urbanperspectivemag.com/2010/12/01/young-new-york-city-girls-are-targets-for-sex-trafficking/.

²⁰Amy Sullivan, "Cracking Down on the Super Bowl Sex Trade," Time 2/6/2011, http://www.time.com/time/nation/article/0,8599,2046568,00.html.

²¹Quoted in Rick Jervis, "Child sex rings spike during Super Bowl week," USAToday 2/1/2011, http://www.usatoday.com/news/nation/2011-01-31-child-prostitution-super-bowl_N.htm.

²²Stassen and Gushee, *Kingdom Ethics*, ch. 17.

²³This list is available at http://afuturenotapast.org/resources/warning-signs/.

²⁴A Future. Not a Past, "Policy Recommendations," online: http://afnap.org/law-and-policy/policy-recommendations/.

²⁵Ibid.

²⁶Stassen and Gushee, *Kingdom Ethics*, ch. 16.

²⁷Tasha Perdue, as quoted in Christie Kerner, "Detroit sex-trafficking victim shares story to bring awareness," online: http://bgnews.com/infocus/detroit-sex-trafficking-victim-shares-story-to-bring-awareness/.

²⁸Women's Funding Network, "Backpage Remains Sex Ad Leader, Girls at Risk," e-newsletter, April 28, 2011.

[29]Aimgroup.com, online: http://library.constantcontact.com/download/get/file/1103423277228-22/EscortAdsMonthlyReport0311.pdf.

[30]Youth Radio, online: http://www.youthradio.org/news/storefront-photo-studios-sell-teens.

9: Those Suffering from Preventable Diseases

[1]Abhijit V. Banerjee and Esther Duflo, *Poor Economics: A Radical Rethinking of the Way to Fight Global Poverty* (New York: Public Affairs, 2011), p. 31.

[2]Ibid., p. 32.

[3]Andi Thomas Sullivan, unpublished journal, June 10, 2006.

[4]Cheston B. Cunha and Burke A. Cunha, "Brief History of the Clinical Diagnosis of Malaria: From Hippocrates to Osler," *Journal of Vector Borne Diseases* 45 (September 2008): 194–99.

[5]Fiammetta Rocco, *Quinine: Malaria and the Quest for a Cure that Changed the World* (New York: HarperCollins Publishers, 2003), pp. 25–54.

[6]"Malaria Fact Sheet N. 94," World Health Organization, April 2010, http://www.who.int/mediacentre/factsheets/fs094/en/.

[7]Ibid.

[8]Letter from Comfort L. Ylonh to Milledge Avenue Baptist Church, Athens, Georgia, undated.

10: Our Muslim Neighbors

[1]http://peace-catalyst.net/programs/love-your-neighbor-dinner.

[2]http://yale.edu/faith/acw/acw-2008-conf.htm.

[3]The Qur'an comprises recitations by Muhammad, believed to come from God, to meet the needs that arose on specific occasions. Some were peaceful; others were not. Therefore either position can be argued by selecting specific verses from the Qur'an or illustrations from history. See J.D Woodberry, "Terrorism, Islam, and Mission: Reflections of a Guest in Muslim Lands," *International Bulletin of Missionary Research* (2002), p. 2.

[4]We do well to avoid stereotyping Muslims based on news sound bites or the reductionism of focusing primarily on religion as the cause of conflicts between Muslim and Christian communities. There are many perspectives in the Muslim community, and even these are changing. Conflicts between Muslim and Christian communities in places such as Indonesia and Sudan have ethnic, economic, and political, as well as religious, roots. See Woodberry, "Terrorism…," p. 6.

[5]Madeleine Albright, *The Mighty and the Almighty* (New York: Harper Perennial, 2007), p. 116.

[6]The Amman Message 2008:16–17. http://ammanmessage.com/media/Amman-Message-pdf-booklet-v-2-5-2-08.pdf.

[7]I often hear the complaint that "moderate" Muslims are not speaking out against terrorism. The fact is that they have done so, and Western media has not acknowledged it. See http://www.peace-catalyst.net/resources/global-issues.

[8]http://www.aalalbayt.org/en/index.html. See also M.H. Kamali, *Freedom of Expression in Islam* (Kuala Lumpur: Ilmiah Publishers, 1998); R. Aslan, *No God But God* (New York: Random House, 2006); and Benazir Bhutto, *Reconciliation: Islam, Democracy, and the West* (New York: HarperCollins, 2008).

[9]Shariah law refers to a legal system based on Islamic principles of jurisprudence. Shariah law addresses many aspects of day-to-day life, including politics, economics, banking, business, contracts, family, sexuality, hygiene, and social issues.

[10]S. Schwartz, *The Other Islam: Sufism and the Road to Global Harmony* (New York: Doubleday, 2008), p. 17.

[11]In emphasizing this, we are not denying that many non-Sufis support reconciliation efforts.

[12]See Philip Jenkins, "Mystical Power: Why Sufi Muslims, for centuries the most ferocious soldiers of Islam, could be our most valuable allies in the fight against extremism," January 25, 2009.

[13]Schwartz, *The Other Islam*, pp. 111, 30.

[14]Mohammad Hashim Kamali, *Freedom of Expression in Islam* (Cambridge: Islamic Text Society, 1997) is an excellent example of a traditionalist addressing a massively important topic (which includes freedom of religion and the law of apostasy).

[15]The chart and commentary are adapted from *Jihad and the Islamic Law of War* (2007): 58–62. http://ammanmessage.com/media/jihad.pdf. According to a Gallup Poll, 7 percent of Muslims are "politically radicalized," but not all in this group commit acts of violence. See J.L. Esposito and D. Mogahed, *Who Speaks for Islam? What a Billion Muslims Really Think* (New York: Gallup, 2007), p. 70.

[16]Christopher L. Heuertz and Christine D. Pohl, *Friendship at the Margins* (Grand Rapids: Eerdmans, 2010), p. 42.

11: People of All Races

[1]Lisa Sharon Harper, *Evangelical Does Not Equal Republican…or Democrat* (New York: The New Press, 2008) pp. 91–93.

[2]Michael Emerson and Christian Smith, *Divided by Faith: Evangelical Religion and the Problem of Race in America* (Oxford: Oxford Press, 2000), p. 68.

[3]Ibid., Introduction.

[4]Ibid., pp. 76–77, 81, 107.

[5]There is much more to be said about the nuances of Emerson and Smith's study and how these findings work their way out in and through the American evangelical church today. To go deeper, I highly recommend Emerson and Smith's *Divided by Faith: Evangelical Religion and the Problem of Race in America*, Emerson's follow up book *United by Faith: The Multiracial Congregation as an Answer to the Problem of Race (Oxford: Oxford University Press, 2004), with Curtis Paul DeYoung, George Yancey, and Karen Chai Kim*, and my first book *Evangelical Does Not Equal Republican…or Democrat*, where I examined the impact of these cultural tools on white evangelicals' engagement with issues of race, gender, and politics.

[6]"Africans in America: Arrival of the First Africans to Virginia Colony," PBS Online: http://www.pbs.org/wgbh/aia/part1/1p263.html.

[7]Taunya Lovell Banks, "Dangerous Woman: Elizabeth Key's Freedom Suit—Subjecthood and Racialized Identity in Seventeen Century Colonial Virginia," Akron Law Review, p. 800. http://digitalcommons.law.umaryland.edu/cgi/viewcontent.cgi?article=1053&context=fac_pubs.

[8]"Africans in America: Arrival of the First Africans to Virginia Colony."

[9]Banks, "Dangerous Woman," p. 800.

[10]"Africans in America: From Indentured Servanthood to Racial Slavery," PBS Online: http://www.pbs.org/wgbh/aia/part1/1narr3.html.

[11]Lawrence R. Tenzer, Ed.D., and A.D. Powell, "White Slavery, Maternal Descent, and the Politics of Slavery in the Antebellum United States," (Originally presented at the University of Nottingham Institute for the study of Slavery, June 30, 2004), http://multiracial.com/site/index2.php?option=com_content&do_pdf=1&id=462.

[12]United States Census of Population and Housing 1790: http://www.census.gov/prod/www/abs/decennial/1790.html.

[13]"Reconstruction Era of the United States," Wikipedia: The Free Library: http://en.wikipedia.org/wiki/Reconstruction_era_of_the_United_States#cite_note-0.

[14]Ibid.

[15]"Lynchings: By Year and Race" (statistics provided by the archives at Tuskeegee Institute), http://law2.umkc.edu/faculty/projects/ftrials/shipp/lynchingyear.html.

[16]See Isabel Wilkerson's *The Warmth of Other Suns: The Epic Story of America's Great Migration* (New York: NY Random House, 2010).

[17]Carol Anderson, *Eyes Off the Prize: The United Nations and the African American Struggle for Human Rights, 1944–1955* (Cambridge: Cambridge University Press, 2003), pp. 4, 124.

[18]Ibid., p. 124.

[19]Hear the live recording of Hubert Humphrey's 1948 Speech on YouTube: http://www.youtube.com/watch?v=8nwIdIUVFm4.

[20]Sarah McCulloh Lemmon, "Ideology of the 'Dixiecrat Movement,'" Social Forces 30, No. 2 (December 1951), pp. 162–171: http://www.jstor.org/pss/2571628.

[21]Robert Siegel and Sheldon Danziger, "Lyndon B. Johnson's War on Poverty: Weeks into Office LBJ Turned Nation's Focus to the Poor," All Things Considered Podcast, January 4, 2004: http://www.npr.org/templates/story/story.php?storyId=1589660.

[22]Carmen DeNavas Walt, Bernadette D. Proctor, and Jessica S. Smith, "Income, Poverty, and Health Insurance Coverage in the United States: 2009," United States Census Bureau, September 2010; http://www.census.gov/prod/2010pubs/p60-238.pdf.

[23]Siegel and Danziger, "Lyndon B. Johnson's War on Poverty."

[24]DeNavas Walt, Proctor, and Smith, "Income, Poverty, and Health Insurance Coverage," p. 56.

[25]David Morgan, "New Census Data Raise Number of Poor to 49 Million," Reuters.com, November 7, 2011: http://www.reuters.com/article/2011/11/07/us-usa-poverty-idUSTRE7A634M20111107.

[26]DeNavas Walt, Proctor, and Smith, "Income, Poverty, and Health Insurance Coverage," p. 59.

[27]Ibid.

[28]Morgan, "New Census Data Raise Number of Poor."

²⁹DeNavas Walt, Proctor, and Smith, "Income, Poverty, and Health Insurance Coverage," p. 58.

12: Women

¹D.A. Carson, R.T. France, J.A. Motyer, and G.J. Wenham, eds., *New Bible Commentary* (Downers Grove, Ill.: IVP Academic, 1994), p. 54, 140.

13: Children

¹For more information about the film, see its Internet Movie Database entry at http://www. imdb.com/title/tt0096928/.

²See Michael McGill, "Child Participation and the Peace Process," *The Barnabas Letter 6:4* (Fort Mill, S.C.: Crisis Care Training International, 2009), available at http://www.crisiscaretraining. org/barnabas-training-newsletters/.

³See Dorothy Boorse, et al., *Loving the Least of These: Addressing a Changing Environment* (Washington, D.C.: National Association of Evangelicals, 2011), available at http://www.nae.net/images/content/ Loving_the_Least_of_These.pdf.

⁴Coalition to Stop the Use of Child Soldiers, "Facts and Figures on Child Soldiers," *Child Soldiers Global Report* (2008), available at http://www.childsoldiersglobalreport.org/content/facts-and-figures-child-soldiers.

⁵Sherry Karabin, "Infanticide, Abortion Responsible for 60 Million Girls Missing in Asia," *Fox News* (17 March 2009), available at http://www.pop.org/2007061375/infanticide-abortion-responsible-for-60-million-girls-missing-in-asia-foxnewscom.

⁶Joyce Ann Mercer, *Welcoming Children: A Practical Theology of Childhood* (St. Louis: Chalice Press, 2005), p. 44.

⁷W.A. Strange, *Children in the Early Church: Children in the Ancient World, the New Testament, and the Early Church* (Eugene, Oreg.: Wipf & Stock, 1996), p. 48.

⁸Ibid., p. 14.

⁹Ibid., p. 10.

¹⁰Ibid., p. 17.

¹¹Ibid., p. 37.

¹²Ibid., p. 50.

¹³Hans-Ruedi Weber, *Jesus and the Children: Biblical Resources for Study and Preaching* (Atlanta: John Knox Press, 1979), p. 16.

¹⁴Strange, *Children in the Early Church*, p. 37.

¹⁵Ibid., p. 48.

¹⁶For a more in-depth analysis of children in these cultures as well as Christian responses to the risks of children in the cultures, see Strange's book, as well as: Everett Ferguson, *Backgrounds of Early Christianity*, 2d ed. (Grand Rapids: William B. Eerdmans, 1987) and George Grant, *Third Time Around: A History of the Pro-Life Movement from the First Century to the Present* (Brentwood, Tenn.: Wogemuth & Hyatt, 1991).

¹⁷Weber, *Jesus and the Children*, p. 15.

¹⁸Ched Myers, *Binding the Strong Man: A Political Reading of Mark's Story of Jesus* (Maryknoll: Orbis Books, 1988), p. 268.

¹⁹Eric Lane, *Special Children? A Theology of Childhood* (London: Grace Publications Trust, 1996), p. 32.

²⁰William Barclay, *Educational Ideals in the Ancient World* (London: Collins, 1959), p. 234.

²¹Mercer, *Welcoming Children*, pp. 51, 53.

²²Strange, *Children in the Early Church*, p. 50.

²³Myers, *Binding the Strong Man*, p. 266.

²⁴Ibid.

²⁵Strange, *Children in the Early Church*, p. 40.

²⁶Ibid., p. 48.

²⁷Glen Stassen and David Gushee, *Kingdom Ethics: Following Jesus in Contemporary Context* (Downers Grove, Ill.: InterVarsity Press, 2003), p. 22.

²⁸Lane, *Special Children*, pp. 32–33.

²⁹Ibid.

³⁰Stassen and Gushee, *Kingdom Ethics*, pp. 22–31.

³¹Ibid., pp. 271–89.

³²Strange, *Children in the Early Church*, p. 64.

[33]Fewell, *Children of Israel*, pp. 27, 105–106.

[34]See my article, "Health-Care Reform – A Pro-Life Victory," *Ethics Daily* (April 19, 2010), available at http://www.ethicsdaily.com/health-care-reform-a-pro-life-victory-cms-15941.

[35]See "A Generation at Risk," *Rainbows* (2003), available at http://www.rainbows.org/statistics. html.

[36]Stassen and Gushee, *Kingdom Ethics*, p. 25.

[37]David Gushee, *Getting Marriage Right* (Grand Rapids: Baker Books, 2004), p. 75.

[38]David Popenoe, *Life Without Father* (Cambridge: Harvard University Press, 1999), pp. 69–71.

[39]Ibid., p. 66, and Elizabeth Marquardt, *Between Two Worlds* (New York: Crown Publishers, 2005), pp. 60–61.

[40]Marquardt, *Between Two Worlds*, p. 17.

[41]Ron Sider, *Just Generosity: A New Vision for Overcoming Poverty in America* (Grand Rapids: Baker Books, 1999), p. 121.

[42]Marquardt, *Between Two Worlds*, p. 65.

[43]Americans for Divorce Reform, "Children of divorce: Psychological, psychiatric, behavioral problems and suicide," available at http://www.divorcereform.org/psy.html.

[44]For examples, see Greg Burch, *Community Children: A Ministry of Hope and Restoration for the Street Dwelling Child* (Colombia: Latin American Mission, 2005), pp. 33, 38.

[45]Michael McGill, "Children Seeking Family in War and Sexual Exploitation," in *Understanding God's Heart for Children*, ed. Douglas McConnell, Jennifer Orona, and Paul Stockley (Colorado Springs: World Vision, 2007), pp. 86–92.

[46]Ray Sanchez, "Deportations Leave Behind Thousands Of Children In Foster Care," *Huffington Post* (November 3, 2011), available online at http://www.huffingtonpost.com/2011/11/02/deportation-immigrant-children-foster-care_n_1072553.html, as well as Child Rights Information Network, "USA: Forced Apart—Families Separated and Immigrants Harmed by United States Deportation Policy," (2007), available online at http://www.crin.org/resources/infoDetail. asp?ID=14050&flag=report.

[47]David Nakamura, "Obama signs defense bill, pledges to maintain legal rights of U.S. citizens," *The Washington Post* (December 31, 2011), available at http://www.washingtonpost.com/politics/obama-signs-defense-bill-pledges-to-maintain-legal-rights-of-terror-suspects/2011/12/31/gIQATzbkSP_story.html?tid=pm_politics_pop.

[48]International Committee of the Red Cross, "Children protected under international humanitarian law" (October 29, 2010), available at http://www.icrc.org/eng/war-and-law/protected-persons/children/overview-protected-children.htm.

[49]UNAIDS, *Report on the Global AIDS Epidemic* (Joint Programme on HIV/AIDS, 2008), p. 163, available at http://viewer.zmags.com/publication/ad3eab7c#/ad3eab7c/165.

[50]Yvette Rattray, "U.N. Treaty limiting parents' rights pushed," Baptist Press (March 18, 2009), available at http://www.bpnews.net/bpnews.asp?id=30092.

[51]McGill, "Child Participation and the Peace Process."

14: The Dying

[1]Thomas E. Reynolds, *Vulnerable Communion* (Grand Rapids: Brazos Press, 2008), p. 51.

[2]Ibid., pp. 54ff.

[3]Glen H. Stassen and David P. Gushee, *Kingdom Ethics: Following Jesus in Contemporary Context* (Downers Grove, Ill.: InterVarsity Press, 2003), p. 239.

[4]This characterization of the Supreme Court comes from interpreting the nearly unanimous decisions of the Court on physician-assisted suicide and euthanasia, and the precedents they created, in 1997. For further analysis, see *Washington v. Glucksberg* and *Vacco v. Quill*.

[5]Reynolds, *Vulnerable Communion*, p.188.

[6]Ibid., p. 191.

[7]Ibid., pp. 240–41.

[8]Paul Ramsey, as quoted in Stassen and Gushee, *Kingdom Ethics*, p. 245.

[9]Ibid., p. 250.

[10]See their concurring opinions in *Washington v. Glucksberg*.

[11]For more information on the political, social, and economic forces that led to the Nazi euthanasia program, see Henry Friedlander's seminal work: Henry Friedlander, *The Origins of Nazi Genocide: From Euthanasia to The Final Solution* (Chapel Hill, N.C.: University of North Carolina Press, 1995).

15: The Global Poor

[1]See Paul Collier, *The Bottom Billion: Why The Poorest Countries Are Failing and What Can Be Done About It* (London: Oxford University Press, 2007).

[2]See Philip Jenkins' important book, *The Next Christendom: The Coming Age of Global Christianity* (London: Oxford University Press, 2002), p. 2.

[3]See "Global Christianity," http://pewforum.org/Christian/Global-Christianity-exec.aspx.

[4]See Andrew Rice, "Mission from Africa," *The New York Times*, April 12, 2009. http://www. nytimes.com/2009/04/12/magazine/12churches-t.html?pagewanted=all.

[5]See Joel Edwards, *An Agenda for Change: A Global Call for Spiritual & Social Transformation* (Grand Rapids: Zondervan, 2008), p. 12.

[6]Adam Hochschild, *Bury the Chains: Prophets and Rebels in the Fight to Free an Empire's Slaves* (Boston: Houghton Mifflin, 2005).

[7]I originally shared this story at http://www.sojo.net/blogs/2010/10/19/global-church-must-hold-politicians-accountable.

[8]"The sun shines bright," *The Economist* (3 December 2011).

[9]Ibid.

[10]Ibid.

[11]See especially Richard Stearns, *The Hole in Our Gospel* (Nashville: Thomas Nelson, 2009), pp. 97–105.

[12]I have reflected on this here: http://sojo.net/blogs/2010/10/26/holding-evangelism-and-social-action-tandem.

[13]See http://www.christianvisionproject.com/2007/08/liberate_my_people.html.

16: Ending the Death Penalty

[1]Although sixteen states do not authorize the death penalty, the federal government does authorize and carry out the death penalty. Thus, the government does put people to death on behalf of all American citizens.

[2]Facts and figures on the death penalty are taken from the Web site of the Death Penalty Information Center, http://www.deathpenaltyinfo.org.

[3]http://www.deathpenaltyinfo.org/death-penalty-international-perspective#interexec.

[4]See Stephen Bright, *Counsel for the Poor: The Death Sentence Not for the Worst Crime but for the Worst Lawyer*, 103 YALE L.J. 1835 (1994).

[5]See studies collected and summarized at http://www.deathpenaltyinfo.org/race-and-death-penalty.

[6]http://www.deathpenaltyinfo.org/innocence-and-death-penalty.

[7]See David Grann, "Did Texas Execute an Innocent Man?" *The New Yorker*, September 7, 2009.

[8]See Web site of the Death Penalty Information Center, http://www.deathpenaltyinfo. org/deterrence-states-without-death-penalty-have-had-consistently-lower-murder-rates#stateswithvwithout.

[9]These are all taken from the Sermon on the Mount, Matthew chapters 5—7. I am persuaded by Walter Wink and Glen Stassen that these statements in the Sermon on the Mount do not counsel passive acceptance of evil. Rather, they are an admonition, not to resist evil with evil means, but instead to use creative nonviolence to resist evil. See Walter Wink, *Engaging the Powers: Discernment and Resistance in a World of Domination*, (Minneapolis: Fortress Press, 1992), pp. 175–94 (1992); Glen Stassen, *Living the Sermon on the Moun (San Francisco: Jossey Bass, 2006.*

[10]See Richard Hays, *The Moral Vision of the New Testament (New York: HarperOne, 1996)*, p. 329.

[11]Philippians 2:8, NRSV.

[12]A Pew Forum survey in 2010 found that support for the death penalty was higher among white evangelical Protestants (74%) than among Americans as a whole (62%), and that support among evangelicals was higher than among mainline Protestants, Roman Catholics, and among African American and Hispanic Christians. http://pewforum.org/Death-Penalty/Public-Opinion-on-the-Death-Penalty.aspx.

[13]Only 31 percent of evangelicals stated that their religion was the most important source of their views on the death penalty. http://pewforum.org/Death-Penalty/Public-Opinion-on-the-Death-Penalty.aspx.

[14]When God saw all that God had created, God declared it "very good" (Gen. 1:31, paraphrase).

[15]Genesis 1:27.

[16]Psalm 8:5.

[17]Romans 3:23.

[18]Solzhenitsyn, *The Gulag Archipelago* (New York: Harper Perennial, 2007).

[19]Matthew 5:45.

[20]Moreover, American culture is saturated with the idea that violence is necessary to save us from violence. Walter Wink has described the "Myth of Redemptive Violence," in which persons believe in the power of violence to right wrongs and to save us from evil; in short, the *redemptive* power of violence. The belief that violence "saves" is so successful because violence simply appears to be the nature of things. It seems inevitable, and it is the last and often the first resort to respond to acts of violence. At bottom, Wink demonstrates the *religious* character of violence. In fact, he goes so far as to assert: "the Myth of Redemptive Violence is the real myth of the modern world. It, and not Judaism or Christianity or Islam, is the dominant religion in our society today." See Wink, *Engaging the Powers*, pp. 13–31.

[21]Matthew 17:5.

17: Making Peace

[1]Genesis 4:23–24, NIV.

[2]Walter Wink, *Engaging the Powers: Discernment and Resistance in a World of Domination (Minneapolis: Fortress Press, 1992),* pp. 175–77.

[3]Ibid., p.176.

[4]Domination and the Arts of Resistance: *(New Haven: Yale University Press, 1992).*

[5]"In a seldom noticed insight, Clarence Jordan has pointed out that the Greek for 'evil' can mean either 'by evil means' or 'the evil person'…the context favors the instrumental 'do not resist by evil means' (Jordan, *Substance of Faith*, 69)." Glen Stassen and David Gushee, *Kingdom Ethics: Following Jesus in Contemporary Context* (Downers Grove: IVP, 2003), p.138.

[6]Wink, *Engaging the Powers*, Willard Swartley, *Covenant of Peace* (Grand Rapids: Eerdmans, 2006), p. 61.

[7]Wink, *Engaging the Powers*, p. 185.

[8]Ibid., p. 375. David Wenham, "Paul's Use of the Jesus Tradition: Three Samples," in *Gospel Perspectives*, vol. 5, *The Jesus Tradition Outside the Gospels*, ed. Wenham (Sheffield: JSOT Press, 1985), 18–19. Wink continues, "The easiest solution, and perhaps the correct one, is to regard Matt. 5:39a as a Matthean addition… But what we *can* say with some confidence is that both 'Do not resist evil violently' and 'Do not return evil for evil' express the same basic insight: the spiritual imperative to resist evil without being made evil in turn," *Engaging the Powers*, p. 375–76.

[9]Wink, *Engaging the Powers*, p. 178.

[10]Lyrics to "Ain't We Got Fun," Raymond B. Egan and Gus Kahn, 1921. Quoted as "The rich get richer and the poor—get children!" in F. Scott Fitzgerald, *The Great Gatsby* (New York: Charles Scribner's Sons, 1925).

[11]Wink, *Engaging the Powers*. Swartley, *Covenant of Peace*, pp. 60–65. Contra Horsley (see note 14 below).

[12]*Papyri greci e latini* 446 (133–37 C.E.), cited by Ramsay MacMullen, *Soldier and Civilian in the Late Roman Empire* (Cambridge: Harvard University Press, 1963), p. 89, n. 42, cited in Wink, *Engaging the Powers*, p. 180.

[13]Josephus, *War* 3.95, cited in Wink, *Engaging the Powers*, p. 373, n. 24.

[14]Richard Horsley, "Ethics and Exegesis: 'Love Your Enemies' and the Doctrine of Nonviolence," in Willard Swartley, ed., *The Love of Enemy and Nonretaliation in the New Testament* (Louisville: Westminster/John Knox Press, 1992), p. 83.

[15]John Howard Yoder, discusses "the four options of Jesus" in his Christian Attitudes to War, Peace, and Revolution (Grand Rapids: Brazos Press, 2009). "…the admiration of 'zeal' (exemplified by the murders committed by Phineas and those instigated by Elijah) was widespread in Judaism from Maccabean times on, that imitation of Phineas and Elijah was often spoken of, and that such thought and practice was closely connected with resistance to foreign rule." Morton Smith, "Zealots and Sicarii: Their Origins and Relation," 64:1 *Harvard Theological Review* (1971): 2: "Josephus lists and distinguishes the revolutionary parties. First, he insists, came the *Sicarii* (254, 262), who set the example of crime and cruelty; then John of Gischala went on to violation of the food laws (264); then Simon ben Giora added treachery and tyranny (265); then the Idumaeans, madness and anarchy (267); and

finally the Zealots emulated every sort of evil and claimed, withal, to practice virtue (268f.). These distinctions are rhetorical and imprecise, but the intention to distinguish the five parties is clear."

[16]*Judas Iscariot as sicarii, definition of sicarii,* Joan E. Taylor, "The Name 'Iskarioth' (Iscariot)" *Journal of Biblical Literature* 129:2 (2010): 367–83. Mark Andrew Brighton, *The Sicarii in Josephus's Judean War: Rhetorical Analysis and Historical Observations* (Atlanta: Society of Biblical Literature, 2009).

[17]Josephus, *Jewish War,* 2.254–56, cited in Nicole Kelley, "The Cosmopolitan Expression of Josephus's Prophetic Perspective in the *Jewish War,*" *Harvard Theological Review* 97:3 (2004): 264. "On the name 'Sicarii,' see *Ant.* 20.186, where Josephus says that they were named after the weapons they carried: 'daggers resembling the scimitars of the Persians in size, but curved and more like the weapons called by the Romans *sicae.*'" Kelley, "The Cosmopolitan Expression," p. 263.

[18]Ada Maria Isasi-Diaz, *Mujerista Theology: A Theology for the Twenty-First Century* (Maryknoll, N.Y.: Orbis Books, 1996).

[19]Peter Ellis, *Matthew: His Mind and His Message (Collegeville, MN: Liturgical Press, 1974),* p. 42: The Sermon on the Mount "is funneled through Matthew 28:16–20 to become the standard of Christian existence for the ongoing community—both Jewish and Gentile—of Matthew's day." Cited in Swartley, *Covenant of Peace,* p. 63.

[20]"Whereas he commanded the women to direct the disciples to Galilee to see him and thus serve as the connecting link between them and his death, burial, and resurrection, he now commands the disciples to make disciples of all peoples (28:19) by baptizing and teaching them all he taught (28:20), so that they are empowered to serve as the authoritative link between all peoples and the teaching, death, burial, and resurrection of Jesus. Because the witness of the women has linked the disciples to the death of Jesus (27:55–56), the universal mission of the disciples to make disciples will expand to 'all peoples' the climactic confession of faith in Jesus' divine sonship by the Gentile soldiers (27:54). This climactic 'a' scene, then, assures the reader of a reliable connection from the Gentiles' confession of faith at the death of Jesus (27:54) to the worship of the women (28:9) and of the disciples (28:17) to the making of all peoples into believing disciples of the risen Jesus (28:19). Through this completed sequence of 'a' scenes (27:55–56, 61; 28:1, 5–10,16–20) the reader has experienced a progressive witnessing to the events of Jesus' death, burial, empty tomb, and resurrection, which culminates in authentic faith in the divine authority of the Jesus who was crucified but is now risen. Through this faith the reader is empowered by the risen Jesus to continue the universal mission of the disciples to make disciples of all peoples." John Paul Heil, "The Narrative Structure of Matthew 27:55—28:20," *Journal of Biblical Literature* 110/3 (1991): 437.

18: Abolishing Nuclear Weapnons

[1]See http://www.tomdispatch.com/post/174870/jonathan_schell_the_bomb_in_the_mind, accessed 5/2/2012.

19: Overcoming Global Warming

[1]McKinsey Global Institute, *The Carbon Productivity Challenge: Curbing Climate Change and Sustaining Economic Growth* (June 2008): p. 7.

[2]Jim Ball, *Global Warming and the Risen Lord: Christian Discipleship and Climate Change* (New Freedom, Pa.: EEN, 2010).

[3]The conclusion that global emissions must peak between 2015–2017 comes from reports from the International Energy Agency (IEA) and the Intergovernmental Panel on Climate Change (IPCC). On the IEA's 2011 report, see my Nov. 17, 2011 EEN blog, "Major Report Says We Are Almost Out of Time to Overcome Global Warming". See also p. 330 and endnote 514 on p. 535 of my book referenced above.

[4]See my book (Ball, *Global Warming...*) for a much more in-depth discussion of the spiritual resources available to us to overcome global warming through our relationship to Christ.

[5]The following story comes from pages 131–33 and pages 143 and following in C. S. Lewis, *The Chronicles of Narnia: Prince Caspian* (New York: HarperTrophy: 1951).

[6]This version of the story of Muya Val as recounted by Dr. Val Shean comes from: (1) personal conversations and communications I have had with Val, (2) a videotaped interview I did with her, and (3) from her presentation at a conference on climate change and the poor in May 2011 in Washington, D.C. sponsored by the National Religious Partnership for the Environment. Dr. Shean's presentation was videotaped. Both my interview and Dr. Shean's presentation can be viewed at www.creationcare.org/video.

20: Reducing Abortion

[1]Throughout this essay I will put the terms "liberal" and "conservative" in scare quotes, indicating my frustration with the inadequacy of these categories for Christians.

[2]Though, as we will see below, that is not a reason to reject legal protection for our prenatal children.

[3]Charles Camosy, *Peter Singer and Christian Ethics: Beyond Polarization* (Cambridge: Cambridge University Press, 2012), Conclusion.

[4]Mary Meehan, "Abortion: The Left Has Betrayed the Sanctity of Life," 44 *The Progressive* (Sept. 1980). See http://groups.csail.mit.edu/mac/users/rauch/nvp/consistent/meehan_progressive. html.

[5]Joseph Cardinal Bernardin and Thomas G. Fuechtmann, *Consistent Ethic of Life* (Kansas City, Mo.: Sheed & Ward, 1988).

[6]Sidney Callahan, "The Consistent Ethic of Life," *University of St. Thomas Law Journal* 2:2 (Spring 2005): 272–73.

[7]Interestingly, the *Catechism of the Catholic Church* connects abandonment of poor (especially when due to greed) to a violation of the fifth commandment, "Thou shalt not kill." Catholic Church, *Catechism of the Catholic Church*, 2d ed., vol. 5–109 (Citta del Vaticano; Washington, D.C.: Libreria Editrice Vaticana; distributed by United States Catholic Conference, 2000a).

[8]As noted above, I despise this binary (and, quite frankly, lazy) way of thinking about our complex theological and political landscape, but given that this is how most Christians see themselves, it serves a temporary organizational purpose to organize the essay in this way. My conclusion, however, is that insights from both approaches are necessary to having a consistent and comprehensive approach to reducing abortion.

[9]"U.S. Stands Apart from Other Nations on Maternity Leave," *USA Today*, http://www.usatoday.com/news/health/2005-07-26-maternity-leave_x.htm.

[10]"Maternity Benefits," *Patient.co.uk*, http://www.patient.co.uk/health/Maternity-Benefits.htm.

[11]Gilda Sedgh, "Legal Abortion Worldwide in 2008: Levels and Recent Trends," Guttmacher Institute Perspectives on Sexual and Reproductive Health 43, no. 3 (Sept. 2011). http://www.guttmacher.org/pubs/journals/4318811.html. As we will see below, there is even more to these numbers than meets the uncritical eye.

[12]Rebecca Wind, http://www.guttmacher.org/pubs/journals/3310607.html. Some may argue that other factors influencing these improved numbers are better public access to contraception, sex education, and universal health care, but see "Abortion Rate Increasing Among Poor Women, Even As It Decreases Among Most Other Groups," Guttmacher Institute, http://www.guttmacher.org/media/nr/2011/05/23/ab.html.

[13]Ibid.

[14]"The Pregnant Women Support Act Hits the Big Time in Health Care Reform," Democrats for Life of America, http://www.democratsforlife.org/index.php?option=com_content.

[15]Gilda Sedgh, "Legal Abortion Worldwide: Incidence and Recent Trends," Guttmacher Institute, http://www.guttmacher.org/pubs/journals/3310607.html.

[16]"An Overview of Abortion in the United States," Guttmacher Institute, http://www.guttmacher.org/presentations/abort_slides.pdf.

[17]RK Jones, l. Finer, and Susheela Singh, "U.S. Abortion Patients, 2008," Guttmacher Institute, http://www.guttmacher.org/pubs/US-Abortion-Patients.pdf.

[18]Ruth Padawer, "The Two Minus One Pregnancy," *The New York Times*, http://www.nytimes.com/2011/08/14/magazine/the-two-minus-one-pregnancy.html?pagewanted=all.

[19]Rebecca Smith, "Three Babies Aborted Every Day Due to Down's Syndrome," Telegraph.co.uk, http://www.telegraph.co.uk/health/healthnews/6440705/Three-babies-aborted-every-day-due-to-Downs-syndrome.html.

[20]Margaret Somerville, "'Deselecting' Our Children," *The Globe and Mail*, http://www.theglobeandmail.com/news/opinions/opinion/deselecting-our-children/article2136096/print/.

[21]"Sweden Rules 'Gender-Based' Abortion Legal," *Huffington Post*, http://www.huffingtonpost.com/2009/05/12/sweden-rules-genderbased-_n_202430.html.

[22]Organizations such as Feminists for Life and Democrats for Life, for instance, are made up of people who believe that a fetus is a human person. Many are even pro-choice despite believing that a fetus is a person. For a detailed argument supporting the claim that a fetus is a person, see Camosy, *Peter Singer and Christian Ethics*, chapter 1.

[23]Mary S. Calderone, "Illegal Abortion as a Public Health Problem," *American Journal of Public Health* (July 1960), 50(7): 949.

[24]Jones RK and Kooistra, K., "Abortion incidence and access to services in the United States, 2008," *Perspectives on Sexual and Reproductive Health*, 2011, 43(1): 41–50.

[25]Jones RK, et al., "Repeat abortion in the United States," *Occasional Report*, New York: Guttmacher Institute, 2006, No. 29.

[26]Daniel Callahan, *Abortion Law, Choice and Morality* (New York: Macmillan, 1970), p. 132–33.

[27]Steven D. Levitt and Stephen J. Dubner, *Freakanomics Intl.: A Rogue Economist Explores the Hidden Side of Everything* (New York: Harper, 2011), p. 138.

[28]Rohini Boddu, "A Review of Abortion in Ireland," *Royal College of Surgeons in Ireland Student Medical Journal* (2011), 4(1): 78–81 (http://www.rcsismj.com/4th-edition/abortion/.

[29]*Case of A, B, and C v. Ireland*, European Court of Human Rights, http://cmiskp.echr.coe.int/tkp197/view.asp?action=html&documentId=878721&portal=hbkm&source=externalbydocnumber&table=F69A27FD8FB86142BF01C1166DEA398649.

[30]Stanley K. Henshaw, "The Incidence of Abortion Worldwide," Guttmacher Institute, http://www.guttmacher.org/pubs/journals/25s3099.html.

[31]Some might say that it is simply Ireland's Catholicism that is primarily or even solely responsible for the low incidence of abortion, but very Catholic countries, such as Italy, have a rate of 11.4 per 1000.

[32]"Fewer Irish Women Opt for Abortion," BBC News, http://news.bbc.co.uk/2/hi/europe/8160806.stm.

[33]The main criminal penalty, in my view, should be paid by the abortion provider, and the mother should have a comparatively small penalty to pay (if any). As mentioned above, women operate within social structures in ways that mitigate their guilt and might even coerce their choices. Furthermore, though it goes beyond the scope of this essay to make the full argument, I believe that equal protection of the laws for prenatal children can be consistent with permitting certain kinds of indirect abortions, including those that are medically indicated and that serve to protect the vital health interests of the mother.

21: Resisting Consumerism

[1]J. Noakes and G. Pridham, eds. *Nazism: A History in Documents and Eyewitness Accounts, 1919–1945* (New York: Schocken Books, 1990).

[2]Jeffrey D. Sachs, *The Price of Civilization: Reawakening American Virtue and Prosperity* (New York: Random House, 2011), 3.

[3]Ibid.

[4]Ibid.

22: Standing Fast Against Torture

[1]Lewis Hanke, *All Mankind Is One* (DeKalb, Ill.: Northern Illinois University Press, 1974), 67.

[2]David P. Gushee, *The Sacredness of Human Life* (Grand Rapids: Eerdmans, 2012).

[3]Marc Thiessen, *Courting Disaster* (Washington: Regnery, 2010).

[4]International Committee of the Red Cross, "ICRC Report on the Treatment of Fourteen 'High Value Detainees' in CIA Custody," February 2007. A report leaked to the press and accessed at http://www.nybooks.com/media/doc/2010/04/22/icrc-report.pdf.

[5]Ibid., p. 26.

[6]Thiessen, *Courting Disaster*, Introduction, chapter 3, and elsewhere.

[7]Ibid., pp. 35–38 and elsewhere.

[8]Ibid., pp. 26–34 and elsewhere.

[9]Ibid., p. 25.

[10]Ibid., p. 35.

[11]Ibid., p. 39.

[12]Ibid., p. 172.

[13]Ibid., p. 46, quoting an interrogator named "Harry."

[14]On training, Ibid., p. 46; involvement of medical professionals, p. 177.

[15]Ibid., pp. 89–90.

[16]Ibid., pp. 232–34.

[17]Ibid., p. 235.

[18]Ibid., pp. 236–37.

[19]Ibid., pp. 129–30.

[20]Ibid., pp. 131–62.

[21]Ali H. Soufan with Daniel Freedman, *The Black Banners* (New York: W.W. Norton, 2011) for the fullest exposition of his experience and perspective.

[22]Ibid., p. 103ff and elsewhere.

[23]CIA report: http://www.aclu.org/torturefoia/released/052708/052708_Special_Review.pdf; 2008 DOJ report: http://www.justice.gov/oig/special/s0805/final.pdf; 2009 DOJ report: http://judiciary.house.gov/hearings/pdf/OPRFinalReport090729.pdf.

[24]From http://harpers.org/archive/2008/12/hbc-90004036.

[25]From the 2006 Senate Select Committee on Intelligence report: "Postwar findings support the DIA February 2002 assessment that Ibn al-Shaykh al-Libi was likely intentionally misleading his debriefers when he said that Iraq provided two al-Qa'ida associates with chemical and biological weapons (CBW) training in 2000… Postwar findings do not support the CIA's assessment that his reporting was credible… No postwar information has been found that indicates CBW training occurred and the detainee who provided the key prewar reporting about this training recanted his claims after the war… CIA's January 2003 version of Iraqi Support for Terrorism described al-Libi's reporting for CBW training "credible," but noted that the individuals who traveled to Iraq for CBW training had not returned, so al-Libi was not in position to know if the training had taken place… In January 2004, al-Libi recanted his allegations about CBW training and many of his other claims about Iraq's links to al-Qa'ida. He told debriefers that, to the best of his knowledge, al-Qa'ida never sent any individuals into Iraq for any kind of support in chemical or biological weapons. Al-Libi told debriefers that he fabricated information while in U.S. custody to receive better treatment and in response to threats of being transferred to a foreign intelligence service which he believed would torture him… He said that later, while he was being debriefed by a (REDACTED) foreign intelligence service, he fabricated more information in response to physical abuse and threats of torture. The foreign government service denies using any pressure during al-Libi's interrogation. In February 2004, the CIA reissued the debriefing reports from al-Libi to note that he had recanted information. A CIA officer explained that while CIA believes al-Libi fabricated information, the CIA cannot determine whether, or what portions of, the original statements or the later recants are true of false." United States Senate Select Committee on Intelligence (September 8, 2006). *Report on Postwar Findings about Iraq's WMD Programs and Links to Terrorism and How they Compare with Prewar Assessments*. pp. 106–108. http://intelligence.senate.gov/phaseiiaccuracy.pdf.

[26]"Educing Information—Interrogation: Science and Art." Intelligence Science Board, Phase I Report (Washington: National Defense Intelligence College, 2006).

[27]Ibid., p. 35.

[28]http://www.washingtonpost.com/wp-dyn/content/article/2009/05/13/AR2009051301281.html and http://www.theatlantic.com/politics/archive/2009/05/zelikow-administration-wanted-to-torture/17504/.

[29]The lawyers who authored those OLC opinions have faced considerable scrutiny. The Justice Department's Office of Professional Responsibility investigated Yoo's work, and completed a report critical of his legal justification for enhanced interrogation techniques. The OPR report concluded that Yoo had "committed 'intentional professional misconduct,'" although the recommendation that he be referred for possible disciplinary proceedings was overruled by another senior Justice Department lawyer. See http://www.nytimes.com/2009/05/06/us/politics/06inquire.html?_r=1.

[30]See http://www.oyez.org/cases/2000-2009/2005/2005_05_184/.

[31]Thiessen, *Courting Disaster*, p. 181.

[32]See the evidence compiled by Michael Peppard, "Religious Torture in the War on Terror," in David P. Gushee, et al, editors, *Religious Faith, Torture, and Our National Soul* (Macon: Mercer University Press, 2010), pp. 229–35.

[33]See http://www.salon.com/news/feature/2007/06/21/cia_sere/print.html.

[34]Thiessen, *Courting Disaster*, p. 102. This was highly secret information for a long time, and consistently denied by government officials. Those who undergo SERE are not supposed to disclose it or what happens during that training.

[35]http://www.foxnews.com/politics/2009/04/30/report-psychologists-responsible-devising-cia-interrogation-methods/

[36]See http://www.propublica.org/article/do-cia-cables-show-doctors-monitoring-torture-528 and http://psychoanalystsopposewar.org/blog/2009/06/18/apa-board-makes-major-statement-on-torture/

[37]Glen Stassen and I make this case repeatedly in our *Kingdom Ethics: Following Jesus in Contemporary Context* (Downers Grove, Ill.: Intervarsity Press, 2003), especially ch. 6.

[38]Thiessen, *Courting Disaster*, p. 137.

[39]David Gushee, "Five Reasons Torture Is Always Wrong," *Christianity Today* (February 2006): 33–37.

[40]Available as David Gushie, "What the Torture Debate Reveals About American Christianity," *Journal of the Society of Christian Ethics* 30, no. 1 (Spring/Summer 2010): 79–98.

[41]Among others, see Mark D. Tooley of the Institute for Religion and Democracy, "The Evangelical Left's Nazi Obsession," http://www.frontpagemag.com/Articles/Read.aspx?GUID=13825700-A2AF-4EEA-91AC-662512B7276D.

[42]Ibid.

[43]Ibid.

[44]Erin Roach, "Ethicist: NAE Torture Declaration 'Irrational.'" March 15, 2007. Here Southeastern Baptist Theological Seminary professor Daniel R. Heimbach is quoted as declaring our work "a diatribe…that threatens to undermine Christian moral witness in contemporary culture by dividing evangelicals..." http:www.bpnews.net/printerfriendly.asp?ID=25190.

[45]This was standard Bush Administration rhetoric, as documented by Jane Mayer, *The Dark Side* (New York: Anchor Books, 2009), 34. One reference to this argument is found in the essay by R. Albert Mohler, Jr., president of Southern Baptist Theological Seminary, "Torture and the War on Terror: We Must Not Add Dirty Rules to Dirty Hands." 20 December, 2005. http://www.albertmohler.com/2005/12/20/torture-and-the-war-on-terror-we-must-not-add-dirty-rules-to-dirty-hands/.

[46]This issue is addressed at length in the most substantive and important critique of the *Evangelical Declaration Against Torture:* Keith Pavlischek, "Human Rights and Justice in an Age of Terror," *Books & Culture* (September 25, 2007).

[47]This is a widely employed critique in all attacks on anti-torture efforts I have seen so far. I address this issue at length in my response to Pavlischek: "Consensus Against Torture: A Response to Keith Pavlischek," http://www.christianitytoday.com/books/web/2007/nov26.html. Here is my concluding paragraph: "So what is the exact definition of the 'torture' that we are 'against'? It is the same 'torture' that is banned without specific rule-oriented or act-oriented definitions by numerous international treaties and conventions which the United States has signed, as well as in the 1992 edition of the U.S. Army Field Manual which simply banned 'acts of violence or intimidation, including physical or mental torture…as a means of or aid to interrogation' (quoted in EDAT, 6.11). And if you are looking for specific rules or acts that this general anti-torture principle precludes, we are 'against' acts banned by the United States Army Field Manual as of its 2006 revision, which specifically include waterboarding, beatings, sexual humiliation, food and water deprivation, mock executions, burnings, and electric shock. If you want more specificity than that, you are on your own." I remain convinced that this relentless call for even more definitional clarity than this represents further evidence of the corrupting effects of the Bush Administration's constant euphemizing, redefining, and lawyering of previously quite clear enough U.S. traditions, laws, and policies. The adoption of this strategy in the name of Christian ethics is shameful.

[48]Many critics claim that we have never adequately defined the line between legitimate coercion and illegitimate torture. The most detailed analysis is in Pavlischek, "Human Rights and Justice."

[49]See Daniel Heimbach's comments, quoted in Erin Roach, "Ethicist: NAE Torture Declaration 'Irrational.'" I think it interesting that we are charged with "substituting passion for reason," as if reason (understood to be casuistic application of Just War theory) is the only plausible or legitimate path to moral knowledge or means of moral analysis in Christian ethics. There is a disturbingly cold, bloodless brand of theology and ethics that has emerged in quadrants of the evangelical community.

[50]R. Albert Mohler considers and ultimately rejects the now famous argument by Harvard University professor Alan Dershowitz that torture should be legalized by statute and implemented through the use of a torture warrant. Instead, Mohler argues that "a categorical ban should be adopted as state policy," but that under extreme circumstances it may be transcended, e.g., overridden, with full accountability. This is certainly preferable to the drift into authorization of torture by statute, and may be the best one can hope for in most nations facing an emergency situation. But it is at least striking that conservative evangelicals who are often quite absolutist in their interpretation of the nature of moral prohibitions, such as bans on abortion or use of embryonic stem cells, become much more flexible on this issue.

[51]"Soft and Hard Just War Theory: A Proposal and Analysis." In William R. Marty and Bruce W. Speck, eds., "Who Is My Neighbor?" *Christian Conduct in a Dangerous World: Proceedings of the 2002 Christianity in the Academy Conference* (Southern Pines, N.C.: Carolinas Press, 2004), pp. 1–8.

[52] James Turner Johnson, "Torture: A Just War Perspective," *Review of Faith and International Affairs* 5, no. 2 (Summer 2007): 29–32.

[53]A methodological claim defended and spelled out thoroughly in Stassen/Gushee, *Kingdom Ethics*, ch. 3.

[54]Quoted in Rodney Stark, *The Rise of Christianity* (New York: HarperOne, 1997), p. 212.

Appendix

[1]Founding policy statements of the New Evangelical Partnership for the Common Good, accessed at http://www.newevangelicalpartnership.org/?q=node/25.